William Henry Davenport Adams

Household Treasury of English Song

Specimens of the English Poets, Chronologically Arranged

William Henry Davenport Adams

Household Treasury of English Song
Specimens of the English Poets, Chronologically Arranged

ISBN/EAN: 9783744771726

Printed in Europe, USA, Canada, Australia, Japan

Cover: Foto ©Thomas Meinert / pixelio.de

More available books at **www.hansebooks.com**

The Household Treasury of English Song.

> .... And though books cannot *make* this mind,
> Which we must bring apt to be set aright;
> Yet do they rectify it in that kind,
> And touch it so, as that it turns that way
> Where judgment lies.   And though we cannot find
> The certain place of truth; yet do they stay
> And entertain us near about the same;
> And give the soul the best delight that may
> Endear it most, and most our spirits enflame
> To thoughts of glory, and to worthy ends.
>   GEORGE DANIEL, *Epistle to the Lady Lucy,*
>   *Countess of Bedford.*

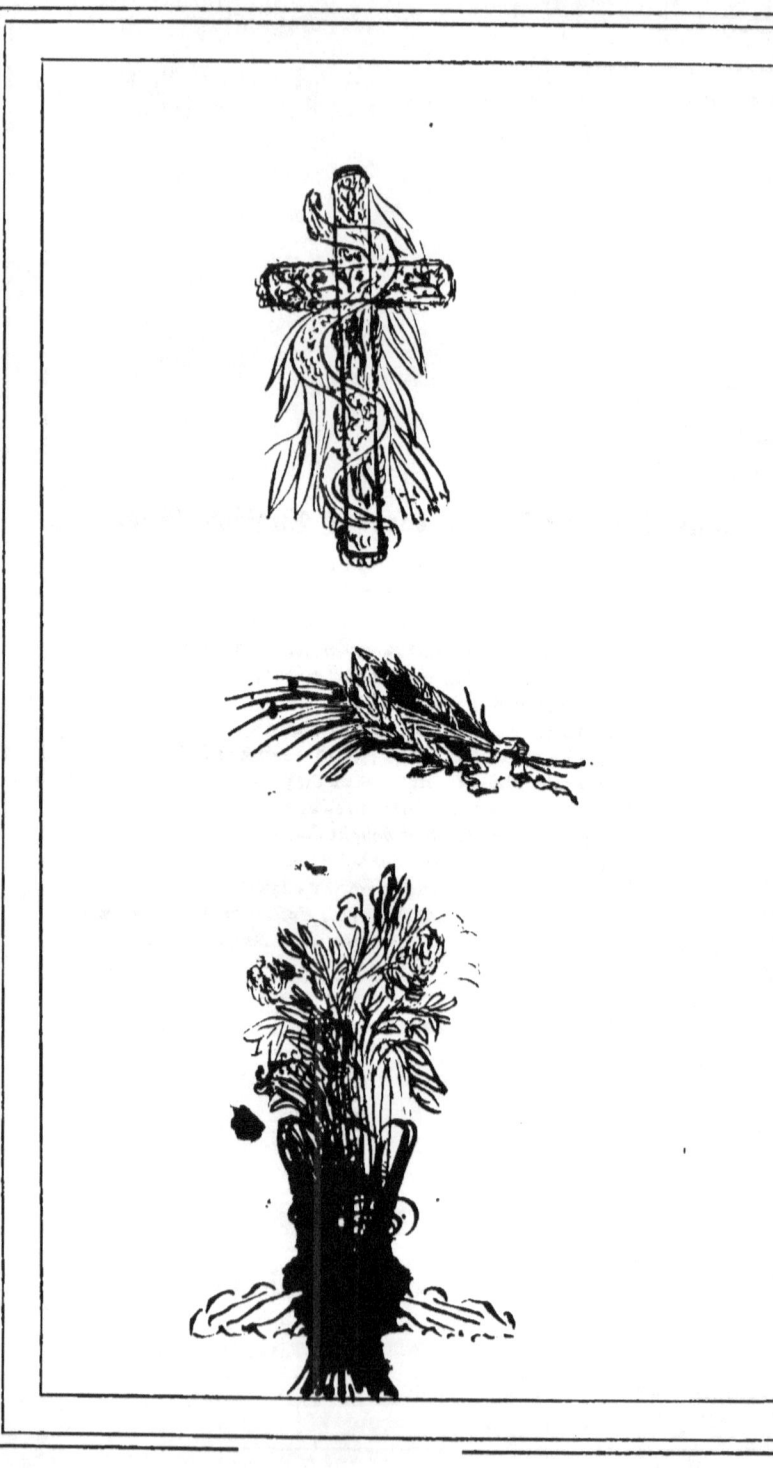

THE
HOUSEHOLD TREASURY
OF
ENGLISH SONG.

Specimens of the English Poets,

CHRONOLOGICALLY ARRANGED;

WITH

BIOGRAPHICAL AND EXPLANATORY NOTES, AND NEARLY
ONE THOUSAND MARGINAL QUOTATIONS.

Freshening life's dusty road with babbling rills
Of song.   GEORGE ELIOT, *The Spanish Gypsy.*

Blessings be with them, and eternal praise,
Who gave us nobler loves, and nobler cares,
THE POETS—who on earth have made us heirs
Of truth and pure delight by heavenly lays!
   WORDSWORTH, *Personal Talk.*

LONDON:
T. NELSON AND SONS, PATERNOSTER ROW;
EDINBURGH; AND NEW YORK.

1872.

THE present volume is designed to furnish youthful readers with a New Manual of English Poetry; a manual which may be of service in their systematic studies, and yet a source of recreation in their leisure hours; while, at the same time, it is intended to supply the tutor and the parent with a poetical text-book of unpretending character but comprehensive scope.

The Compiler, in order to carry out these objects, has endeavoured to extend his selection of extracts over the widest possible range. He has sought to introduce almost every distinguished name in English poetry, and has, therefore, frequently been compelled to confine his specimens to a few lines, which, he is willing to admit, can give the reader no just idea of an author's genius. But in the narrow compass of a book of extracts it is impossible to do justice to the many sides of a great poet's intellect; and if the "fancy" of Shakspeare is fairly represented, his "imagination" or his "philosophic insight" must be neglected. It seems desirable, therefore, in a book intended for the young, that the greatest possible number of authors should be introduced, rather than the supposed choicest specimens of an illustrious few; and the Compiler believes that the youthful reader who carefully peruses the following pages will at all events acquire a tolerably correct knowledge of the wealth and variety of our poetic literature. Familiar with the names of its immortal "lights," he may afterwards proceed to a fuller study of the works which have secured their enduring renown.

In his choice of extracts the Compiler has been influenced by a desire to engage the attention and fix the interest of the young; and, consequently, few purely didactic pieces have been introduced. He has also been anxious to include a large number suitable for *being committed to memory*, or *read* aloud— the latter the only way by which the young ear can be properly trained, and made sensible of the true melody of verse.

To increase the educational value of the volume, the extracts have been arranged chronologically, and brief biographical and explanatory notes appended. It is divided into Four Parts :— the first ranging from 1316 to 1668; the second from 1668 to 1765; the third from 1765 to 1867; and the fourth being devoted to Living Authors. By very young readers or learners, the first two books may be passed over, until they have made themselves familiar with the more modern contents of the last two.

A novel feature of the present volume is the introduction of nearly one thousand Marginal Quotations—each quotation being literally a "pearl of price," which shines with an undying lustre. The reader is recommended to commit as many as possible of these choice phrases and "household words" to memory. Most of them enjoin, in striking language, some truth well worthy of being borne in mind. Others are remarkable for their felicity of expression or imagery. Thus they may be used as hints for pleasant discussion in the domestic circle, or as subjects for "themes" and "essays" by the student of English composition. And, at all times, they will serve to "point a moral" or "adorn a tale;" to refresh the mind with agreeable recollections of favourite poets, just as the dried flower or leaf reminds the traveller of the scenes of wonder and beauty visited by him in the happy past.

In the Table of Contents references are given to the best biographies (known to the Compiler) of the poets represented in the following pages, as well as to a few accredited critical authorities, whose remarks will assist the reader in forming an estimate of their excellencies and errors.

The preparation of this volume has been a labour of love, and every care has been taken to render it worthy of its subject. That there are many deficiencies, nevertheless, the Compiler must needs admit, and any suggestions towards its improvement he will most gladly consider. Yet he would fain hope that the "HOUSEHOLD TREASURY OF ENGLISH SONG" may do "yeoman's service," in promoting among the young an intelligent love of, and a familiar acquaintance with, the vast poetical wealth of our immortal literature.

In conclusion, the Compiler has to express his acknowledgments to the various publishers and authors who have courteously waived their copyright claims on his application; among others, to Messrs. Macmillan, F. Ellis, Arnold, R. Browning, W. Allingham, W. C. Bennett, B. W. Procter, His Grace the Archbishop of Dublin, the Right Hon. Lord Lytton, Lord Houghton, Alfred Tennyson, the Rev. Charles Kingsley, Miss Jean Ingelow, Mrs. E. D. Bullock, and Mr. A. Strahan. He has to regret that in some few instances he was less successful.

PREFACE.

A supplementary volume, for the use of older scholars, and devoted entirely to the poets of the present century, is in preparation.

W. H. D. A.

---o---

NOTE: AUTHORITIES.

FOR the convenience of the young student, a list is subjoined of a few critical authorities, whose careful perusal will enable him to detect the true from the false, the gold from the alloy, and to form a correct and comprehensive judgment of our Poetical Literature.

Thomas Warton, *History of English Poetry;* Hazlitt, *Lectures on English Poetry,* and *On the Elizabethan Dramatists;* Thomas De Quincey, *Critical Essays;* Lord Jeffrey, *Contributions to the Edinburgh Review;* S. T. Coleridge, *Biographia Literaria;* Hartley Coleridge, *Marginalia;* Professor Shairp, *Studies in Poetry and Philosophy;* Rev. Frederick William Robertson, *Lectures and Addresses;* Henry Taylor, *Essay on Poetry,* prefixed to *Philip van Artevelde;* Professor Craik, *History of English Literature;* Hallam, *Introduction to the History of Literature, &c.;* Morley, *English Writers;* James Hannay, *A Course of English Literature;* Carlyle, *Miscellaneous Essays;* Professor Wilson, *Recreations of Christopher North,* and *Essays;* Leigh Hunt, *The Indicator, The Seer,* and *Men, Women, and Books;* J. Hain Friswell, *Essays on English Writers;* E. S. Dallas, *The Gay Science;* Sir Egerton Brydges, *Censura Literaria; Guesses at Truth,* by the brothers Julius and Augustus Hare; Sir F. H. Doyle, *Lectures on Poetry;* and Arthur Helps, *Friends in Council.* Admirable monographs on our great poets frequently appear in the leading Reviews, as the *Edinburgh, Quarterly, Westminster, North British,* and *British and Foreign;* and in some of the principal weeklies, *The Spectator, Saturday Review, Athenæum, &c.*

PART I.

FROM JOHN BARBOUR, A.D. 1316, TO SIR JOHN DENHAM, A.D. 1668.

John Barbour, A.D. 1316—1395.
[*Life*, in Irving's *Lives of the Scottish Poets*: see also his poem of *The Brus*, published by the Spalding Club.]
THE BATTLE OF BANNOCKBURN, ... 3

Geoffrey Chaucer, A.D. 1328—1400.
[For *Life*, see Tod, Godwin, Sir Harris Nicolas, Singer, Craik's *English Literature*, Morley's *English Writers*.]
THE GOOD PARSON, ... 4

James I., of Scotland, A.D. 1374—1437.
[For *Life*, see J. Hill Burton's *History of Scotland*.]
A GARDEN, ... 6

William Dunbar, A.D. 1465—1530.
[*Life*, by Laing: see also Alexander Smith's *Dreamthorpe*; Warton's *History of Poetry*.]
GOOD GIVING AND ILL GIVING, ... 7

Sir Thomas Wyatt, A.D. 1503—1542.
[*Life*, by Dr. Nott and Robert Bell.]
PLEASURE BLENDS WITH EVERY PAIN, ... 9

Henry Howard, Earl of Surrey, A.D. 1517—1546-47.
[*Life*, in Froude's *History of England*.]
THE HAPPY SEASON OF LIFE, ... 9

CONTENTS.

Edmund Spenser, A.D. 1553—1599.
[*Life*, by Dr. Todd, Rev. J. Mitford, and J. P. Collier.]

UNA AND THE LION,	11
ENCHANTED MUSIC,	14
MAY,	15

Sir Philip Sidney, A.D. 1554—1586.
[*Life*, by Lord Zouch, H. Fox Bourne, and Julius Lloyd.]

SLEEP,	15

John Lylye, A.D. 1563-64—1601.
[See Craik's *English Literature*, and Morley's *English Literature*.]

SONGS OF BIRDS,	16

Christopher Marlowe, A.D. 1563-64—1593.
[*Life*, by Rev. Alexander Dyce; Lamb's *English Dramatists*.]

THE MIND'S PROGRESS,	17

Thomas Nash, A.D. 1564—1601.
[*Life*, in J. P. Collier's *Pierce Penniless*, and I. D'Israeli's *Calamities of Authors*.]

SPRING,	18

Sir Walter Raleigh, A.D. 1552—1618.
[*Life*, by Oldys, P. Tytler, M. Napier, J. A. St. John, and Edward Edwards.]

THE HEAVENLY PILGRIMAGE,	19

Joshua Sylvester, A.D. 1563—1618.

THE SOUL'S ERRAND (*also ascribed to Raleigh*),	20

William Shakspeare, A.D. 1564—1616.
[*Life*, by Rowe, Drake, Malone, Guizot, J. P. Collier, Charles Knight, J. O. Halliwell, Philaret Chasles, Rev. A. Dyce, and Howard Staunton. *Criticism*: Philaret Chasles, Dr. Johnson, Dr. Gervinus, Dr. Ulrici, Goethe, R. W..Emerson, Thomas Carlyle, Hallam, Mrs. Jameson, Hazlitt, Thomas De Quincey, and S. T. Coleridge.]

UNDER THE GREENWOOD TREE,	23
A WINTER SONG,	24

CONTENTS.

A Sea Dirge,	25
Music and Moonlight,	26
A Morning Song,	27
Morning,	27
Sunrise,	27
A Fool in the Forest,	28
England,	29
Life,	30
Queen Mab,	30
Ariel's Song,	31
A Precipice,	32
What Time does,	33
A Funeral Song,	33

Michael Drayton, A.D. 1563—1631.
[*Life*, in Anderson's and Chalmers' *British Poets*.]

The Fairy Palace,	34
The Fairy Queen's Chariot,	35
The Battle of Agincourt,	37

Thomas Dekker, A.D. 1570—1638-39.
[*Life*: see his *Plays*, edited by Dyce.]

The Happy Heart,	42

Sir John Davies, A.D. 1570—1626.
[*Life*, by George Chalmers.]

Here and There,	42

John Fletcher, A.D. 1579—1625.
[*Life*, by Rev. A. Dyce: see C. Lamb's *English Dramatists*, and Leigh Hunt's *Beaumont and Fletcher*.]

The Dawn,	43
Self-Reliance,	44

Sir Henry Wotton, A.D. 1568—1639.
[*Life*, by Izaak Walton.]

A Happy Life,	44

CONTENTS.

Ben Jonson, A.D. 1574—1637.
[*Life*, by William Gifford, and B. W. Procter.]

STARS AND FLOWERS,	45
TO CYNTHIA—THE MOON,	46
LIFE AND DEATH,	47
ROBIN GOODFELLOW (*authorship doubtful*),	47

George Herbert, A.D. 1593—1632.
[*Life*, by Izaak Walton.]

A VIRTUOUS SOUL,	50

Thomas Carew, A.D. 1589—1639.
[See Hallam's *History of Literature*, and Chalmers' *British Poets*.]

WOMAN'S TRUE BEAUTY,	50

John Webster, A.D. 1585—1654.
[*Life*, see Rev. A. Dyce's edition of his *Plays*; Hazlitt's *Lectures on the Elizabethan Dramatists*.]

A LAND DIRGE,	51

Sir William Davenant, A.D. 1605—1668.
[*Life*, in Anderson's *British Poets*.]

IN PRAISE OF SOLITUDE,	51

William Browne, A.D. 1590—1645.
[*Life*, in Anderson's *British Poets*.]

A LANDSCAPE,	53

Robert Herrick, A.D. 1591—1674.
[*Life*, in Anderson's *British Poets*, and Dr. Drake's *Literary Hours*.]

TO BLOSSOMS,	54
A WARNING AGAINST PROCRASTINATION,	55
TO DAFFODILS,	56

Henry King, Bishop of Chichester, A.D. 1591—1669.

SIC VITA—SUCH IS LIFE,	56

John Shirley, A.D. 1596—1666.
[*Life*, by Rev. A. Dyce, in Gifford's edition of his Works.]

DEATH THE LEVELLER,	57

Richard Lovelace, A.D. 1618—1658.
TRUE FREEDOM IS IN THE MIND, ... 59

John Milton, A.D. 1608—1674.
[*Life*, and *Criticism*, by Lord Macaulay, Dr. Channing, Sir Egerton Brydges, Rev. W. Stebbing, James Montgomery, Thomas Keightley, and Professor Masson.]
L'ALLEGRO, ... 59
ON SHAKSPEARE, ... 62
ON MAY MORNING, ... 62
FAME, ... 64
SATAN'S ADDRESS TO THE SUN, ... 64
THE GARDEN OF EDEN, ... 68

Sir John Denham, A.D. 1615—1668.
[*Life*, in Johnson's, Chalmers', and Anderson's *British Poets*.]
THE THAMES, ... 69

PART II.
FROM ABRAHAM COWLEY, A.D. 1618, TO DR. EDWARD YOUNG, A.D. 1765.

Abraham Cowley, A.D. 1618—1667.
[*Life*, by Bishop Sprat, and Dr. Johnson.]
A KING'S GARDEN, ... 73
ON DELAYS, ... 74
THE GRASSHOPPER, ... 74

Andrew Marvell, A.D. 1620—1678.
[*Life*, by Captain Thompson, and Hartley Coleridge.]
THE SONG OF THE EMIGRANTS IN BERMUDA, ... 75

Richard Crashaw, A.D. 1625—1650.
[*Life*, by P. Phillips, and in Dr. Anderson's *British Poets*.]
THE SONG OF THE NIGHTINGALE, ... 77

John Dryden, A.D. 1631—1701.
[*Life*, by Dr. Johnson, Malone, and Sir W. Scott: see Hazlitt's *Lectures on English Poetry*.]
A CHARACTER: THE COURTIER, ... 79
THE GOOD PARSON, ... 80

Dr. Edward Young, A.D. 1681—1765.

[*Life*, by Rev. J. Mitford, Dr. Doran, and Rev. G. Gilfillan; also by Dr. Johnson and Dr. Anderson.]

THOUGHTS ON TIME, ... 82

---o---

PART III.

FROM ALEXANDER POPE, A.D. 1688, TO ALEXANDER SMITH, A.D. 1830.

Alexander Pope, A.D. 1688—1744.

[*Life*, by W. Lisle Bowles, William Roscoe, and R. Carruthers: see Professor Craik's *English Literature* and Rev. C. Kingsley's *Miscellanies*.]

A CHARACTER: THE PHILANTHROPIST, ... 87
A FOREST SCENE, ... 89

James Thomson, A.D. 1700—1748.

[*Life*, by Dr. Murdock, and Sir Harris Nicolas: see Professor Wilson's *Recreations of Christopher North*.]

THE CARAVAN IN THE DESERT, ... 91
RULE BRITANNIA, ... 93

Samuel Johnson, A.D. 1709—1784.

[*Life*, by James Boswell, and Sir J. Hawkins: see Thomas Carlyle's *Miscellanies* and *Hero-Worship*.]

A ROYAL MADMAN: CHARLES XII. OF SWEDEN, ... 94

Thomas Gray, A.D. 1716—1771.

[*Life*, by Dr. Mitford, and Rev. W. Mason.]

ODE TO THE SPRING, ... 95

William Collins, A.D. 1720—1756.

[*Life*, by Dr. Johnson, Rev. A. Dyce, and Moy Thomas.]

AN EPITAPH FOR HEROIC WARRIORS, ... 98
HASSAN; OR, THE CAMEL-DRIVER, ... 98

Oliver Goldsmith, A.D. 1728—1774.

[*Life*, by Prior, Washington Irving, Sir W. Scott, and John Forster: see De Quincey's *Miscellanies*.]

ENGLISH COUNTRY LIFE: THE VILLAGE SCHOOLMASTER AND THE VILLAGE INN, ... 101

William Cowper, A.D. 1731—1800.

[*Life*, by Hayley, Southey, Grimshawe, and Sir Harris Nicolas.]

BOADICEA, ... 104
THE SOLITUDE OF ALEXANDER SELKIRK, ... 107
LOSS OF THE ROYAL GEORGE, ... 109
A WINTER EVENING, ... 111

William Falconer, A.D. 1732—1770.

[*Life*, by Robert Carruthers.]

THE SHORES OF GREECE, ... 115

Robert Burns, A.D. 1754—1796.

[*Life*, by James Currie, J. G. Lockhart, Allan Cunningham, Professor Wilson, Thomas Carlyle, Rev. P. Hately Waddell, and Alexander Smith.]

DOMESTIC HAPPINESS, ... 121
THE PEASANT'S EVENING PRAYER, ... 121
TO A MOUNTAIN DAISY, ... 124

William Blake, A.D. 1757—1827.

[*Life*, by Alexander Gilchrist, and Algernon Swinburne: see *Quarterly Review*, vol. cxvii.]

THE TIGER, ... 126

Rev. George Crabbe, A.D. 1754—1832.

[*Life*, by his Son: see Lord Jeffrey's *Essays*, and *St. James' Magazine*, February 1869.]

THE DYING SAILOR, ... 127

Joanna Baillie, A.D. 1762—1851.

[See *Life*, prefixed to *Dramatic Works*, edition 1853.]

A SAILOR'S SONG, ... 129
A SERENADE, ... 130

Samuel Rogers, A.D. 1763—1855.

[See his *Recollections*; Hayward's and Lord Jeffrey's *Essays*.]

A WISH,	132
GINEVRA,	133

James Hogg, A.D. 1770—1835.

[*Life*, by Professor Wilson.]

THE SKYLARK,	136

Sir Walter Scott, A.D. 1771—1832.

[*Life*, by J. G. Lockhart: see Lord Jeffrey's *Essays*; Carlyle's *Miscellanies*; F. T. Palgrave, *Globe Edition of Scott*.]

MELROSE ABBEY,	137
THE QUARREL BETWEEN MARMION AND THE DOUGLAS,	139

Samuel Taylor Coleridge, A.D. 1772—1834.

[*Life*, by Gilman: see De Quincey's *Works*, Hazlitt's *Lectures on Poetry*, Professor Shairp's *Studies in Poetry and Philosophy*, and *Quarterly Review* for 1868.]

THE ALBATROSS,	142
THE BEST PRAYER,	143

William Wordsworth, A.D. 1770—1850.

[*Life*, by Canon Wordsworth, and Rev. Paxton Hood: see also De Quincey's *Works*, Hazlitt's *Lectures*, George Brimley's *Essays*, Professor Shairp's *Studies in Poetry and Philosophy*, and Rev. F. W. Robertson's *Lectures and Addresses*.]

A PERFECT WOMAN,	144
THE DANISH BOY,	145
THE FOUNTAIN,	147
WE ARE SEVEN,	150
TO THE DAISY,	152
TO A BUTTERFLY,	154
THE REDBREAST AND THE BUTTERFLY,	155
TO THE SMALL CELANDINE,	158
SIMON LEE THE OLD HUNTSMAN,	160

Thomas Campbell, A.D. 1777—1844.

[*Life*, by Dr. Beattie: see also Lord Jeffrey's *Essays*.]

LORD ULLIN'S DAUGHTER,	164
BATTLE OF THE BALTIC,	166
MEN OF ENGLAND,	169

HOHENLINDEN,	170
TO THE RAINBOW,	171

James Montgomery, A.D. 1771—1854.
[*Life*, by Holland and Everett: see also Lord Jeffrey's *Essays*.]

THE AURORA BOREALIS,	174

Thomas Moore, A.D. 1779—1852.
[*Life*, by Earl Russell: see Hazlitt's *Lectures*, and Lord Jeffrey's *Essays*.]

THE MINSTREL BOY,	176
REMEMBRANCE,	176

Leigh Hunt, A.D. 1784—1859.
[See his *Autobiography* and *Letters*, edited by his Son.]

SUMMER,	177
ABOU-BEN-ADHEM,	179
THE GLOVE AND THE LIONS,	180

Henry Kirke White, A.D. 1785—1806.
[*Life*, by Robert Southey, and Sir Harris Nicolas.]

THE CITIES OF THE PAST,	181

Allan Cunningham, A.D. 1785—1842.
[See edition of *Poems*, 1847.]

A SEA-SONG,	182

Robert Southey, A.D. 1774—1843.
[*Life*, by Caroline Southey, and C. T. Browne.]

THE HOLLY-TREE,	184
BISHOP BRUNO,	185
A MOONLIGHT NIGHT,	188
HENRY V. AND THE HERMIT OF DREUX,	189

George Gordon, Lord Byron, A.D. 1788—1824.
[*Life*, by Thomas Moore, J. Galt, Sir Egerton Brydges: see also Countess Guiccioli's *Recollections of Lord Byron*, A. C. Swinburne's Preface to Moxon's Miniature Edition, Lord Jeffrey's *Essays*, Professor Wilson's *Recreations*, &c.]

NAPOLEON BONAPARTE,	192
NIGHT BEFORE THE BATTLE OF WATERLOO,	195

CONTENTS.

Rev. Charles Wolfe, A.D. 1791—1823.
The Burial of Sir John Moore, ... 198

Percy Bysshe Shelley, A.D. 1792—1824.
[*Life*, by Hogg, Captain Medwin, Trelawney, and Mrs. Shelley.]
To the Night, ... 199
The Cloud, ... 201
To a Skylark, ... 204

Mrs. Felicia Dorothea Hemans, A.D. 1793—1835.
[*Life*, by H. F. Chorley: see also Professor Wilson's *Recreations* and Lord Jeffrey's *Essays*.]
Ivan the Czar, ... 209
Henry I. after the Death of his Son, ... 212
The Landing of the Pilgrim Fathers in New England, .. 213
Cœur de Lion at the Bier of his Father, ... 215
The Voice of Spring, ... 219

William Motherwell, A.D. 1797—1835.
[*Life*, by M'Conochy.]
Facts from Fairyland, ... 221

John Keats, A.D. 1796—1821.
[*Life*, by Lord Houghton: see also Lord Jeffrey's *Essays*, Thomas De Quincey's *Works*, Hazlitt's *Lectures*, Leigh Hunt's *Imagination and Fancy*, and Professor Craik's *English Literature*.]
Robin Hood, ... 223

Lord Macaulay, A.D. 1800—1859.
[*Life*, by Rev. F. Arnold: see J. Hutchinson Stirling's *Essays*.]
The Spanish Armada, ... 229
The Battle of Ivry, ... 231

Letitia Elizabeth Landon (Mrs. Maclean), A.D. 1802—1838.
[*Life*, by Laman Blanchard.]
Hannibal's Oath, ... 234

Elizabeth Barrett Browning, A.D. 1809—1861.
[See Bayne's *Essays*; Professor Craik's *English Literature*.]
The Romance of the Swan's Nest, ... 235
A Dead Rose, ... 236

Arthur Hugh Clough, A.D. 1819—1861.
[*Life*, by F. T. Palgrave, prefixed to his *Poems*: see *Fortnightly Review*, December 1868.]

INCITEMENT TO PERSEVERANCE, ... 240
TO A SLEEPING CHILD, ... 241

Ralph Waldo Emerson, born 1803.
[See *North British Review*, No. xciv.]

THE MOUNTAIN AND THE SQUIRREL, ... 242
THE HUMBLE-BEE, ... 244

Adelaide Anne Procter, A.D. 1825—1864.
[*Life*, by Charles Dickens, prefixed to her *Legends and Lyrics*.]

THE MESSAGE (*abridged*), ... 246
A DOUBTING HEART, ... 247

Rev. John Keble, A.D. 1800—1867.
[*Life*, by Sir J. Coleridge: see Professor Shairp's *Studies in Poetry and Philosophy*.]

THE BOOK OF NATURE, ... 249

Alexander Smith, A.D. 1830—1867.
[*Life*, by Patrick P. Alexander: see Kingsley's *Miscellanies*.]

BARBARA, ... 250

———o———

PART IV.
FROM B. W. PROCTER, A.D. 1790, TO WILLIAM MORRIS.

Bryan Waller Procter, born 1790.

THE RETURN OF THE ADMIRAL, ... 255
THE OWL, ... 257
THE STORMY PETREL, ... 259

Walter Cullen Bryant, born 1794.
[See *North British Review*, No. xcii.]

MARCH, ... 261

Lord Lytton, born 1805.

THE ANGEL AND THE CHILD, ... 262

Mrs. Mary Howitt, born 18—.

BIRDS IN SUMMER, ...	263
THE VOICE OF SPRING, ...	265

Henry Wadsworth Longfellow, born 1807.

THE REAPER AND THE FLOWERS, ...	267
THE CHILDREN'S HOUR, ...	268
THE VILLAGE BLACKSMITH, ...	270
A SPRING LANDSCAPE, ...	272
THE WRECK OF THE HESPERUS, ...	273

R. C. Trench, Archbishop of Dublin, born 1807.

AUTUMN, ...	277
ENGLAND, ...	279
XERXES AT THE HELLESPONT, ...	280
THE SPILT PEARLS, ...	281
THE LENT JEWELS, ...	283

J. G. Whittier, born 1808.

HOPE, ...	284
THE FROST SPIRIT, ...	285

Lord Houghton, born 1809.

[See *Quarterly Review*, vol. cxviii.]

THE VALUE OF THE HOURS, ...	287

Alfred Tennyson, born 1810.

[See George Brimley's *Essays*, Rev. Charles Kingsley's *Miscellanies*, and E. C. Tainsh's *Studies in Tennyson*.]

THE LORD OF BURLEIGH, ...	288
LITTLE BIRDIE, ...	292
THE CHARGE OF THE LIGHT BRIGADE, ...	293
THE TOURNAMENT, ...	295

Robert Browning, born 1812.

[See J. T. Nettleship's *Essays on R. Browning's Poetry*; *Quarterly Review*, vol. cxviii.; *Edinburgh* and *Westminster Reviews*.]

HOW THEY BROUGHT THE GOOD NEWS FROM GHENT TO AIX, ..	298

Charles Mackay, born 1812.

TUBAL CAIN, ...	300
YOUTH'S WARNING, ...	302

Rev. Charles Kingsley, born 1819.

THE SANDS OF DEE,	303
THE STARLINGS,	304
THE THREE FISHERS,	305
EARL HALDAN'S DAUGHTER,	306
A FAREWELL,	307

James Russell Lowell, born 1819.

THE FOUNTAIN,	307

William Cox Bennett, born 1820.

THE SEASONS,	309
BABY MAY,	310

George MacDonald, born 1826.

[See *British and Foreign Review*, January 1868.]

LITTLE WHITE LILY,	312
THE SHADOWS,	314

Gerald Massey, born 1828.

THE FIGHTING TEMERAIRE,	315

William Allingham.

ROBIN REDBREAST: A CHILD'S SONG,	317
OUTWARD BOUND,	319
HOMEWARD BOUND,	320

Robert Buchanan, born 1841.

SUMMER MOON, O SUMMER MOON,	322
IRIS THE RAINBOW,	324

Jean Ingelow, born about 1830.

THE WARBLING OF BLACKBIRDS,	326

Sir Francis Hastings Doyle.

THE PRIVATE OF THE BUFFS,	327

Matthew Arnold, born 1822.

APOLLO AND MARSYAS,	329

CONTENTS.

Elizabeth D. Cross (Mrs. Bullock).
A CROSS IN EACH ONE'S LOT, ... 332

George Eliot (Miss Evans), born about 1820.
A GYPSY ENCAMPMENT, ... 333

William Morris.
A SONG OF APRIL, ... 335

---o---

A SCORE OF SONNETS.

THE LOVELINESS OF TRUTH, ..	.. William Shakspeare,	336
A COMPARISON AND A MORAL, ..	.. William Drummond,	337
ON THE LATE MASSACRE IN PIEDMONT,	John Milton, ..	338
DEATH NOT THE CONQUEROR, ..	.. Dr. John Donne, ..	339
IN MEMORY OF A DEPARTED FRIEND, ..	Thomas Gray, ..	340
TO THE RIVER LODDON,	.. Thomas Warton, ..	341
EVENING, ...	.. William Wordsworth,	341
WORLDLINESS, ..	.. William Wordsworth,	343
THE FIRST MAN, ...	.. Hartley Coleridge, ..	343
THE BELLS, ...	.. Rev. W. Lisle Bowles,	344
THE THRUSH'S NEST, ..	.. John Clare, ...	345
THE GRASSHOPPER AND THE CRICKET, ..	Leigh Hunt, ..	346
THE GRASSHOPPER AND THE CRICKET, ..	John Keats, ..	347
TO AILSA ROCK, ...	.. John Keats, ..	347
THE EVENING CLOUD, ..	.. John Wilson, ..	347
FALSE POETS AND TRUE, ..	.. Thomas Hood, ..	348
SPRING, ...	.. Ebenezer Elliott, ..	349
NOT DEATH, BUT LOVE, ..	.. E. Barrett Browning,	349
WORLDLY PLACE, ...	.. Matthew Arnold, ..	350
A PRAYER FOR SUMMER, ..	.. David Gray, ..	351

Index of First Lines.

A blue-eyed child, that sits amid the noon,	.. *Bennett*, ..	.. 309
Abou-Ben-Adhem—may his tribe increase!	.. *Leigh Hunt*,	.. 179
A chieftain to the Highlands bound, ..	.. *Campbell*,	.. 164
A cloud lay cradled near the setting sun,	.. *Wilson*, ..	.. 347
A fool, a fool! I met a fool i' the forest, ..	.. *Shakspeare*,	.. 28
Again the violet of our early days, ..	.. *Elliott*, ..	.. 349
Ah, what a weary race my feet have run,	.. *T. Warton*,	.. 341
And now there came both mist and snow,	.. *Coleridge*, ..	.. 142
And the night was dark and calm,	.. *Landon*, ..	.. 234
A parish priest was of the pilgrim train, ..	.. *Dryden*, ..	.. 80
Art thou poor, yet hast thou golden slumbers? ..	*Dekker*, ..	.. 42
Art thou the bird whom man loves best,	.. *Wordsworth*,	.. 155
As a beam o'er the face of the waters may glow,	*Moore*, ..	.. 176
A simple child, ...	*Wordsworth*,	.. 150
As the sky-brightening south wind clears the day,	*M. Arnold*,	.. 329
A thousand miles from land are we, ..	.. *Procter*, ..	.. 259
A true good man there was of religion, ..	.. *Chaucer*, ..	.. 4
Attend all ye who list to hear, ...	.. *Macaulay*,	.. 226
Avenge, O Lord, thy slaughtered saints,	.. *Milton*, ..	.. 338
A wet sheet and a flowing sea, ...	.. *Cunningham*,	.. 182
A wilful, headlong river, ...	.. *Cross*, ..	.. 332
Begin, be bold, and venture to be wise, ..	.. *Cowley*, ..	.. 74
Believe not that your inner eye, ...	.. *Houghton*,	.. 287
Beside yon straggling fence that skirts the way,	*Goldsmith*,	.. 101
Between the dark and the daylight, ..	.. *Longfellow*,	.. 268
Between two sister moorland rills, ..	.. *Wordsworth*,	.. 145
Beware, exulting youth, beware, ...	.. *Mackay*, ..	.. 302
Bird of the wilderness, ...	.. *Hogg*, ..	.. 136
Bishop Bruno awoke in the dead midnight,	.. *Southey*, ..	.. 185
Breathed hot from all the boundless furnace,	.. *Thomson*, ..	.. 91
Burly, dozing humble-bee, ...	.. *Emerson*,	.. 244
But all our praises why should lords engross? ..	*Pope*, ..	.. 87

INDEX OF FIRST LINES.

Call for a robin redbreast, and the wren,	*Webster*,	51
Calm is now that stormy water,	*Trench*,	280
Cheeks as soft as July peaches,	*Bennett*,	310
Clink! clink! clink! goes our windlass,	*Allingham*,	319
Come forth, come forth, the gentle Spring,	*Jonson*,	45
Come, sleep, O sleep, the certain knot of peace,	*Sidney*,	15
Come unto these yellow sands,	*Shakspeare*,	31
Death, be not proud, though some have callèd thee,	*Donne*,	339
Early in spring time, on raw and windy mornings,	*Kingsley*,	304
Eftsoons they heard a most melodious sound,	*Spenser*,	14
Even in a palace, life may be led well,	*M. Arnold*,	359
Fair daffodils, we weep to see,	*Herrick*,	56
Fair pledges of a fruitful tree,	*Herrick*,	54
Fair stood the wind for France,	*Drayton*,	37
Fame is the spur that the clear spirit doth raise,	*Milton*,	64
Fear no more the heat of the sun,	*Shakspeare*,	33
For who did ever yet in honour, wealth,	*Davies*,	42
Full fathom five thy father lies,	*Shakspeare*,	25
Full many a glorious morning have I seen,	*Shakspeare*,	27
Gather ye rosebuds while ye may,	*Herrick*,	55
Give me my scallop-shell of quiet,	*Raleigh*,	19
Go, soul, the body's guest,	*Raleigh*,	20
Good-bye, good-bye to Summer,	*Allingham*,	317
Green little vaulter on the sunny grass,	*Leigh Hunt*,	346
Hail to thee, blithe Spirit!	*Shelley*,	204
Half a league, half a league,	*Tennyson*,	293
Happy insect! what can be,	*Cowley*,	74
Hark, hark! the lark at heaven's gate sings,	*Shakspeare*,	27
He called his friend, and prefaced with a sigh,	*Crabbe*,	127
He comes—he comes—the frost spirit comes!	*Whittier*,	285
He passed unquestioned through the camp,	*Southey*,	189
He prayeth best who loveth best,	*Coleridge*,	143
He sat in silence on the ground,	*Mrs. Hemans*,	209
He that loves a rosy cheek,	*Carew*,	50
Head the ship for England!	*Allingham*,	320
Hearken, thou craggy ocean-pyramid,	*Keats*,	347
Her chariot ready strait is made,	*Drayton*,	35
Her supple breast thrills out,	*Crashaw*,	77
His courtiers of the Caliph crave,	*Trench*,	281
How beautiful is night!	*Southey*,	188

INDEX OF FIRST LINES.

—How fearful,	Shakspeare,	32
How gallantly, how merrily,	Procter,	255
How happy is he born and taught,	Wotton,	44
How pleasant the life of a bird must be,	Howitt,	263
How sleep the brave who sink to rest,	Collins,	98
—How sweet the moonlight sleeps upon this bank!	Shakspeare,	26
How sweet the tuneful bells responsive peal,	Bowles,	344
I am coming, I am coming!	Howitt,	265
I am monarch of all I survey,	Cowper,	107
I bring fresh showers for the thirsting flowers,	Shelley,	201
I come, I come! ye have called me long,	Hemans,	219
I had a message to send her,	A. A. Procter,	246
I saw the little boy,	Surrey,	9
I sprang to the stirrup, and Joris, and he,	R. Browning,	298
I thought once how Theocritus had sung,	E. B. Browning,	349
I've watched you now a full half-hour,	Wordsworth,	154
If thou shouldst ever come by choice or chance,	Rogers,	133
If thou wouldst view fair Melrose aright,	Scott,	137
Immortal Athens first, in ruin spread,	Falconer,	115
In her ear he whispers gaily,	Tennyson,	288
In schools of wisdom all the day was spent,	Trench,	283
In silent horror, o'er the boundless waste,	Collins,	98
In the hollow tree, in the gray old tower,	Procter,	257
In the sweet shire of Cardigan,	Wordsworth,	160
In vain to me the smiling mornings shine,	Gray,	340
Into the sunshine,	Lowell,	307
It is a beauteous evening, calm and free,	Wordsworth,	341
It is a glorious tale to tell,	Massey,	315
It was a roundel seated on a plain,	Browne,	53
It was Earl Haldan's daughter,	Kingsley,	306
It was the point of noon,	Tennyson,	295
It was the schooner Hesperus,	Longfellow,	273
King Francis was a hearty king,	Leigh Hunt,	180
Last night, among his fellow roughs,	Doyle,	327
Like the falling of a star,	King,	56
Lips, lips, open!	Clough,	241
Little Ellie sits alone,	E. B. Browning,	235
Little White Lily,	MacDonald,	312
Lo, here the gentle lark, weary of rest,	Shakspeare,	27
Lo! where the rosy-bosomed hours,	Gray,	95
Look how the flower which lingeringly doth fade,	Drummond,	337
Look how the lark soars upward and is gone,	Hood,	348

INDEX OF FIRST LINES.

Man is his own star, and the soul that can,	*Fletcher,*	44
Men of England! who inherit,	*Campbell,*	169
Methinks I see great Diocletian walk,	*Cowley,*	73
'Mid the cloud-enshrouded haze,	*R. Buchanan,*	324
Midnight hath told his hour; the moon, yet young,	*Montgomery,*	174
Mine be a cot beside the hill,	*Rogers,*	132
More swift than lightning can I fly,	*Ben Jonson,*	47
My eye, descending from the Hill, surveys,	*Denham,*	69
My fairest child, I have no song to give you,	*Kingsley,*	307
My little boy, with pale round cheeks,	*MacDonald,*	314
Nature, that formed us of four elements,	*Marlowe,*	17
No! those days are gone away,	*Keats,*	223
Not a drum was heard, not a funeral note,	*Wolfe,*	198
Not far advanced was morning day,	*Scott,*	139
Not proud Olympus yields a nobler sight,	*Pope,*	89
Now glory to the Lord of Hosts,	*Macaulay,*	231
Now stir the fire, and close the shutters fast,	*Cowper,*	111
Now the bright morning star, day's harbinger,	*Milton,*	62
Now was there made, fast by the Towris wall,	*James I.,*	6
O fair mid-spring, besung so oft and oft,	*Morris,*	335
O Rose, who dares to name thee?	*E. B. Browning,*	239
O thou, that with surpassing glory crowned,	*Milton,*	64
O Winter, wilt thou never, never go,	*David Gray,*	351
Of Nelson and the North,	*Campbell,*	166
Oh, how much more doth beauty beauteous seem,	*Shakspeare,*	336
Oh, Mary, go and call the cattle home,	*Kingsley,*	303
Oh, reader! hast thou ever stood to see,	*Southey,*	184
Oh, then, I see, Queen Mab hath been with you,	*Shakspeare,*	30
Old Tubal Cain was a man of might,	*Mackay,*	300
On Linden, when the sun was low,	*Campbell,*	170
On the Sabbath day,	*Alex. Smith,*	250
On what foundation stands the warrior's pride?	*Johnson,*	94
One day, nigh weary of the irksome way,	*Spenser,*	11
Pansies, lilies, kingcups, daisies,	*Wordsworth,*	158
Peace, Freedom, Happiness, have loved to wait,	*Trench,*	279
Queen and Huntress, chaste and fair,	*Jonson,*	46
Say not, the struggle nought availeth,	*Clough,*	240
See, the day begins to break,	*Fletcher,*	43
She was a phantom of delight,	*Wordsworth,*	144
So on he fares, and to the borders comes,	*Milton,*	68

INDEX OF FIRST LINES.

Some gives for pride and glory vain, ...	Dunbar, ...	7
Some of their chiefs were princes of the land, ..	Dryden, ...	79
Spring, the sweet Spring, ...	Nash, ...	18
Stone walls do not a prison make, ...	Lovelace, ...	59
Straight mine eye hath caught new pleasures, ..	Milton, ...	59
Summer Moon, O summer Moon, ...	R. Buchanan, ..	322
Sweet Day! so cool, so calm, so bright, ..	Herbert, ...	50
Swiftly walk over the western wave, ...	Shelley, ...	199
The bark that held a prince went down, ...	Hemans, ...	212
The breaking waves dashed high, ...	Hemans, ...	213
The cheerfu' supper done, wi' serious face, ..	Burns, ...	121
The glories of our blood and state, ...	Shirley, ...	57
—The green trees whispered low and mild, ..	Longfellow, ..	272
The Minstrel Boy to the war is gone, ...	Moore, ...	176
The mouths we used to read of, ...	Leigh Hunt, ..	177
The Mountain and the Squirrel, ...	Emerson, ...	242
The night is mother of the day, ...	Whittier, ..	284
The poetry of earth is never dead, ...	Keats, ...	346
The ports of death are sins; of life, good deeds,	Jonson, ...	47
The stormy March has come at last, ...	Bryant, ...	261
The world is too much with us; late and soon, ..	Wordsworth, ..	343
Then came fair May, the fairest maid on ground,	Spenser, ...	15
There is a book who runs may read, ...	Keble, ...	249
There is a Reaper whose name is Death, ..	Longfellow, ..	267
There was a sound of revelry by night, ..	Byron, ...	195
Thine, Autumn, is unwelcome lore, ...	Trench, ...	277
This is Moorish land, ...	George Eliot, ..	333
This palace standeth in the air, ...	Drayton, ...	34
—This royal throne of kings, this sceptered isle, ..	Shakspeare, ..	29
Three fishers went sailing away to the west, ..	Kingsley, ...	305
Thrice happy he who by some shady grove, ..	Davenant, ..	51
Thus were they bound on either side, ...	Barbour, ...	3
Tiger, tiger, burning bright, ...	Blake, ...	126
~Time's glory is to calm contending kings, ..	Shakspeare, ..	33
'Tis done—but yesterday a king, ...	Byron, ...	192
Toll for the brave!	Cowper, ...	109
To make a happy fireside clime, ...	Burns, ...	121
To-morrow, and to-morrow, and to-morrow, ..	Shakspeare, ..	30
Torches were blazing clear, ...	Hemans, ...	215
Triumphal arch, that fill'st the sky, ...	Campbell, ..	171
Under a spreading chestnut tree, ...	Longfellow, ..	270
Under the greenwood tree, ...	Shakspeare, ..	23
Up! quit thy bower! late wears the hour, ..	Joanna Baillie, ..	130
Upon a barren steep, ...	Lytton, ...	262

INDEX OF FIRST LINES.

Venomous thorns, that are so sharp and keen, ..	Wyatt, ...	9
We talked with open heart and tongue, ...	Wordsworth, ..	147
We waste, not use our time; we breathe, not live,	Young, ...	82
Wee, modest, crimson-tippèd flower, ...	Burns, ...	124
What bird so sings, yet so does wail?	Lylye, ...	16
What does little Birdie say?	Tennyson, ..	292
What needs my Shakspeare, ...	Milton, ...	62
What was't awakened first the untried ear, ..	H. Coleridge, ..	343
When Britain first, at Heaven's command, ..	Thomson, ..	93
When icicles hang by the wall, ...	Shakspeare, ..	24
When I hear the waters fretting, ...	Ingelow, ...	326
When the British warrior queen, ...	Cowper, ...	104
Where are the swallows fled?	A. A. Procter, ..	247
Where is Rome?	Kirke White, ..	181
Where the remote Bermudas ride, ...	Marvell, ...	75
While clouds on high are riding, ...	Joanna Baillie,..	129
With little here to do or see, ...	Wordsworth, ..	152
Within a thick and spreading hawthorn bush, ..	Clare, ...	345
Wouldst thou know of me, ...	Motherwell, ..	221

Index of Marginal Quotations.

The figures indicate the pages; and the figures within brackets the number of quotations from the same author occurring on any particular page. The date of birth and death is given of those authors who are not included in the Table of Contents.

Addison, Joseph (author of "The Campaign," *b.* 1672; *d.* 1719), 21; 22.
Akenside, Mark (author of "Pleasures of the Imagination," *b.* 1721; *d.* 1770), 16; 247; 345; 347.
Allingham, William, 308; 309 (3); 310 (3).
Arnold, Matthew, 333 (2); 334; 336.

Bailey, Philip James (author of "Festus," *b.* 1816), 3; 9; 28; 56; 57.
Baillie, Joanna, 292.
Barbour, John (*b.* 1316; *d.* 1395), 59.
Barton, Bernard (*b.* 1784; *d.* 1849), 281.
Beaumont, Francis (dramatist, *b.* 1586; *d.* 1616), 15.
Blair, Robert (author of the "Grave," *b.* 1699; *d.* 1747), 165.
Bowles, Rev. William Lisle (author of "Sonnets," *b.* 1762; *d.* 1850), 76; 286.
Browning, Elizabeth Barrett, 236 (3); 237 (2); 238 (2); 239 (4).
Browning, Robert, 267; 298; 299 (4); 302 (3).
Bryant, William Cullen (American poet, *b.* 1797), 249 (2); 287.
Buchanan, Robert, 25.
Burns, Robert, 121 (3); 122 (4); 123 (4); 124 (3); 125 (3); 227.
Butler, Samuel, 229; 285.
Byron, George Gordon Noel, Lord, 9; 14; 21; 32; 33; 47; 57; 120; 129 (2); 183; 194 (3); 195 (3); 196 (2); 197 (3); 198 (4); 227; 234; 260 (3); 264 (2); 265 (2); 266; 345.

Campbell, Thomas, 45; 94 (2); 129; 164 (3); 165 (2); 166 (4); 167 (4); 168 (2); 169 (3); 170 (2); 171 (3); 172 (3); 173 (3).
Carew, Thomas, 18.
Chaucer, Geoffrey, 4; 59.
Churchill, Charles (author of the "Rosciad," *b.* 1731; *d.* 1764), 45; 240.
Clough, Arthur Hugh, 115; 241; 242.
Coleridge, Hartley (*b.* 1796; *d.* 1849), 286; 334.
Coleridge, Samuel Taylor, 7; 10; 142 (3); 143 (3); 181; 230; 249; 255; 265 (2); 317; 319; 346.
Collins, William, 50; 98 (2); 99 (3); 100 (4).
Cotton, Charles (*b.* 1630; *d.* 1687), 42; 44; 118; 183; 328.

Cowley, Abraham, 20; 42; 73 (3); 74 (3); 75 (4); 117; 269; 278; 283 (3); 307; 340.
Cowper, William, 13; 24; 29; 43; 53 (2); 59; 76; 104; 105 (4); 106 (4); 107 (3); 108 (3); 109 (3); 110 (4); 111 (3); 112 (4); 113 (4); 114 (3); 116; 263; 271.
Crabbe, Rev. George, 127 (4); 128 (3).
Crashaw, Richard, 77 (3); 78 (3).
Croly, Rev. George (author of "Salathiel," *b.* 1780; *d.* 1860), 46.

Davenant, Sir William, 55; 278; 327; 338.
Davies, Sir John (*b.* 1570; *d.* 1626), 5.
Denham, Sir John, 10; 43; 44; 69 (3); 70 (3).
Dekker, Thomas, 58.
Dobell, Sydney (author of "Balder," *b.* 1824), 18; 137.
Drayton, Michael, 35 (3); 36 (3); 37 (3); 38; 39 (3).
Dryden, John, 5; 7; 10; 15; 21; 22; 32; 47; 76; 79 (4); 80 (4); 81 (3); 82; 115; 229; 232; 247; 322.
Drummond, William (*b.* 1585; *d.* 1649), 16.
Dunbar, William, 7.

Eliot, George, 324.
Elliott, Ebenezer (author of "Corn Law Rhymes," *b.* 1781; *d.* 1842), 241; 242.
Emerson, Ralph Waldo, 118; 327.

Forster, John (Essayist, *b.* 1812), 285.

Gay, John (author of "Fables," &c., *b.* 1688; *d.* 1732), 51; 282.
Goldsmith, Oliver, 5; 101 (3); 102 (3); 103 (4); 104 (2); 126.
Gray, Thomas, 95 (2); 96 (3); 97 (4); 98; 99; 346; 351.

Habington, William (author of "Castara," *b.* 1605; *d.* 1645), 325; 327.
Halleck, Fitz-Green (American poet, *b.* 1795), 232.
Heber, Bishop Reginald (*b.* 1783; *d.* 1826), 316.
Hemans, Mrs. Felicia Dorothea, 25; 58; 129; 178; 209 (4); 210 (3); 211 (3); 212 (3); 213 (2); 214 (2); 215 (3); 216 (3); 217 (3); 218 (3); 219 (3); 220 (4).
Herbert, George, 45; 50 (2).
Herrick, Robert, 20; 43; 119; 230; 234; 240; 261; 267; 279; 339.
Heywood, Thomas, 43.
Holmes, Oliver Wendell (American poet, *b.* 1809), 284.
Holyday, Barton (author of "A Survey of the World," *b.* 1593; *d.* 1661), 326; 341; 349.
Hood, Thomas, 226 (3); 307.
Howitt, Mrs. Mary, 54.
Hunt, Leigh, 23; 179 (4); 258; 329.

Johnson, Samuel, 9; 30; 95 (2).
Jonson, Ben, 6; 48 (4); 49 (4).

Keats, John, 3; 24; 46; 51; 181; 223 (4); 224 (3); 225 (3); 232; 249; 321; 329 (2); 330; 331 (3); 332 (2); 333; 350.
Keble, Rev. John, 45; 54; 280; 281; 318; 319 (2).
King, Henry, 325; 327; 342; 343; 344.
Kingsley, Rev. Charles, 303; 304 (2); 306 (2).

Lamb, Charles (*b.* 1775; *d.* 1834), 280.
Landon, Letitia Elizabeth, 8; 178; 230; 235 (2); 280.
Logan, John (author of "The Cuckoo," *b.* 1748; *d.* 1788), 17.
Longfellow, Henry Wadsworth, 21; 54; 57; 180; 261; 267 (2); 268 (2); 269; 270 (2); 271; 272 (2); 273; 274 (2); 275 (3); 276 (2); 277 (2).
Lytton, Lord, 28; 58; 233; 262 (3); 303.

MacDonald, George, 311 (3); 312 (2); 313 (2); 314 (2); 315 (3).
Mackay, Charles, 55; 266; 300 (2); 301.
Marlowe, Christopher, 17.
Marvell, Andrew, 6.
Massey, Gerald, 250; 316 (3); 317.
Milton, John, 7; 15; 26; 27; 28; 52; 58; 60 (4); 61 (3); 62 (4); 63 (4); 64 (4); 65 (3); 66 (4); 67 (4); 68 (3); 126; 180.
Montgomery, James, 19; 174 (2); 175 (3); 322.
Moore, Thomas, 176 (4); 177 (3); 256; 321; 323.
Morris, William, 335 (3).
Motherwell, William, 221 (3); 222 (3).

Nicoll, Robert (Scotch poet, *b.* 1814; *d.* 1837), 279.
Norris, John (*b.* 1657; *d.* 1711), 59; 165; 231.
Norton, Hon. Mrs. Caroline (author of "The Lady of La Garaye," *b.* 1808), 255.

Otway, Edward (dramatist, *b.* 1651; *d.* 1685), 8.

Parnell, Thomas (author of "The Hermit," *b.* 1679; *d.* 1718), 349.
Patmore, Coventry (author of "The Angel in the House," *b.* 1823), 337 (2).
Pollok, Robert (author of "The Course of Time," *b.* 1799; *d.* 1827), 183.
Pope, Alexander, 31; 42; 50; 51; 87 (3); 88 (3); 89 (3); 90 (3); 91 (3); 116; 248 (3); 286; 328; 336; 347; 348.
Prior, Matthew (author of "Alma," *b.* 1664; *d.* 1721), 12.
Procter, Bryan Waller, 25; 255; 282; 317.

Quarles, Francis (author of "The Emblems," *b.* 1592; *d.* 1644), 22; 116; 240; 273; 341.

Raleigh, Sir Walter, 23; 31; 53.
Rogers, Samuel, 9; 132 (2); 133 (4); 134 (4); 135 (3); 136.

Roscommon, Earl of (*b.* 1633; *d.* 1684), 8.
Rossetti, Christina (author of " The Prince's Progress "), 117.

Scott, Sir Walter, 131 (2); 138 (4); 139(3); 140 (2); 141 (3); 227; 257 (2); 259; 320.
Shakspeare, William, 3; 4; 8; 14; 19; 20 (2); 22; 27 (3); 29; 32; 33; 34; 38 (3); 39; 40 (4); 41 (4); 54; 228; 229; 231 (2); 233 (2); 245 (3); 246 (2); 268; 303; 305; 318; 326; 342.
Shelley, Percy Bysshe, 18; 30; 47; 119; 120; 137; 199 (4); 200 (4); 201 (3); 202 (3); 203 (3); 204 (2); 205 (3); 206 (3); 207 (3); 208 (3); 228; 284.
Sidney, Sir Philip, 46.
Smith, Alexander (author of "Edwin of Deira," *b.* 1830, *d.* 1867), 23; 53; 251 (2); 252 (2); 305; 317.
Southey, Robert, 19; 26; 31; 184 (3); 185 (3); 186 (2); 187 (3); 188 (3); 189 (3); 190 (3); 191 (4); 192 (3); 193 (3); 318.
Southwell, Robert, 55; 56 (3); 117; 244 (3); 325.
Spenser, Edmund, 6; 11; 12 (2); 13 (3); 16; 51; 126 (2); 180; 228; 308; 322; 330; 343; 344.
Swinburne, Algernon Charles (author of "Atalanta in Calydon," &c., *b.* 1843), 250.

Taylor, Henry (author of "Philip Van Artevelde," *b.* 1805), 119; 234.
Tennyson, Alfred, 3; 11; 14; 24; 26; 29 (2); 30; 31; 33; 34; 44; 94; 118; 240; 284; 288 (3); 289 (4); 290 (3); 291 (2); 292 (3); 293 (2); 294; 295 (4); 296 (4); 297 (2); 306; 320; 321.
Thomson, James, 18; 24; 28; 46; 92 (3); 93 (3); 348.
Trench, Richard Chenevix, 294; 298; 301; 305.

Vaughan, Henry (*b.* 1621; *d.* 1695), 234; 337; 338; 339.

Waller, Edmund, 76; 228; 246; 322.
Webster, Thomas (dramatist of the 17th century), 137; 293.
White, Henry Kirke, 181 (2); 182 (3).
Whittier, John Greenleaf, 263; 287; 324.
Wilson, John (author of "Isle of Palms," &c., *b.* 1785; *d.* 1854), 26.
Wither, George (*b.* 1588; *d.* 1667), 340.
Wordsworth, William, 11; 17; 19; 37; 52; 130 (4); 131; 136 (2); 144 (2); 145 (4); 146 (2); 147 (4); 148 (4); 149 (4); 150 (3); 151 (4); 152 (3); 153 (3); 154 (2); 155 (2); 156 (4); 157 (4); 158 (4); 159 (3); 160 (3); 161 (3); 162 (4); 163 (3); 227; 243 (2); 256 (2); 257; 258; 259 (2); 263; 273; 278; 319; 323; 350; 351.
Wotton, Sir Henry, 246.

Young, Edward, 4; 15; 33; 44; 52; 55; 57; 82 (2); 83 (4); 231; 232; 233; 268; 278; 323.

PART · I.

FROM

JOHN BARBOUR, A.D. 1316,

TO

SIR JOHN DENHAM, A.D. 1668.

"A THING OF BEAUTY IS A JOY FOR EVER."—KEATS.

THE CHILDREN'S
TREASURY OF ENGLISH SONG.

THE BATTLE OF BANNOCKBURN.

[EDWARD II. was defeated on the field of Bannockburn, near Stirling, by the Scotch, under Robert Bruce, on the 24th of June 1313. The English lost ten thousand, the Scotch four thousand.—*See J. Hill Burton's "History of Scotland," Tytler's "Lives of the Scottish Worthies," and Dr. Lingard's "History of England."*]

THUS were they bound on either side;
And Englishmen, with mickle pride,
That were intill their avaward*
To the battle that Sir Edward †
Governt and led, held straight their way.
The horse with spurs hastened they,
And prickit upon them sturdily;
And they met them richt hardily.
Sae that, at their assembly there,
Sic a frushing of spears were,
That far away men micht it hear,
That at that meeting forouten ‡ were.
Were steeds stickit mony ane,
And mony gude man borne down and slain. . . .
Their micht men hear mony a dint,
And wappins § upon armours stint.

* Vanguard.   † Sir Edward Bruce.
‡ That were without, or away from the battle.   § Weapons.

"THE POET IN A GOLDEN CLIME WAS BORN."—TENNYSON.

4   THE GOOD PARSON.

And see tumble knichts and steeds,
And mony rich and royal weeds
Defoullit foully under feet.
Some held on loft; some tint* the seat.
A lang time thus fechting they were;
That men nae noise micht hear there;
Men heard noucht but granes and dints,
That flew fire, as men flays on flints.
They foucht ilk ane sae eagerly,
That they made nae noise nor cry,
But dang on other at their micht,
With wappins that were burnist bricht.

[JOHN BARBOUR, Archdeacon of Aberdeen, 1316–1395 (dates doubtful), author of a rhyming historical chronicle, "The Bruce," from which I give an extract in illustration of his style and language.]

—o—

THE GOOD PARSON.†

TRUE good man there was of religion,
 Pious and poor—the parson of a town.
 But rich he was in holy thought and work;
And thereto a right learnèd man; a clerk
That Christ's pure gospel would sincerely preach,
And his parishioners devoutly teach.
Benign he was, and wondrous diligent,
And in adversity full patient,
As proven oft; to all who lacked a friend.
Loth for his tithes to ban or to contend.
At every need much rather was he found
Unto his poor parishioners around

* Held, or kept.
† The reader should compare this passage (from the "Canterbury Pilgrimage") with Dryden's paraphrase.—See *post.*

THE GOOD PARSON.

Of his own substance and his dues to give:
Content on little, for himself, to live.
  Wide was his cure; the houses far asunder,
Yet never failed he, or for rain or thunder,
Whenever sickness or mischance might call,
The most remote to visit, great or small,
And staff in hand, on foot, the storm to brave.
  This noble ensample to his flock he gave,
That first he wrought, and afterward he taught.
The word of life he from the gospel caught;
And well this comment added he thereto—
If that gold rusteth, what shall iron do?
And if the priest be foul on whom we trust,
What wonder if the unlettered layman lust?
And shame it were in him the flock should keep,
To see a sullied shepherd and clean sheep.
For sure a priest the sample ought to give,
By his own cleanness, how his sheep should live.
  He never set his benefice to hire,
Leaving his flock acombered in the mire,
And ran to London cogging at St. Poul's,
To seek himself a chauntery for souls,
Or with a brotherhood to be enrolled;
But dwelt at home, and guarded well his fold,
So that it should not by the wolf miscarry.
He was a shepherd, and no mercenary.
  Tho' holy in himself, and virtuous,
He still to sinful men was mild and piteous:
Not of reproach imperious or malign;
But in his teaching soothing and benign.
To draw them on to heaven, by reason fair
And good example, was his daily care.
But were there one perverse and obstinate,
Were he of lofty or of low estate,

Him would he sharply with reproof astound.
A better priest is nowhere to be found.

[GEOFFREY CHAUCER, the Morning Star of English Poetry, author of the immortal "Canterbury Pilgrimage" (a series of tales supposed to be told by a party of pilgrims on their way to Thomas à-Becket's shrine in Canterbury Cathedral), "The Flower and the Leaf," and other poems, was born in London in 1328, died in 1400.]

———o———

A GARDEN.

[JAMES I. of Scotland was imprisoned in the Tower of London for upwards of eighteen years. The garden which lay before his chamber window, and where he first saw his future queen, Lady Joan Beaufort,* he thus describes:—]

NOW was there made, fast by the Towris wall,
A garden fair; and in the corners set
Ane arbour green, with wandis long and small
Railèd about, and so with treës set
Was all the place, and hawthorn hedges knet,
That lyf was none walking there forbye,†
That might within scarce any wight espy,

So thick the boughis and the leavis green
Beshaded all the alleys that there were,
And mids of every arbour might be seen
The sharpè greenè sweetè juniper,
Growing so fair with branches here and there,
That, as it seemèd to a lyf without,
The boughis spread the arbour all about.

  * "The dusky Tower
  Whence King James beheld his lady
   Sitting in the castle bower;
  Birds around her sweetly singing,
   Fluttering on the kindled spray."—W. E. AYTOUN.
† None of the passers-by could look within.

GOOD GIVING AND ILL GIVING. 7

And on the smallè greenè twistis* sat
The little sweetè nightingale, and sung
So loud and clear, the hymnis consecrat
Of lovis use, now soft, now loud among,
That all the gardens and the wallis rung
Right of their song.

(JAMES I., 1374-1437, author of "The King's Quhair" (or Book), and
"Christis Kirk on the Greene.")

GOOD GIVING AND ILL GIVING.

SOME gives for pride and glory vain,
   Some gives with grudging and with pain,
     Some gives in prattick† for supplie,‡
Some give for twice as gude again:
     In Giving suld Discretion be.

Some gives for thank, and some for threat,
Some gives money, and some gives meat,
   Some gives wordis fair and slie;

* Twigs.   † Trading.   ‡ The *ie* must be pronounced as if written *ee*.

"GIFTS ARE THE BEADS OF MEMORY'S ROSARY."—L. E. L.

GOOD GIVING AND ILL GIVING.

And gifts from some may na man treit :
    In Giving suld Discretion be.

Some is for gift sae lang required,
While that the craver be sae tired,
  That, ere the gift delivered be,
The thank is frustrate and expired :
    In Giving suld Discretion be.

Some in his giving is so large
That all o'erladen is his barge;
  Then vice and prodigalitie
There of his honour does discharge :
    In Giving suld Discretion be.

Some to the rich gives his gear
That might his giftis weel forbear,
  And, though the poor for fault* suld die,
His cry not enters in his ear :
    In Giving suld Discretion be.

Some gives to them can ask and plain,†
Some gives to them can flatter and feign,
  Some gives to men of honestie,
And halds all janglers at disdain :
    In Giving suld Discretion be.

[WILLIAM DUNBAR, of whose "bold music" Langhorne speaks, and whom Thomas Campbell pronounced "a poet of a high order," was born about 1465, died about 1530. His works, of which the principal are "The Thistle and the Rose," and "The Dance of the Seven Deadly Sins," have been edited by David Laing, and criticised, with true appreciation, by Alexander Smith, in his "Dreamthorpe."]

    * Want.   † Lament.

"RICH GIFTS WAX POOR WHEN GIVERS PROVE UNKIND."—SHAKSPEARE.

"THERE IS NO STERNER MORALIST THAN PLEASURE."—BYRON.

THE HAPPY SEASON OF LIFE.

PLEASURE BLENDS WITH EVERY PAIN.

VENOMOUS thorns, that are so sharp and keen,
    Bear flowers, we see, full fresh and fair of hue:
Poison is also put in medicine,
And unto man his health doth oft renew:
The fire that all things eke consumeth clean
    May hurt and heal: then, if that this be true,
I trust some time my *harm* may be my *health*,
Since every woe is joinèd with some wealth.

[Sir THOMAS WYATT, 1503–1542. His poems have been edited by Mr. Robert Bell.]

———o———

THE HAPPY SEASON OF LIFE.

I SAW the little boy,
    In thought how oft that he
    Did wish of God, to 'scape the rod,
A tall young man to be:

The young man eke that feels
    His bones with pains opprest,
How he would be a rich old man,
    To live and lie at rest:

The rich old man that sees
    His end draw on so sore,
How he would be a boy again,
    To live so much the more.

Whereat full oft I smiled,
    To see how all these three,

From boy to man, from man to boy,
  Would chop and change degree:

And musing thus, I think
  The case is very strange,
That man from wealth to live in woe
  Doth ever seek to change.

Thus thoughtful as I lay,
  I saw my withered skin,
How it doth shew my dented thews,
  The flesh was worn so thin;

And eke my toothless chaps,
  The gates of my right way,
That opes and shuts as I do speak,
  Do thus unto me say:

The white and hoarish hairs,
  The messengers of age,
That shew, like lines of true belief,
  That this life doth assuage;

Bids thee lay hand and feel
  Them hanging on thy chin,
The which do write two ages past,
  The third now coming in.

Hang up, therefore, the bit
  Of thy young wanton time,
And thou that therein beaten art
  The happiest life define:

Whereat I sighed, and said,—
  Farewell my wonted joy;

Truss up thy pack and trudge from me,
To every little boy;

And tell them thus from me:
Their time most happy is,
*If to their time they reason had
To know the truth of this.**

[HENRY HOWARD, Earl of Surrey, born 1517, executed by order of Henry VIII., January 21, 1546–7. (See J. A. Froude's "History of England," vol. iv.) He wrote numerous sonnets and love poems, and translated part of Virgil's "Æneid."]

―――o―――

UNA AND THE LION.†

ONE day, nigh weary of the irksome way,
From her unhasty beast she did alight;
And on the grass her dainty limbs did lay
In secret shadow, far from all men's sight;
From her fair head her fillet she undight,
And laid her stole aside: Her angel's face,
As the great eye of heaven, shinèd bright,
And made a sunshine in the shady place; ‡
Did never mortal eye behold such heavenly grace.

It fortunèd,§ out of the thickest wood
A ramping lion rushèd suddenly,
Hunting full greedy after salvage blood:
Soon as the royal virgin he did spy,
With gaping mouth at her ran greedily,

* Youth (so says the poet) would be the happiest season of life, if only the young had sense enough to know it.
† From "The Faery Queen," book i., canto iii.
‡ The reader should note the exquisite beauty of this line.
§ It happened.

UNA AND THE LION.

"FOR OF THE SOUL THE BODY FORM DOTH TAKE;

"IT IS THE MIND THAT MAKETH GOOD OR ILL, THAT MAKETH WRETCH OR HAPPY, RICH OR POOR."—SPENSER.

"AS LAMPS BURN BRIGHTEST WITH UNCONSCIOUS LIGHT, SO MODEST EASE IN BEAUTY SHINES MOST BRIGHT."—PRIOR.

To have at once devoured her tender corse:
But to the prey when as he drew more nigh,
His bloody rage assuagèd with remorse,
And with the sight amazed, forgat his furious force.

Instead thereof he kissed her weary feet,
And licked her lily hands with fawning tongue;
As he her wrongèd innocence did weet.
Oh, how can beauty master the most strong,
And simple truth subdue avenging wrong!
Whose yielded pride and proud submissiön,
Still dreading death when she had markèd long,
Her heart 'gan melt in great compassiön:
And drizzling tears did shed for pure affectiön.

FOR SOUL IS FORM, AND DOTH THE BODY MAKE."—SPENSER.

UNA AND THE LION.

" The lion, lord of every beast in field,"
Quoth she, "his princely puissance doth abate,
And mighty proud to humble weak does yield,
Forgetful of the hungry rage, which late
Him pricked, with pity of my sad estate:
But he, my lion, and my noble lord,
How does he find in cruel heart to hate
Her, that him loved, and ever most adored
As the god of my life? Why hath he me abhorred?"...

The lion would not leave her desolate,
But with her went along, as a strong guard
Of her chaste person, and a faithful mate
Of her sad troubles and misfortunes hard:
Still when she slept he kept both watch and ward;
And when she waked he waited diligent,
With humble service to her will prepared:
From her fair eyes he took commandèment,
And even by her looks conceivèd her intent.*

[EDMUND SPENSER, born at London in 1553, died 1599. Author of "The Faery Queen," "The Shepherd's Calendar," and other poems. "Three things," says Leigh Hunt, "must be conceded to the objectors against this divine poet: first, that he wrote a good deal of allegory; second, that he has a great many superfluous words; third, that he was very fond of alliteration. The answer is, that his genius not only makes amends for all, but overlays them, and makes them beautiful with 'riches fineless.' When acquaintance with him is once begun, he repels none but the anti-poetical. Others may not be able to read him continuously: but more or less, and as an enchanted stream 'to dip into,' they will read him always."]

* Una is the personification of Truth. Mrs. E. B. Browning thus alludes to the above passage:—
"Mindful oft
Of thee, whose genius walketh mild and soft
As *Una's lion, chainless though subdued,
Beside thy purity of womanhood.*"
And Keats speaks of—
" Lovely Una in a leafy nook."

ENCHANTED MUSIC.

EFTSOONS they heard a most melodious sound
Of all that might delight a dainty ear,
Such as, at once, might not on living ground,
Save in this paradise, be heard elsewhere:
Right hard it was for wight which did it hear
To weet * what manner music that might be,
For all that pleasing is to living ear
Was there consorted in one harmony—
Birds, voices, instruments, winds, waters, all agree.

The joyous birds, shrouded in cheerful shade,
Their notes unto the voice attempered sweet:

* Guess.

SLEEP.

Th' angelical, soft, trembling voices made
To th' instruments divine respondence meet;
The silver-sounding instruments did meet
With the base murmur of the water's fall;
The water's fall, with difference discreet,
Now soft, now loud, unto the wind did call;
The gentle warbling wind low answerèd to all.

[EDMUND SPENSER. I give the foregoing passage as a specimen of what Coleridge calls "the indescribable sweetness and fluent projections of his verse."]

MAY.

WHEN came fair May, the fairest maid on ground,
Decked all with dainties of her season's pride,
And throwing flowers out of her lap around:
Upon two brethren's shoulders she did ride,
The Twins of Leda;* which, on either side,
Supported her, like to their sovereign queen.
Lord! how all creatures laughed when her they spied,
And leaped and danced as they had ravished been;
And Cupid's self about her fluttered all in green.

[EDMUND SPENSER. See p. 11.]

SLEEP.

COME, Sleep, O Sleep, the certain knot of peace,
The baiting-place of wit, the balm of woe,
The poor man's wealth, the prisoner's release,
The indifferent judge between the high and low.

* Castor and Pollux, the "Dioscuri" of Greek mythology.

SONGS OF BIRDS.

With shield of proof shield me from out the prease
Of those fierce darts Despair at me doth throw;
Oh, make in me those civil wars to cease:
I will good tribute pay, if thou do so.

[Sir PHILIP SIDNEY, poet, courtier, knight, whose life has been said to be " poetry put in action," was born at Penshurst, in Kent, in 1554, died 1586. His chief works are the " Defence of Poesy," and the prose romance of " The Arcadia."]

———o———

SONGS OF BIRDS.

WHAT bird so sings, yet so does wail?
Oh, 'tis the ravished nightingale.
"Jug, jug, jug, jug, teren"—she cries,
And still her woes at midnight rise.

Brave prick-song! who is't now we hear?
None but the lark so shrill and clear;
Now at heaven's gate she claps her wings,
The morn not waking till she sings.

THE MIND'S PROGRESS.

Hark, hark! with what a pretty note,
Poor robin redbreast tunes his throat;
Hark how the jolly cuckoos sing,
"Cuckoo!" to welcome in the spring!
"Cuckoo!" to welcome in the spring!

[JOHN LYLYE, born in Kent in 1563—some writers say 1554—died in 1601. He was the author of nine plays, and some prose novels, one of which, termed "Euphues," introduced an affected style known as *Euphuism*, ridiculed by Shakspeare, and, let us add, by Sir Walter Scott in his romance of "The Abbot." The foregoing lyric occurs in his drama of "Alexander and Campaspe."]

——o——

THE MIND'S PROGRESS.

NATURE, that formed us of four elements,*
Warring within our breasts for regiment,†
Doth teach us all to have aspiring minds:
Our souls, whose faculties can comprehend -
The wondrous architecture of the world,
And measure every wandering planet's course,
Still climbing after knowledge infinite,
And always moving as the restless spheres,
Will us to wear ourselves, and never rest
Until we reach the ripest fruit of all.

[CHRISTOPHER MARLOWE, one of the greatest of our early dramatists, author of "Tamburlaine the Great"—from which the above extract is taken—"The Jew of Malta," "Life and Death of Dr. Faustus," &c., was born at Canterbury in February 1563-4, and died 1593.]

* Alluding to a fancy of the old philosophers that in man the four elements —earth, air, fire, and water—mingled.
† Supremacy.

SPRING.

SPRING.

PRING, the sweet Spring, is the year's pleasant king;
Then blooms each thing, then maids dance in a ring,
Cold doth not sting, the pretty birds do sing,
    Cuckoo, jug-jug, pu-we, to-witta-woo!

The palm and may make country houses gay,
Lambs frisk and play, the shepherds pipe all day,
And we hear aye birds tune this merry lay,
    Cuckoo, jug-jug, pu-we, to-witta-woo!

The fields breathe sweet, the daisies kiss our feet,
Young lovers meet, old wives a-sunning sit,
In every street these tunes our ears do greet,
    Cuckoo, jug-jug, pu-we, to-witta-woo!
      Spring! the sweet spring!

[T. NASH, an old Elizabethan poet and dramatist, born 1564, died 1601.]

THE HEAVENLY PILGRIMAGE.

GIVE me my scallop-shell of quiet,
　　My staff of faith to walk upon;
My scrip of joy, immortal diet;
　　My bottle of salvation;
My gown of glory, hope's true gage—
And thus I'll take my pilgrimage.

Blood must be my body's 'balmer,
　　No other balm will there be given;
Whilst my soul, like quiet palmer,*
　　Trav'lleth tow'rds the land of Heaven:
O'er the silver mountains
　　Where spring the nectar fountains.

There will I kiss the bowl of bliss,
　　And drink mine everlasting fill
Upon every milken hill.
My soul will be a-dry before;
But after, it will thirst no more.

Then, by that happy blissful day,
　　More peaceful pilgrims I shall see
That have cast off their rags of clay,
　　And walk apparelled fresh like me.

[Sir WALTER RALEIGH, equally famous as poet, historian, courtier, adventurer, and statesman, was born in 1552, beheaded October 29, 1618. It is said that he wrote the poem from which the preceding verses are extracted during his imprisonment in the Tower in 1603, and immediately after he had been sentenced to death by corrupt judges.—*See his Life*, by *P. F. Tytler, Macvey Napier, J. A. St. John, and E. Edwards*.]

* The pilgrims who travelled to the Holy Sepulchre at Jerusalem were sometimes called "palmers," from their carrying a palm-branch in their hats.

THE SOUL'S ERRAND.

O, soul, the body's guest,
  Upon a thankless errand!
Fear not to touch the best;
  The truth shall be thy warrant.
Go, since I needs must die,
And give the world the lie.

Say to the Court—it glows
  And shines like rotten wood;
Say to the Church—it shows
  What's good, and doth no good:
If Court and Church reply,
Then give them both the lie.

Tell Potentates—they live
  Acting by others' action,
Not loved unless they give,
  Not strong but by affection.
If Potentates reply,
Give Potentates the lie.

Tell men of high condition,
  That manage the Estate,
Their purpose is ambition,
  Their practice—only hate.
And if they once reply,
Then give them all the lie.

Tell them that brave it most,
  They beg for more by spending

Who, in their greatest cost,
  Like nothing but commending:
And if they make reply,
Then give them all the lie.

Tell Zeal—it wants devotion;
  Tell Love—it is but lust;
Tell Time—it is but motion;
  Tell Flesh—it is but dust.
And wish them not reply,
For thou must give the lie.

Tell Age—it daily wasteth;
  Tell Honour—how it alters;
Tell Beauty—how she blasteth;
  Tell Favour—how it falters.
And as they shall reply,
Give every one the lie.

Tell Wit—how much it wrangles
  In tickle points of niceness;
Tell Wisdom—she entangles
  Herself in over-wiseness.
And when they do reply,
Straight give them both the lie.

Tell Physic—of her boldness;
  Tell Skill—it is pretention;
Tell Charity—of coldness;
  Tell Law—it is contention.
And as they do reply,
So give them all the lie.

THE SOUL'S ERRAND.

Tell Fortune—of her blindness;
   Tell Nature—of decay;
Tell Friendship—of unkindness;
   Tell Justice—of delay.
And if they will reply,
Then give them all the lie.

Tell Arts—they have no soundness,
   But vary by esteeming;
Tell Schools—they want profoundness,
   And stand so much on seeming.
If Arts and Schools reply,
Give Arts and Schools the lie.

Tell Faith—it's fled the city;
   Tell how the Country erreth;
Tell—Manhood shakes off pity;
   Tell—Virtue least preferreth.
And if they do reply,
Spare not to give the lie.

So when thou hast, as I
   Commanded thee, done blabbing,
Because to give the lie
   Deserves no less than stabbing,
Stab at thee who that will,
No stab the soul can kill.

[Sir WALTER RALEIGH. This has also been ascribed to JOSHUA SYLVESTER, born 1563, died 1618.]

UNDER THE GREENWOOD TREE.

UNDER the greenwood tree
Who loves to lie with me,
And turn his merry note
Unto the sweet bird's throat,
Come hither, come hither, come hither:
Here shall he see
No enemy
But winter and rough weather.

Who doth ambition shun
And loves to live i' the sun,

"THEN COMES THE FATHER OF THE TEMPEST FORTH."—THOMSON.

A WINTER SONG.

> Seeking the food he eats,
>   And pleased with what he gets,
> Come hither, come hither, come hither:
>   Here shall he see
>   No enemy:
>   But winter and rough weather.

[W. SHAKSPEARE, born 1564, died 1616. This exquisite song is sung by *Amiens*, a character in the play of "As You Like It."]

———o———

A WINTER SONG.

WHEN icicles hang by the wall,
　　And Dick the shepherd blows his nail,
And Tom bears logs into the hall,
　　And milk comes frozen home in pail;
When blood is nipped, and ways be foul,
Then nightly sings the staring owl,
　　　　Tuwhoo!
Tuwhit! tuwhoo! a merry note,
While greasy Joan doth keel* the pot.

When all around the wind doth blow,
　　And coughing drowns the parson's saw,
And birds sit brooding in the snow,
　　And Marian's nose looks red and raw;
When roasted crabs hiss in the bowl,
Then nightly sings the staring owl,
　　　　Tuwhoo!
Tuwhit! tuwhoo! a merry note,
While greasy Joan doth keel the pot.

[W. SHAKSPEARE. This song occurs in the play of "Love's Labour's Lost."]

* Skim.

"AH! BITTER CHILL IT WAS; THE OWL, FOR ALL HIS FEATHERS, WAS A-COLD."—KEATS.

"ALONE, AND WARMING HIS FIVE WITS, THE WHITE OWL IN THE BELFRY SITS."—TENNYSON.

"AND WINTER, RULER OF THE INVERTED YEAR."—COWPER.

A SEA DIRGE.

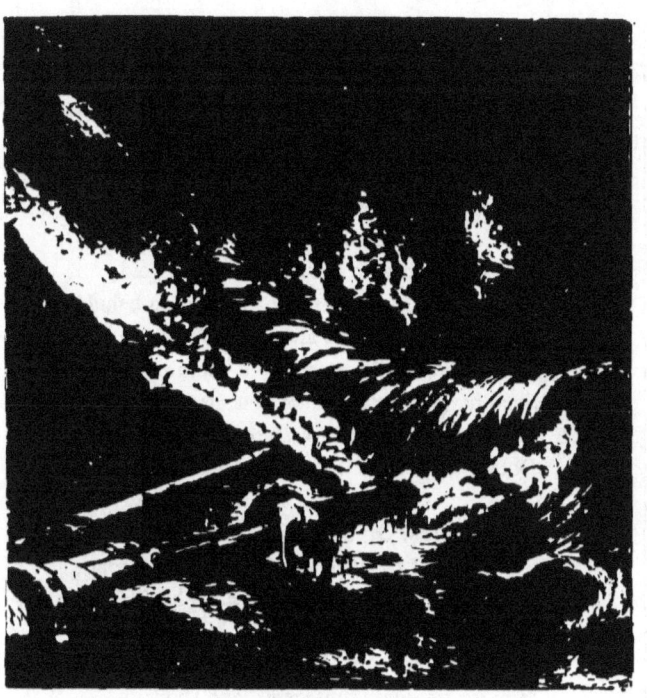

A SEA DIRGE.

FULL fathom five thy father lies:
    Of his bones are coral made;
   Those are pearls that were his eyes:
  Nothing of him that doth fade,
  But doth suffer a sea-change
  Into something rich and strange.
  Sea-nymphs hourly ring his knell:
    Ding, dong!
  Hark! now I hear them,—
    Ding, dong, bell.

[W. SHAKSPEARE. From the play of "The Tempest."]

MUSIC AND MOONLIGHT.

HOW sweet the moonlight sleeps upon this bank!
Here will we sit, and let the sounds of music
Creep in our ears: soft stillness and the night
Become the touches of sweet harmony.
           Look how the floor of heaven
Is thick inlaid with patines* of bright gold;
There's not the smallest orb which thou behold'st
But in his motion like an angel sings,†
Still quiring to the young-eyed cherubins;
Such harmony is in immortal souls;
But whilst this muddy vesture of decay
Doth grossly close it in, we cannot hear it.
           The poet
Did feign that Orpheus drew trees, stones, and floods; ‡
Since nought so stockish, hard, and full of rage,
But music for the time doth change his [its] nature.
The man that hath no music in himself,
Nor is not moved with concord of sweet sounds,
Is fit for treasons, stratagems, and spoils;
The motions § of his spirit are dull as night,
And his affections dark as Erebus:
Let no such man be trusted.

[WILLIAM SHAKSPEARE. From "The Merchant of Venice."]

* Small plates.
† Pythagoras and his followers taught that the planets performed their revolutions to the sound of majestic music—the music of the spheres—which originated in themselves.
‡ According to the Greek mythology, the skill of Orpheus in music was so remarkable that he could make even trees and rocks to follow him. This story is beautifully told by Virgil. A similar fancy is related of Amphion, and has been celebrated by Tennyson in a graceful ballad. Older readers are also referred to Horace, in his "Epis. Ad Pisonem."
§ Conceptions, or ideas.

SUNRISE.

A MORNING SONG.

HARK, hark! the lark at heaven's gate sings,*
    And Phœbus 'gins arise,
    His steeds to water at those springs
On chaliced flowers that lies;
And winking Mary-buds begin
    To ope their golden eyes;
With everything that pretty bin :—
    My lady sweet, arise :
        Arise, arise!

[WILLIAM SHAKSPEARE. From the play of "Cymbeline."]

———o———

MORNING.

FULL many a glorious morning have I seen
    Flatter the mountain-tops with sovereign eye,
    Kissing with golden face the meadows green,
Gilding pale streams with heavenly alchemy;
Anon permit the basest clouds to ride
With ugly rack on his celestial face,
And from the forlorn world his image hide,
Stealing unseen to west with this disgrace.

[WILLIAM SHAKSPEARE. These lines are extracted from Sonnet xxxiii.]

———o———

SUNRISE.

LO! here the gentle lark, weary of rest,
    From his moist cabinet mounts up on high,
    And wakes the morning from whose silver breast
The sun ariseth in its majesty;

* Compare with John Lylye's "Songs of Birds," p. 16.

A FOOL IN THE FOREST.

Who doth the world so gloriously behold,
The cedar-tops and hills seem burnished gold.

[WILLIAM SHAKSPEARE. From the poem of "Venus and Adonis."]

A FOOL IN THE FOREST.

A FOOL, a fool! I met a fool i' the forest,
A motley fool; a miserable world!
As I do live by food, I met a fool;
Who laid him down and basked him in the sun,
And railed on Lady Fortune in good terms,
In good set terms—and yet a motley fool.
"Good morrow, fool," quoth I. "No, sir," quoth he,
"Call me not fool till heaven hath sent me fortune:"

"ENGLAND, WITH ALL THY FAULTS I LOVE THEE STILL."—COWPER.

ENGLAND.

And then he drew a dial from his poke,
And, looking on it with lack-lustre eye,
Says, very wisely, "It is ten o'clock:
Thus may we see," quoth he, "how the world wags:
'Tis but an hour ago since it was nine,
And after one hour more 'twill be eleven;
And so from hour to hour we ripe and ripe,
And then from hour to hour we rot and rot;
And thereby hangs a tale." When I did hear
The motley fool thus moral on the time,
My lungs began to crow like chanticleer,
That fools should be so deep-contemplative,
And I did laugh sans intermission
An hour by his dial. O noble fool!
A worthy fool! Motley's the only wear.

[WILLIAM SHAKSPEARE. This is spoken by *Jaques* in the play of "As You Like It."]

———o———

ENGLAND.

THIS royal throne of kings, this sceptered isle,
This earth of majesty, this seat of Mars,
This other Eden, demi-paradise;
This fortress, built by Nature for herself,
Against infection and the hand of war;
This happy breed of men, this little world;
This precious stone set in a silver sea,
Which serves it in the office of a wall,
Or as a moat defensive to a house,
Against the envy of less happier lands,—
This blessèd spot, this earth, this realm, this England.

[WILLIAM SHAKSPEARE. From the play of "Henry V."]

"LIKE LITTLE BODY WITH A MIGHTY HEART."—SHAKSPEARE.

LIFE.

TO-MORROW, and to-morrow, and to-morrow,
Creeps in this petty pace from day to day
To the last syllable of recorded time;
And all our yesterdays have lighted fools
The way to dusty death. Out, out, brief candle!
Life's but a walking shadow; a poor player,
That struts and frets his hour upon the stage,
And then is heard no more: it is a tale
Told by an idiot, full of sound and fury,
Signifying nothing.

[WILLIAM SHAKSPEARE. From the play of "Macbeth."]

―o―

QUEEN MAB.

OH, then, I see, Queen Mab hath been with you.
She is the fairies' midwife, and she comes
In shape no bigger than an agate-stone
On the fore-finger of an alderman,
Drawn with a team of little atomies
Athwart men's noses as they lie asleep:
Her waggon-spokes made of long-spinners' legs;
The cover, of the wings of grasshoppers;
The traces, of the smallest spider's web;
The collars, of the moonshine's watery beams;
Her whip, of cricket's bone; the lash, of film;
Her waggoner, a small gray-coated gnat,
Not half so big as a round little worm
Pricked from the lazy finger of a maid;

ARIEL'S SONG.

Her chariot is an empty hazel-nut,
Made by the joiner squirrel, or old grub,
Time out of mind the fairies' coach-maker.
And in this state she gallops night by night
Through lovers' brains, and then they dream of love!
O'er courtiers' knees, that dream on courtsies straight;
O'er lawyers' fingers, who straight dream on fees;
O'er ladies' lips, who straight on kisses dream;
Which oft the angry Mab with blisters plagues,
Because their breaths with sweetmeats tainted are.
Sometime she gallops o'er a courtier's nose,
And then dreams he of smelling out a suit;
And sometime comes she with a tithe-pig's tail,
Tickling a parson's nose as a' lies asleep,
Then dreams he of another benefice;
Sometime she driveth o'er a soldier's neck,
And then dreams he of cutting foreign throats,
Of breaches, ambuscadoes, Spanish blades,
Of healths five fathom deep; and then anon
Drums in his ear; at which he starts and wakes,
And, being thus frighted, swears a prayer or two
And sleeps again.
[WILLIAM SHAKSPEARE. From "Romeo and Juliet."]

———o———

ARIEL'S SONG.

COME unto these yellow sands,
    And then take hands:
Courtsied when you have and kissed,
    (The wild waves whist,*)
Foot it featly here and there;
And, sweet sprites, the burden bear.

    * Hushed, silent.

"THERE IS SOCIETY, WHERE NONE INTRUDES,

A PRECIPICE.

Hark, hark!
Bow, wow.
The watch-dogs bark:
Bow, wow.
Hark, hark! I hear
The strain of strutting chanticleer
Cry, Cock-a-doodle-dow.

[WILLIAM SHAKSPEARE. From "The Tempest."]

---o---

A PRECIPICE.

HOW fearful
And dizzy 'tis, to cast one's eyes so low!
The crows and choughs that wing the midway air
Scarce show so gross as beetles: half-way down
Hangs one that gathers samphire—dreadful trade!
Methinks he seems no bigger than his head:
The fishermen, that walk upon the beach,
Appear like mice; and yon tall anchoring bark,
Diminished to her cock; her cock, a buoy

BY THE DEEP SEA, AND MUSIC IN ITS ROAR."—BYRON.

"FROM THE DREAD SUMMIT OF THIS CHALKY BOURN LOOK UP A-HEIGHT."—SHAKSPEARE.

"AND SEES THE OCEAN AT SO GREAT A DISTANCE, IT LOOKS AS IF THE SKIES WERE SUNK BENEATH HIM."—DRYDEN.

Almost too small for sight: the murmuring surge,
That on the unnumbered idle pebbles chafes,
Cannot be heard so high.—I'll look no more,
Lest my brain turn, and the deficient sight
Topple down headlong.

[WILLIAM SHAKSPEARE. From "King Lear." The locality described is generally identified with Shakspeare's Cliff, Dover.]

WHAT TIME DOES.

IME'S glory is to calm contending kings;
    To unmask falsehood and bring truth to light;
    To stamp the seal of time in agèd things;
To wake the morn, and sentinel the night;
To wrong the wronger till he render right;
    To ruinate proud buildings with thy hours,
    And smear with dust their glittering golden towers;

To fill with worm-holes stately monuments;
To feed oblivion with decay of things;
To blot old books, and alter their contents;
To pluck the quills from ancient ravens' wings;
To dry the old oak's sap, and cherish springs;
    To spoil antiquities of hammered steel,
    And turn the giddy round of Fortune's wheel.

[WILLIAM SHAKSPEARE. From "Lucrece."]

A FUNERAL SONG.

EAR no more the heat o' the sun,
    Nor the furious winter's rages;
Thou thy worldly task hast done,
    Home art gone, and ta'en thy wages.

THE FAIRY PALACE.

Fear no more the frown o' the great,
   Thou art past the tyrant's stroke;
Care no more to clothe and eat;
   To thee the reed is as the oak.

Fear no more the lightning-flash,
   Nor the all-dreaded thunder-stone;
Fear not slander, censure rash:
   Thou hast finished joy and moan.

[WILLIAM SHAKSPEARE. From "Cymbeline."]

---o---

THE FAIRY PALACE.

THIS palace standeth in the air,
   By necromancy placèd there,
   That it no tempests needs to fear,
      Which way soe'er it blow it:
And somewhat southward tow'rd the noon,
Whence lies a way up to the moon,
And thence the Fairy can as soon
   Pass to the earth below it.

The walls of spiders' legs are made,
Well morticèd and finely laid,
He was the master of his trade,
   It curiously that builded:
The windows of the eyes of cats,
And for the roof, instead of slats,
Is covered with the skins of bats,
   With moonshine that are gilded.

Hence Oberon, him sport to make
(Their rest when weary mortals take,
And none but only fairies wake),
  Descendeth for his pleasure:
And Mab, his merry queen, by night
Bestrides young folks that lie upright
(In elder times the mare that hight),*
  Which plagues them out of measure.

[MICHAEL DRAYTON, born at Atherston, in Warwickshire, in 1563, died 1631. In his epitaph by Quarles he is styled "a memorable poet of his age." His works were, "The Shepherd's Garland," "Barons' Wars," "England's Heroical Epistles," "The Poly-Olbion," and "Nymphidia, the Court of Fayrie," from which the foregoing extract is taken.]

---0---

THE FAIRY QUEEN'S CHARIOT.

HER chariot ready strait is made,
  Each thing therein is fitting laid,
  That she by nothing might be stayed,
    For nought must her be letting: †
Four nimble gnats the horses were,
Their harnesses of gossamer,
Fly Cranion, her charioteer,
  Upon the coach-box getting.

Her chariot of a snail's fine shell,
Which for the colours did excel,
The fair Queen Mab becoming well,
  So lovely was the limning: ‡
The seat the soft wool of the bee,
The cover (gallantly to see)

* *Hight*—that is, called. The mare alluded to is the unpleasant nocturnal visitor known as the nightmare.
† *Letting*—that is, impeding, hindering.
‡ *Limning*—that is, painting.

THE FAIRY QUEEN'S CHARIOT.

The wing of a pied* butterflie,—
I trow, 'twas simple trimming.

The wheels composed of crickets' bones,
And daintily made for the nonce,†
For fear of rattling on the stones
   With thistle-down they shod it:
For all her maidens much did fear,
If Oberon had chanced to hear
That Mab his queen should have been there,
   He would not have abode it.

She mounts her chariot with a trice,
Nor would she stay for no advice
Until her maids, that were so nice,
   To wait on her were fitted:
But ran herself away alone;
Which when they heard, there was not one
But hasted after to be gone,
   As she had been diswitted.

Hop, and Mop, and Drop so clear,
Pip, and Trip, and Skip, that were
To Mab, their sovereign dear,
   Her special maids of honour:
Fib, and Tib, and Pinck, and Pin,
Tick, and Quick, and Fill, and Fin,
Tit, and Nit, and Wap, and Win,
   The train that wait upon her.

Upon a grasshopper they got,
And what with amble and with trot,

* *Pied*—that is, parti-coloured.
† Pronounced as if spelt *nones*—that is, for the occasion.

For hedge nor ditch they sparèd not,
But after her they hie them :
A cobweb over them they throw,
To shield the wind if it should blow ;
Themselves they wisely could bestow,
Lest any should espy them.

[MICHAEL DRAYTON. See p. 35.]

———o———

THE BATTLE OF AGINCOURT.

[This great battle was fought on the 25th of October 1415, by an English army of 8000 men under Henry V., against a French force of between 50,000 and 60,000 under the Dukes of Orleans and Bourbon, and the Constable D'Albret.]

FAIR stood the wind for France,
When we our sails advance,
Nor now to prove our chance
Longer will tarry;
But, putting to the main,
At Kaux, the mouth of Seine,
With all his martial train,
Landed King Harry.

And taking many a fort,
Furnished in warlike sort,
Marched towards Agincourt
In happy hour ;
Skirmishing day by day
With those that stopped his way,
Where the French gen'ral lay
With all his power ;

Which, in his height of pride,
King Henry to deride,

THE BATTLE OF AGINCOURT.

His ransom to provide
   To the King sending;
Which he neglects the while,
As from a nation vile,
But, with an angry smile,
   Their fall portending.

And, turning to his men,
Quoth our brave Henry then,—
"Though they to one be ten,
   Be not amazèd;
Yet have we well begun,
Battles so bravely won
Have ever to the sun
   By fame been raisèd.

And for myself," quoth he,
"This my full rest shall be;
England, ne'er mourn for me,
   Nor more esteem me:
Victor I will remain,
Or on this earth be slain,
Never shall she sustain
   Loss to redeem me.

Poictiers and Cressy tell,
When most their pride did swell,
Under our swords they fell;
   No less our skill is,
Than when our grandsire great,
Claiming the regal seat,
By many a warlike feat,
   Lopped the French lilies."

The Duke of York so dread,
The eager vaward led;
With the main Henry sped,
   Amongst his henchmen;
Excester had the rear,
A braver man not there;
O Lord, how hot they were
   On the false Frenchmen!

They now to fight are gone,—
Armour on armour shone,
Drum now to drum did groan,
   To hear was wonder;
That with the cries they make,
The very earth did shake,
Trumpet to trumpet spake,
   Thunder to thunder.

Well it thine age became,
O noble Erpingham,
Which did the signal aim
   To our hid forces;
When from a meadow by,
Like a storm suddenly,
The English archery
   Struck the French horses.

With Spanish yew so strong,
Arrows a cloth-yard long,
That like to serpents stung,
   Piercing the weather;
None from his fellow starts,
But, playing manly parts,
And like true English hearts,
   Stuck close together.

"ENGLAND NE'ER LOST A KING OF SO MUCH WORTH."—SHAKSPEARE.

THE BATTLE OF AGINCOURT.

When down their bows they threw,
And forth their bilbows drew,
And on the French they flew,
  Not one was tardy;
Arms were from shoulders sent,
Scalps to the teeth were rent,
Down the French peasants went—
  Our men were hardy.

This while our noble king,
His broadsword brandishing,

"VIRTUE HE HAD, DESERVING TO COMMAND."—SHAKSPEARE.

THE BATTLE OF AGINCOURT.

Down the French host did ding,
As to o'erwhelm it;
And many a deep wound lent,
His arms with blood besprent,
And many a cruel dent
Bruisèd his helmet.

Glo'ster, that duke so good,
Next of the royal blood,
For famous England stood,
With his brave brother,
Clarence, in steel so bright,
Though but a maiden knight,
Yet in that furious fight
Scarce such another.

Warwick in blood did wade,
Oxford the foe invade,
And cruel slaughter made,
Still as they ran up;
Suffolk his axe did ply,
Beaumont and Willoughby
Bare them right doughtily,
Ferrers and Fanhope.

Upon Saint Crispin's day
Fought was this noble fray,
Which fame did not delay
To England to carry;
Oh, when shall Englishmen
With such acts fill a pen,
Or England breed again
Such a King Harry?

[MICHAEL DRAYTON.]

THE HAPPY HEART.

ART thou poor, yet hast thou golden slumbers?
O sweet content!
Art thou rich, yet is thy mind perplexèd?
O punishment!
Dost thou laugh to see how fools are vexèd
To add to golden numbers, golden numbers?
O sweet content, O sweet, O sweet content!
   Work apace, apace, apace, apace;
   Honest labour bears a lovely face;
Then hey nonny nonny, hey nonny nonny!

Canst drink the waters of the crispèd spring?
O sweet content!
Swimm'st thou in wealth, yet sink'st in thine own tears?
O punishment!
Then he that patiently want's burden bears
No burden bears, but is a king, a king!
O sweet content, O sweet, O sweet content!
   Work apace, apace, apace, apace;
   Honest labour bears a lovely face;
Then hey nonny nonny, hey nonny nonny!

[T. DEKKER, a dramatist of high merit born 1570, died about 1638-39.]

———o———

HERE AND THERE.

FOR who did ever yet in honour, wealth,
   Or pleasure of the sense, contentment find?
Who ever ceased to wish when he had health,
   Or, having wisdom, was not vexed in mind?

"CONTENT'S A KINGDOM, AND I WEAR THE CROWN."—HEYWOOD.

THE DAWN. 43

Then, as a bee which among weeds doth fall,
   Which seem sweet flowers with lustre fresh and gay,
She lights on that, and this, and tasteth all,
   But, pleased with none, doth rise and soar away.

So, when the soul finds here no true content,
   And, like Noah's dove, can no sure footing take,
She doth return from whence she first was sent,
   And flies to him that first her wings did make.

[Sir JOHN DAVIES, author of a philosophical poem, "On the Soul of Man," wrote in numbers (says Southey) which, for precision and clearness, and felicity and strength, have never been surpassed. Born 1570, died 1626.]

THE DAWN.

SEE, the day begins to break,
   And the light shoots like a streak
Of subtle fire. The wind blows cold,
While the morning doth unfold.

[JOHN FLETCHER, dramatist, born at Rye, 1579, died 1625. I think his finest work is "The Faithful Shepherdess," whence these lines are taken.]

"WHERE WILL AT EASE, AND HAPPY, LIVE CONTENT."—DENHAM.

SELF-RELIANCE.

MAN is his own star, and the soul that can
  Render an honest and a perfect man,
  Commands all light, all influence, all fate;
Nothing to him falls early, or too late.
Our acts our angels are, or good or ill,
Our fated shadows that walk by us still.

[JOHN FLETCHER.]

A HAPPY LIFE.

HOW happy is he born and taught
    That serveth not another's will;
  Whose armour is his honest thought,
    And simple truth his utmost skill!

Whose passions not his masters are,
    Whose soul is still prepared for death;
  Not tied unto the world with care
    Of public fame, or private breath;

Who envies none that chance doth raise
    Or vice; who never understood
  How deepest wounds are given by praise;
    Nor rules of state, but rules of good:

Who hath his life from rumours freed,
    Whose conscience is his strong retreat;
  Whose state can neither flatterers feed,
    Nor ruin make accusers great;

"I MADE A POSY WHILE THE DAY RAN BY."—HERBERT.

STARS AND FLOWERS.

Who God doth late and early pray
More of his grace than gifts to lend;
And entertains the harmless day
With a well-chosen book or friend;

—This man is freed from servile bands
Of hope to rise, or fear to fall;
Lord of himself, though not of lands;
And having nothing, yet hath all.

[Sir H. WOTTON, poet, statesman, and diplomatist, born 1568, died 1639.]

———o———

STARS AND FLOWERS.

Zephyrus. COME forth, come forth, the gentle Spring,
And carry the glad news I bring
To Earth, our common mother:
It is decreed by all the gods,
That heaven of earth shall have no odds,
But one shall love another.

Their glories they shall mutual make,
Earth look on heaven for heaven's sake,
Their honours shall be even:
All emulation cease, and jars—
Jove will have Earth to have her stars
And lights, no less than Heaven.

Spring. It is already done, in flowers
As fresh and new as are the hours,
By warmth of yonder sun:

"SWEET NURSLINGS OF THE VERNAL SKIES."—KEBLE.

"WITH HOW SAD STEPS, O MOON, THOU CLIMB'ST THE SKIES."—SIDNEY.

TO CYNTHIA—THE MOON.

But will be multiplied on us,
If from the breath of Zephyrus
Like favour we have won.

[BEN JONSON, second only to Shakspeare among English dramatists, was born in 1574, died in 1637. Besides his eighteen plays, he wrote several masques—from one of which, "Chloridia," the above extract is taken—and miscellaneous poems, collected under the titles of "The Forest," and "Underwoods."]

TO CYNTHIA—THE MOON.

QUEEN and Huntress, chaste and fair,
Now the sun is laid asleep,
Seated in thy silver chair,
State in wonted manner keep:
Hesperus entreats thy light,
Goddess excellently bright.

Earth, let not thy envious shade
Dare itself to interpose;

"HOW LIKE A QUEEN COMES FORTH THE LOVELY MOON!"—CROLY.

Cynthia's shining orb was made
    Heaven to clear, when day did close :
      Bless us then with wishèd sight,
      Goddess excellently bright.

Lay thy bow of pearl apart,
    And thy crystal shining quiver;
Give unto the flying hart
    Space to breathe, how short soever :
      Thou that mak'st a day of night,
      Goddess excellently bright.

[BEN JONSON. From the play of "Cynthia's Revels."]

LIFE AND DEATH.

THE ports of death are sins; of life, good deeds;
    Through which our merit leads us to our meeds.
    How wilful blind is he, then, that would stray,
And hath it in his powers to make his way!
This world death's region is, the other life's;
And here it should be one of our first strifes
So to front death, as men might judge us past it :
For good men but *see* death, the wicked *taste* it.

[BEN JONSON. From the "Epigrams."]

ROBIN GOODFELLOW.

MORE swift than lightning can I fly
    About this aëry welkin soon,
    And in a minute's space descry
    Each thing that's done below the moon :

There's not a hag
   Or ghost shall wag,
Or cry, "'Ware goblin!" where I go;
   But Robin I
   Their feats will spy,
And send them home with ho! ho! ho!

Where'er such wanderers I meet,
   As from their night sports they trudge home,
With counterfeiting voice I greet,
   And call on them with me to roam.
      Through woods, through lakes,
      Through bogs, through brakes;
Or else unseen with them I go
      All in the nick,
      To play some trick,
And frolic it with ho! ho! ho!

Sometimes I meet them like a man,
   Sometimes an ox, sometimes a hound;
And to a horse I turn me can,
   And trip and trot about them round;
      But if, to ride,
      My back they stride,
More swift than any wind I go;
      O'er hedge and lands,
      Through pools and ponds,
I whirry, laughing, ho! ho! ho!

When lads and lasses merry be
   With possets and rich juncates fine,
Unseen of all the company,
   I eat their cakes and sip their wine.

"STAND FORTH, BRIGHT FAYS, AND TUNE YOUR LAYS."—BEN JONSON.

ROBIN GOODFELLOW.

"HE THAT'S COMPELLED TO GOODNESS MAY BE GOOD, BUT 'TIS BUT FOR THAT FIT."—BEN JONSON.

"HE THAT IS AFFECTED WITH THE LEAST INJURY IS LESS THAN IT."—BEN JONSON.

  And to make sport,
   I puff and snort,
And out the candle I do blow;
  And maids I kiss,—
   They shriek, "Who's this?"
I answer nought but ho! ho! ho!

Yet now and then, the maids to please,
 At midnight I card up their wool;
And while they sleep and take their ease,
 With wheel to threads their flax I pull.
   I grind at will
   Their malt up still,
I dress their hemp and spin their tow;
   If any walk,
   And would me talk,
I wend me, laughing, ho! ho! ho!

The men do traps and engines set
 In loopholes where the vermines creep,
Who from their fields and houses get
 Their ducks and geese, and lambs and sheep;
   I spy the gin
   And enter in,
And seem a vermin taken so:
   But when they there
   Approach me near,
I leap out laughing, ho! ho! ho!

   [Attributed to BEN JONSON.]

"I MUST GO DANCE ABOUT THE FOREST NOW."—BEN JONSON.

A VIRTUOUS SOUL.

SWEET Day! so cool, so calm, so bright,
    The bridal of the earth and sky;
    The dews shall weep thy fall to-night,
        For thou must die.

Sweet Rose! when here, angry and brave,
Bids the rash gazer wipe his eye;
Thy root is ever in its grave,
    And thou must die.

Sweet Spring! full of sweet days and roses,
A box where sweets compacted lie,
Thy music shows ye have your closes,
    And all must die.

Only a sweet and virtuous soul,
Like seasoned timber, never gives;
But, though the whole world turn to coal,
    Then chiefly lives.

[GEORGE HERBERT, born at Montgomery Castle, in Wales, in 1593, author of "The Temple, or Sacred Poems and Private Ejaculations," died at Bemerton, where he was rector, in 1632.]

WOMAN'S TRUE BEAUTY.

HE that loves a rosy cheek,
    Or a coral lip admires,
    Or from star-like eyes doth seek
    Fuel to maintain his fires;
As old Time makes these decay,
So his flames must waste away.

"NATURE IN VARIOUS MOULDS HAS BEAUTY CAST."—GAY.

IN PRAISE OF SOLITUDE.

> But a smooth and stedfast mind,
>   Gentle thoughts and calm desires;
> Hearts, with equal love combined,
>   Kindle never-dying fires.
> Where these are not, I despise
> Lovely cheeks, or lips, or eyes.

[THOMAS CAREW, the author of many elegant songs and ballads, died about 1639.]

A LAND DIRGE.*

ALL for a robin redbreast, and the wren,
  Since o'er shady groves they hover,
  And with leaves of flowers do cover
The friendless bodies of unburied men.
Call unto his funeral dole
The ant, the field-mouse, and the mole,
To rear him hillocks that shall keep him warm.
And when gay tombs are robbed, sustain no harm:
But keep the wolf far thence, that's foe to men,
For with his nails he'll dig them up again.†

[J. WEBSTER, an old dramatist, born 1585, died 1654. The Dirge is taken from his tragedy of "The Duchess of Malfy."]

IN PRAISE OF SOLITUDE.

THRICE happy he who by some shady grove,
  Far from the clamorous world, doth live his own.‡
Thou solitary, who is not alone,
But doth converse with that Eternal Love.

* The reader should compare this with Shakspeare's "Sea Dirge."
† Alluding to the wolf's habit of plundering the graves of the dead.
‡ That is, lives on his own resources.

"'TIS NOT A LIP, OR EYE, WE BEAUTY CALL."—POPE.

"FOR SOLITUDE SOMETIMES IS BEST SOCIETY,

IN PRAISE OF SOLITUDE.

"HOW DIVINE TO ROAM AT LARGE AMONG UNPEOPLED GLENS!"—WILLIAM WORDSWORTH.

"FOR LOST TO VIRTUE THEY, WHO THINK IT SOLITUDE TO BE ALONE."—EDWARD YOUNG.

Oh, how more sweet is bird's harmonious moan,
   Or the hoarse sobbings of the widowed dove,
Than those smooth whisperings near a prince's throne
   Which good make doubtful, do the ill approve!
Oh, how more sweet is zephyr's wholesome breath,
   And sighs embalmed which new-born flowers unfold,
Than that applause vain honour doth bequeath!
   How sweet are streams to poisons drunk in gold!

AND SHORT RETIREMENT URGES SWEET RETURN."—MILTON.

"GOD MADE THE COUNTRY, AND MAN MADE THE TOWN."—COWPER.

A LANDSCAPE.

The world is full of horrors, troubles, slights:
Woods' harmless shades have only true delights.

[Sir WILLIAM DAVENANT, a Scotch poet, born in 1605, died in 1668. Author of "The Flowers of Zion," "Wandering Muses," and numerous sonnets, epigrams, and lyrics.]

A LANDSCAPE.

IT was a roundel seated on a plain,
That stood as sentinel unto the main,
Environed round with trees and many an arbour,
Wherein melodious birds did nightly harbour:

"THE LIGHTS AND SHADOWS ON THE LANDSCAPE'S FACE."—A. SMITH.

TO BLOSSOMS.

And on a bough within the quick'ning spring,
Would be a-teaching of their young to sing;
Whose pleasing notes the tirèd swain have made
To steal a nap at noontide in the shade.
Nature herself did there in triumph ride,
And made that place the ground of all her pride.
Whose various show'rs deceived the rasher eye,
In taking them for curious tapestry.
A silver spring forth of a rock did fall,
That in a drought did serve to water all.
Upon the edges of a grassy bank,
A tuft of trees grew circling in a rank,
As if they seemed their sports* to gaze upon,
Or stood as guard against the wind and sun :
So fair, so fresh, so green, so sweet a ground,
The piercing eyes of heaven yet never found.

[WILLIAM BROWNE, a descriptive poet of great excellence, born at Tavistock in 1590, died about 1645. His principal works are, "Britannia's Pastorals"—from which the foregoing extract is taken—"The Shepherd's Pipe," and "The Inner Temple Masque."]

TO BLOSSOMS.

FAIR pledges of a fruitful tree,
  Why do you fall so fast?
  Your date is not so past
But you may stay yet here awhile,
  To blush and gently smile,
    And go at last.

What! were ye born to be
  An hour or half's delight
  And so to bid good night?

* The sports of some merry maidens who made this their place of meeting.

'Tis pity Nature brought ye forth
Merely to show your worth,
And lose you quite.

But you are lovely leaves, where we
May read how soon things have
Their end, though ne'er so brave:
And after they have shown their pride,
Like you, awhile, they glide
Into the grave.

[ROBERT HERRICK, one of the most beautiful of English lyrical poets, born in London, 1591, died at the vicarage of Dean Prior, Devonshire, 1674; wrote "Noble Numbers," and the "Hesperides, or Works both Human and Divine." His songs are distinguished by their happy expression and graceful flow.]

---o---

A WARNING AGAINST PROCRASTINATION.

GATHER ye rosebuds while ye may,
    Old Time is still a-flying;
And this same flower that smiles to-day,
To-morrow will be dying.

The glorious lamp of heaven, the sun,
    The higher he's a-getting,
The sooner will his race be run,
    And nearer he's to setting.

That age is best which is the first,
    When youth and blood are warmer;
But being spent, the worse, and worst
    Times, still succeed the former.

[ROBERT HERRICK. From the "Hesperides."]

TO DAFFODILS.

FAIR daffodils, we weep to see
    You haste away so soon;
As yet the early rising sun
Has not attained his noon:
    Stay, stay,
Until the hastening day
    Has run
But to the even song;
And having prayed together, we
Will go with you along.

We have short time to stay, as you;
    We have as short a spring;
As quick a growth to meet decay
As you, or any thing:
    We die
As your hours do; and dry
    Away
Like to the summer's rain,
Or as the pearls of morning dew,
Ne'er to be found again.

[ROBERT HERRICK. From the "Hesperides."]

SIC VITA—SUCH IS LIFE.

LIKE the falling of a star,
    Or as the flights of eagles are;
    Or like the fresh spring's gaudy hue,
Or silver drops of morning dew;

Or like a wind that chafes the flood,
Or bubbles which on water stood :
Even such is man—whose borrowed light
Is straight called in, and paid to-night.
The wind blows out, the bubble dies;
The spring entombed in autumn lies;
The dew dries up, the star is shot;
The flight is past—and man forgot.

[HENRY KING, Bishop of Chichester, a religious poet of great sweetness, born 1591, died October 1, 1669.]

DEATH THE LEVELLER.

THE glories of our blood and state
    Are shadows, not substantial things;
There is no armour against fate;
Death lays his icy hand on kings :
    Sceptre and crown
    Must tumble down,
And in the dust be equal made
With the poor crooked scythe and spade.

Some men with swords may reap the field,
    And plant fresh laurels where they kill :
But their strong nerves at last must yield;
    They tame but one another still :
    Early or late
    They stoop to fate,
And must give up their murmuring breath
When they, pale captives, creep to death.

The garlands wither on your brow;
    Then boast no more your mighty deeds;

"THOU HAST ALL SEASONS FOR THINE OWN, O DEATH!"—MRS. HEMANS.

DEATH THE LEVELLER.

Upon Death's purple altar now
  See where the victor-victim bleeds;
    Your heads must come
    To the cold tomb;
  Only the actions of the just
  Smell sweet, and blossom in their dust.

[J. SHIRLEY, a dramatist, born 1596, died 1666. The song which we extract from the play of "The Contention of Ajax and Ulysses," is said to have been a great favourite with Charles II.]

"THERE'S A LEAN FELLOW BEATS ALL CONQUERORS."—DEKKER.

TRUE FREEDOM IS IN THE MIND.

STONE walls do not a prison make,
    Nor iron bars a cage;
    Minds innocent and quiet take
    That for a hermitage:
If I have freedom in my love,
    And in my soul am free;
Angels alone, that soar above,
    Enjoy such liberty.

[RICHARD LOVELACE, a cavalier-poet, born 1618, died 1658. His poetical works consist of odes, sonnets, and songs.]

———o———

L'ALLEGRO.

STRAIGHT mine eye hath caught new pleasures,
    While the landscape round it measures:
    Russet lawns and fallow gray,
    Where the nibbling flocks do stray;
Mountains, on whose barren breast
The lab'ring clouds do often rest;
Meadows trim with daisies pied,
Shallow brooks and rivers wide;
Towers and battlements it sees
Bosomed high in tufted trees,
Where perhaps some beauty lies,
The cynosure of neighb'ring eyes.
    Hard by a cottage chimney smokes,
From betwixt two aged oaks,
Where Corydon and Thyrsis, met,
Are at their sav'ry dinner set
Of herbs, and other country messes,
Which the neat-handed Phillis dresses:

And then in haste her bower she leaves,
With Thestylis to bind the sheaves;
Or, if the earlier season lead,
To the tanned haycock in the mead.
    Sometimes, with secure delight,
The upland hamlets will invite,
When the merry bells ring round,
And the jocund rebecks sound
To many a youth and many a maid,
Dancing in the chequered shade;
And young and old come forth to play
On a sunshine holiday.
Till the livelong daylight fail;
Then to the spicy nut-brown ale,
With stories told of many a feat,
How fairy Mab the juncates ate;
She was pinched and pulled, she said,
And he, by friar's lantern led;
Tells how the grudging goblin sweat
To earn his cream-bowl duly set,
When in one night, ere glimpse of morn,
His shadowy flail had threshed the corn,
That ten day-labourers could not end;
Then lies him down the lubber fiend,
And, stretched out all the chimney's length,
Basks at the fire his hairy strength,
And, cropful, out of doors he flings,
Ere the first cock his matin rings.
Thus done the tales, to bed they creep,
By whisp'ring winds soon lulled asleep.
    Towered cities please us then,
And the busy hum of men,
Where throngs of knights and barons bold,
In weeds of Peace high triumphs hold,

L'ALLEGRO.

With store of ladies, whose bright eyes
Rain influence, and judge the prize
Of wit or arms, while both contend
To win her grace, whom all commend.
There let Hymen oft appear
In saffron robe, with taper clear,
And Pomp, and Feast, and Revelry,
With Mask and antique Pageantry;
Such sights as youthful poets dream
On summer eves by haunted stream.
Then to the well-trod stage anon,
If Jonson's learnèd sock be on,
Or sweetest Shakspeare, Fancy's child,
Warble his native wood-notes wild.
  And ever against eating cares,
Lap me in soft Lydian airs,
Married to immortal verse,
Such as the meeting soul may pierce,
In notes, with many a winding bout
Of linkèd sweetness long drawn out,
With wanton heed, and giddy cunning;
The melting voice through mazes running,
Untwisting all the chains that tie
The hidden soul of harmony;
That Orpheus' self may heave his head
From golden slumber on a bed
Of heaped Elysian flowers, and hear
Such strains as would have won the ear
Of Pluto, to have quite set free
His half-regained Eurydice.

[JOHN MILTON, 1608–1674, our greatest epic poet and one of our finest prose writers, author of "Paradise Lost," "Paradise Regained," "Comus," "Samson Agonistes," "Areopagitica," and other noble works in prose and poetry. We extract the above from the fine pastoral of "L'Allegro."]

ON SHAKSPEARE.

WHAT needs my Shakspeare for his honoured bones,
　　The labour of an age in pilèd stones?
　　Or that his hallowed reliques should be hid
Under a star-y-pointing pyramid?
Dear son of Memory, great heir of Fame!
What need'st thou such weak witness of thy name?
Thou, in our wonder and astonishment,
Hast built thyself a live-long monument.
For whilst, to the shame of slow-endeavouring Art,
Thy easy numbers flow; and that each heart
Hath, from the leaves of thy unvalued * book,
Those Delphic† lines with deep impression took;
Then thou, our fancy of itself bereaving,
Dost make us marble with too much conceiving;
And, so sepúlchred, in such pomp dost lie,
That kings for such a tomb would wish to die.

[JOHN MILTON. Written in 1630.]

―――o―――

ON MAY MORNING.

NOW the bright morning star, day's harbinger,
　　Comes dancing from the east, and leads with her
　　The flow'ry May, who from her green lap throws
The yellow cowslip and the pale primrose.
　　Hail, beauteous May, that doth inspire
　　Mirth and youth and warm desire!

* That is—*invaluable*. Shakspeare uses the word "unvalued" with the same meaning.
† *Delphic*—oracular. Delphi, in Greece, was the seat of a famous oracle of Apollo.

"LET THERE BE LIGHT! AND LIGHT WAS OVER ALL."—MILTON.

ON MAY MORNING. 63

Woods and groves are of thy dressing,
Hill and dale doth boast thy blessing.
Thus we salute thee with our early song,
And welcome thee, and wish thee long.

[JOHN MILTON. From his "Poems on Several Occasions."]

"MANY ARE THE SAYINGS OF THE WISE, EXTOLLING PATIENCE AS THE TRUEST FORTITUDE."—MILTON.

"TO KNOW, THAT WHICH ABOUT US LIES IN DAILY LIFE, IS THE PRIME WISDOM."—MILTON.

"HOW CHARMING IS DIVINE PHILOSOPHY!"—MILTON.

FAME.

FAME is the spur that the clear spirit doth raise
 (That last infirmity of noble minds)
 To scorn delights and live laborious days:
But the fair guerdon when we hope to find,
And think to burst out into sudden blaze,
Comes the blind Fury with the abhorrèd shears,
And slits the thin-spun life. "But not the praise,"
Phœbus replied, and touched my trembling ears;
"Fame is no plant that grows on mortal soil,
Nor in the glistering foil
Set off to the world, nor in broad rumour lies;
But lives and spreads aloft by those pure eyes,
And perfect witness of all-judging Jove;
As he pronounces lastly on each deed,
Of so much fame in heaven expect thy meed."

[JOHN MILTON. From his monody entitled "Lycidas." Shelley's "Adonais," Tennyson's "In Memoriam," Milton's "Lycidas," and Matthew Arnold's "Thyrsis," are the four noblest elegiac poems in any language.]

―――o―――

SATAN'S ADDRESS TO THE SUN.

O THOU, that with surpassing glory crowned
 Look'st from thy sole dominion like the God
 Of this new world; at whose sight all the stars
Hide their diminished heads; to thee I call,
But with no friendly voice; and add thy name,
O Sun, to tell thee how I hate thy beams,
That bring to my remembrance from what state
I fell, how glorious once—above thy sphere;

SATAN'S ADDRESS TO THE SUN. 65

Till pride and worse ambition threw me down,
Warring in heaven against heaven's matchless king.
Ah, wherefore? He deserved no such return
From me, whom he created what I was
In that bright eminence, and with his good
Upbraided none, nor was his service hard.
What could be less than to afford him praise,
The easiest recompense, and pay him thanks?

SATAN'S ADDRESS TO THE SUN.

How due!—yet all his good proved ill in me,
And wrought but malice; lifted up so high,
I 'sdained subjection, and thought one step higher
Would set me highest, and in a moment quit
The debt immense of endless gratitude,
So burdensome still paying, still to owe:
Forgetful what from him I still received;
And understood not that a grateful mind
By owing owes not, but still pays, at once
Indebted and discharged: what burden then?
Oh, had his powerful destiny ordained
Me some inferior angel, I had stood
Then happy; no unbounded hope had raised
Ambition! Yet why not?—some other power
As great might have aspired, and me, though mean,
Drawn to his part; but other powers as great
Fell not, but stand unshaken, from within
As from without, to all temptations armed.
Hadst thou the same free will and power to stand?
Thou hadst: whom hast thou, then, or what to accuse,
But Heaven's free love dealt equally to all?
Be then his love accurst; since love or hate,
To me alike, it deals eternal woe:
Nay, cursed be thou; since against his thy will
Chose freely what it now so justly rues.
Me miserable!—which way shall I fly
Infinite wrath and infinite despair?
Which way I fly is hell; myself am hell;
And in the lowest deep a lower deep,
Still threatening to devour, me opens wide;
To which the hell I suffer seems a heaven.
Oh, then at last relent; is there no place
Left for repentance, none for pardon left?
None left but by submission; and that word

SATAN'S ADDRESS TO THE SUN.

Disdain forbids me, and my dread of shame
Among the spirits beneath, whom I seduced
With other promises and other vaunts
Than to submit, boasting I could subdue
The Omnipotent.   Ay me! they little know
How dearly I abide that boast so vain;
Under what torments inwardly I groan,
While they adore me on the throne of hell.
With diadem and sceptre high advanced,
The lower still I fall; only supreme
In misery: such joy ambition finds.
But say I could repent, and could obtain
By act of grace my former state; how soon
Would height recall high thoughts, how soon unsay
What feigned submission swore!   Ease would recant
Vows made in pain, as violent and void.
For never can true reconcilement grow
Where wounds of deadly hate have pierced so deep;
Which would but lead me to a worse relapse
And heavier fall: so should I purchase dear
Short intermission bought with double smart.
This knows my Punisher; therefore as far
From granting he, as I from begging peace:
All hope excluded thus, behold, instead
Of us outcast, exiled, his new delight,
Mankind, created, and for him this world.
So farewell hope; and with hope, farewell fear:
Farewell remorse: all good to me is lost;
Evil, be thou my good; by thee at least
Divided empire with heaven's king I hold,
By thee, and more than half perhaps will reign;
As man ere long and this new world shall know.

[JOHN MILTON. From "Paradise Lost."]

THE GARDEN OF EDEN.

So on he fares, and to the borders comes
Of Eden, where delicious Paradise,
Now nearer, crowns with her enclosure green,
As with a rural mound, the champaign head
Of a steep wilderness, whose hairy sides
With thicket overgrown, grotesque and wild,
Access denied; and overhead up-grew
Insuperable height of loftiest shade,
Cedar and pine, and fir, and branching palm,
A sylvan scene, and as the ranks ascend,
Shade above shade, a woody theatre
Of stateliest view. Yet higher than their tops
The verd'rous wall of Paradise up-sprung:
Which to our general sire gave prospect large
Into his nether empire neighb'ring round.
And higher than that wall a circling row
Of goodliest trees, loaden with fairest fruit,
Blossoms and fruit at once of golden hue,
Appeared, with gay enamelled colours mixed;
On which the sun more glad impressed his beams
Than in fair evening cloud, or humid bow,
When God hath showered the earth; so lovely seemed
That landscape; and of pure, now purer air
Meets his approach, and to the heart inspires
Vernal delight and joy, able to drive
All sadness but despair; now gentle gales
Fanning their odoriferous wings, dispense
Native perfumes, and whisper whence they stole
Those balmy spoils: as when to them who sail
Beyond the Cape of Hope, and now are past
Mozambic, off at sea north-east winds blow

Sabean odours from the spicy shore
Of Araby the blest; with such delay
Well pleased they slack their course, and many a
    league,
Cheered with the grateful smell, old Ocean smiles.

[JOHN MILTON. From "Paradise Lost."]

THE THAMES.

MY eye, descending from the Hill, surveys,
    Where Thames among the wanton valleys strays;
    Thames, the most loved of all the ocean's sons,
By his old sire, to his embraces runs,
Hasting to pay his tribute to the sea,
Like mortal life to meet eternity;
Though with those streams he no remembrance hold,
Whose foam is amber, and their gravel gold:
His genuine and less guilty wealth t' explore,
Search not his bottom but survey his shore,
O'er which he kindly spreads his spacious wing,
And hatches plenty for the ensuing spring;
And then destroys it with too fond a stay,
Like mothers who their infants overlay;
Nor with a sudden and impetuous wave,
Like profuse kings, resumes the wealth he gave.
No unexpected inundations spoil
The mower's hopes, nor mock the ploughman's toil,
But god-like his unwearied bounty flows;
First loves to do, then loves the good he does.
Nor are his blessings to his banks confined,
But free or common as the sea or wind;

THE THAMES.

When he, to boast or to disperse his stores,
Full of the tributes of his grateful shores,
Visits the world, and in his flying towers
Brings home to us, and makes both Indies ours:
Finds wealth where 'tis, bestows it where it wants,
Cities in deserts, woods in cities, plants.
So that to us no thing, no place, is strange,
While his fair bosom is the world's exchange.
Oh, could I flow like thee! and make thy stream
My great example, as it is my theme;
Though deep, yet clear, though gentle, yet not dull;
Strong without rage, without o'erflowing, full.

[Sir JOHN DENHAM, chiefly known to posterity by his poem of "Cooper's Hill" (near Chertsey, Surrey), in which the foregoing vigorous and energetic lines occur. Born 1615, died 1668.]

PART · II.

FROM

ABRAHAM COWLEY, A.D. 1618,

TO

EDWARD YOUNG, A.D. 1765.

PART II.

A KING'S GARDEN.

METHINKS I see great Diocletian* walk
  In the Salonian garden's noble shade,
  Which by his own imperial hands was made;
I see him smile, methinks, as he does talk
With the ambassadors, who come in vain
To entice him to a throne again.
"If I, my friends," said he, "should to you show
All the delights which in these gardens grow,
'Tis likelier much that you should with *me* stay,
Than 'tis that *you* should carry me away:
And trust me not, my friends, if every day
I walk not here with more delight
Than ever, after the most happy fight,
In triumph to the Capitol I rode,
To thank the gods, and to be thought myself a god."

[ABRAHAM COWLEY, born in London in 1618, died at Chertsey in 1667. Those who read him "must be contented to admire rather than to be pleased." He overloads his poems with conceits, which we may praise for their ingenuity, but feel in their abundance to be wearisome. His principal works are a sacred poem, "The Davideis," his "Books of Plants," "Anacreontics," and "Elegiac Poems." The foregoing extract is from "The Garden."]

* The Emperor Diocletian abdicated sovereignty on the 1st of May 305, and retired to his birth-place in Dalmatia, where he spent the remainder of his life in the cultivation of his garden, refusing all solicitations to resume imperial honours. He died at Salona about 312–313.

ON DELAYS.

BEGIN, be bold, and venture to be wise;
He who defers this work from day to day,
Does on a river's bank expecting stay,
Till the whole stream which stopped him should be gone,
That runs, and as it runs, for ever will run on.

[ABRAHAM COWLEY. From the Latin.]

THE GRASSHOPPER.

HAPPY insect! what can be
In happiness compared to thee?
Fed with nourishment divine,
The dewy morning's gentle wine!
Nature waits upon thee still,
And thy verdant cup does fill;
'Tis filled wherever thou dost tread,
Nature's self's thy Ganymede.
Thou dost drink, and dance, and sing,
Happier than the happiest king!
All the fields which thou dost see,
All the plants belong to thee,
All that summer hours produce,
Fertile made with early juice:
Man for thee does sow and plough;
Farmer he and landlord thou!
Thou dost innocently joy,
Nor does thy luxury destroy.
The shepherd gladly heareth thee,
More harmonious than he.
Thee, country minds with gladness hear,
Prophet of the ripened year:

Thee Phœbus loves and does inspire;
Phœbus is himself thy sire.
To thee, of all things upon earth,
Life is no longer than thy mirth.
Happy insect! happy thou,
Dost neither age nor winter know:
But when thou'st drunk, and danced, and sung
Thy fill, the flowery leaves among
(Voluptuous and wise withal,
Epicurèan animal),
Sated with the summer feast
Thou retir'st to endless rest.

[ABRAHAM COWLEY.]

―――o―――

THE SONG OF THE EMIGRANTS IN BERMUDA.

WHERE the remote Bermudas* ride
In the ocean's bosom unespied,
From a small boat that rowed along
The listening winds received this song.

" What should we do but sing His praise
That led us through the watery maze,
Where He the huge sea-monsters macks
That lift the deep upon their backs,
Unto an isle so long unknown,
And yet far kinder than our own?
He lands us on a grassy stage,
Safe from the storms, and prelate's rage : †

* The Bermuda Islands, discovered by Bermudez, a Spaniard, in 1527, are situated between the Gulf of Mexico and the North Atlantic Ocean, in lat. 32° 20′ N. They number five hundred, but are mostly rocks.
† These emigrants are supposed to have quitted England to avoid persecution on account of their religious faith.

76 THE SONG OF THE EMIGRANTS IN BERMUDA.

He gave us this eternal spring
Which here enamels everything,
And sends the fowls to us in care
On daily visits through the air.
He hangs in shades the orange bright
Like golden lamps in a green night,
And does in the pomegranates close
Jewels more rich than Ormus* shows :
He makes the figs our mouths to meet,
And throws the melons at our feet;
But apples, plants of such a price,
No tree could ever bear them twice.
With cedars chosen by his hand
From Lebanon he stores the land;
And makes the hollow seas that roar
Proclaim the ambergris on shore.
He cast (of which we rather boast)
The Gospel's pearl upon our coast;
And in these rocks for us did frame
A temple where to sound His name.
Oh, let our voice His praise exalt
Till it arrive at heaven's vault,
Which then perhaps rebounding, may
Echo beyond the Mexique bay !"

Thus sung they in the English boat,
A holy and a cheerful note :
And all the way, to guide their chime,
With falling oars they kept the time.

[ANDREW MARVELL, poet and statesman, remarkable for his integrity, manliness, and high sense of honour, born 1620, died 1678.]

* Ormus, in the Persian Gulf, famous for its pearls.

THE SONG OF THE NIGHTINGALE.

[From a poem entitled "Music's Duel," founded on a Latin poem by Strada.]

HER supple breast thrills out
    Sharp airs, and staggers in a warbling doubt
    Of dallying sweetness, hovers o'er her skill,
And folds in waved notes, with a trembling bill,
The pliant series of her slippery song;
Then starts she suddenly into a throng
Of short thick sobs, whose thund'ring volleys float
And roll themselves over her lubric throat
In panting murmurs, stilled out of her breast;

THE SONG OF THE NIGHTINGALE.

That ever-bubbling spring; the sugared nest
Of her delicious soul, that there does lie
Bathing in streams of liquid melody;
Music's best seed-plot; where, in ripened airs,
A golden-headed harvest fairly rears
His honey-dropping tops, ploughed by her breath
Which there reciprocally laboureth
In that sweet soil, it seems a holy quire
Founded to th' name of great Apollo's lyre;
Whose silver roof rings with the sprightly notes
Of sweet-lipped angel-imps, that swell their throats
In cream of morning Helicon,* and then
Prefer soft anthems to the ears of men,
To woo them from their beds, still murmuring
That men can sleep while they their matins sing—
Most divine service†—whose so early lay
Prevents‡ the eyelids of the blushing day.

There might you hear her kindle her soft voice,
In the close murmur of a sparkling noise;
And lay the groundwork of her hopeful song,
Still keeping in the forward stream so long,
Till a sweet whirlwind—striving to get out—
Heaves her soft bosom, wanders round about,
And makes a pretty earthquake in her breast,
Till the fledged notes at length forsake their nest,
Fluttering in wanton shoals, and to the sky,
Winged with their own wild echoes, prattling fly.
She opes the flood-gate, and lets loose a tide
Of streaming sweetness, which in state doth ride
On the waved back of every swelling strain,
Rising and falling in a pompous train,

---

* A mountain in Greece, whose fountains of Aganippe and Hippocrene are sacred to Apollo and the Muses.

† An allusion to the "matins," or morning service of the Roman Church

‡ *Prevents*—used in its ancient sense of "anticipates."

And while she thus discharges a shrill peal
Of flashing airs, she qualifies their zeal
With the cool epode* of a graver note;
Thus high, thus low, as if her silver throat
Would reach the brazen voice of War's hoarse bird;
Her little soul is ravished, and so poured
Into loose ecstacies, that she is placed
Above herself, Music's enthusiast.

[RICHARD CRASHAW, a poet of deep devotional feeling and wonderful richness of expression, was born in London about 1625—the exact date is uncertain—and died in Italy in 1650. His chief works are, "Steps to the Temple," "The Delights of the Muses," and a version of Marino's "Sospetto d'Herode."]

A CHARACTER.

THE COURTIER.

[Designed as a portrait of George Villiers, Duke of Buckingham, one of the favourites of Charles II.]

OME of their chiefs were princes of the land;
In the first rank of these did Zimri stand:
A man so various, that he seemed to be
Not one, but all mankind's epitome:
Stiff in opinions, always in the wrong;
Was everything by starts, and nothing long;
But, in the course of one revolving moon,
Was chemist, fiddler, statesman, and buffoon:
Then all for women, painting, rhyming, drinking,
Besides ten thousand freaks that died in thinking.
Blest madman, who could every hour employ,
With something new to wish, or to enjoy!
Railing and praising were his usual themes;
And both, to show his judgment, in extremes:

* *Epode* (Επωδος), a lyric poem in which long and short stanzas alternate; here employed in the sense of "contrast."

So over violent, or over civil,
That every man with him was god or devil.
In squandering wealth was his peculiar art:
Nothing went unrewarded but desert.
Beggared by fools, whom still he found too late;
He had his jest, and they had his estate.

[JOHN DRYDEN, 1631-1701, a famous master of nervous, energetic, and manly verse, author of "Religio Laici," "The Hind and the Panther" (from which our extract is taken), "Annus Mirabilis," and numerous odes and plays, the satire of "Mac Flecknoe," and an English translation of Virgil.]

---o---

THE GOOD PARSON.*

A PARISH priest was of the pilgrim train;
An awful, reverend, and religious man.
His eyes diffused a venerable grace,
And charity itself was in his face.
Rich was his soul, though his attire was poor
(As God hath clothed his own ambassador),
For such on earth his blessed Redeemer bore.
Of sixty years he seemed; and well might last
To sixty more, but that he lived too fast;
Refined himself to soul, to curb the sense;
And made almost a sin of abstinence.
Yet had his aspect nothing of severe,
But such a face as promised him sincere.
Nothing reserved or sullen was to see,
But sweet regards and pleasing sanctity:
Mild was his accent, and his action free.
With eloquence unnate his tongue was armed;
Though harsh the precept, yet the people charmed.

* Compare this description with Chaucer's, p. 4.

THE GOOD PARSON.

For, letting down the golden chain from high,
He drew his audience upward to the sky.
    He taught the gospel rather than the law;
And forced himself to drive, but loved to draw.
For fear but freezes minds: but love, like heat,
Exalts the soul sublime, to seek her native seat,
To threats the stubborn sinner oft is hard,
Wrapped in his crimes, against the storm prepared;
But, when the milder beams of mercy play,
He melts, and throws his cumbrous cloak away.
Lightning and thunder (heaven's artillery)
As harbingers before th' Almighty fly:
Those but proclaim his style, and disappear;
The stiller sound succeeds, and God is there.
Wide was his parish; nor contracted close
In streets, but here and there a straggling house;
Yet still he was at hand, without request,
To serve the sick, to succour the distressed:
Tempting, on foot, alone, without affright,
The dangers of a dark tempestuous night.
    All this the good old man performed alone,
Nor spared his pains; for curate he had none,
Nor durst he trust another with his care;
Nor rode himself to Paul's, the public fair,
To chaffer for preferment with his gold,
Where bishoprics and sinecures are sold.
But duly watched his flock, by night and day;
And from the prowling wolf redeemed the prey:
And hungry sent the wary fox away.
    The proud he tamed, the penitent he cheered:
Nor to rebuke the rich offender feared.
His preaching much, but more his practice wrought
(A living sermon of the truths he taught);

For this by rules severe his life he squared,
That all might see the doctrines which they heard:
For priests, he said, are patterns for the rest
(The gold of heaven, who bear the God impressed):
But when the precious coin is kept unclean,
The sovereign's image is no longer seen.
If they be foul on whom the people trust,
Well may the baser brass contract a rust.
   Such was the saint; who shone with every grace,
Reflecting, Moses like, his Maker's face.

[JOHN DRYDEN. A paraphrase upon Chaucer.]

―――o―――

THOUGHTS ON TIME.

WE waste, not use our time; we breathe, not live;
   Time wasted is existence; used, is life:
   And bare existence man, to live ordained,
Wrings and oppresses with enormous weight.
And why? since time was given for use, not waste,
Enjoined to fly, with tempest, tide, and stars,
To keep his speed, nor ever wait for man.
Time's use was doomed a pleasure, waste a pain,
That man might feel his error if unseen,
And, feeling, fly to labour for his cure;
Nor blundering, split on idleness for ease.

We push Time from us, and we wish him back;
Life we think long and short; death seek and shun.
Oh, the dark days of vanity! while
Here, how tasteless! and how terrible when gone!
Gone!. they ne'er go; when past, they haunt us still:

THOUGHTS ON TIME.

The spirit walks of every day deceased,
And smiles an angel, or a fury frowns.
Nor death nor life delight us. If time past,
And time possessed, both pain us, what can please?
That which the Deity to please ordained,
Time used. The man who consecrates his hours
By vigorous effort, and an honest aim,
At once he draws the sting of life and death:
He walks with nature, and her paths are peace.

'Tis greatly wise to talk with our past hours,
And ask them what report they bore to heaven,
And how they might have borne more welcome news.
Their answers form what men experience call;
If wisdom's friend her best, if not, worst foe.

But why on Time so lavish is my song:
On this great theme kind Nature keeps a school
To teach her sons herself. Each night we die—
Each morn are born anew; each day a life
And shall we kill each day? If trifling kills,
Sure vice must butcher. Oh, what heaps of slain
Cry out for vengeance on us! time destroyed
Is suicide, where more than blood is spilt.

[EDWARD YOUNG, born 1681, died 1765, author of numerous poetical, dramatic, and religious works, but chiefly remembered for his noble poem, "The Night Thoughts," from which the above extracts are taken. His style is remarkable for sententiousness, gravity, antithetical force, and a well-sustained elevation.]

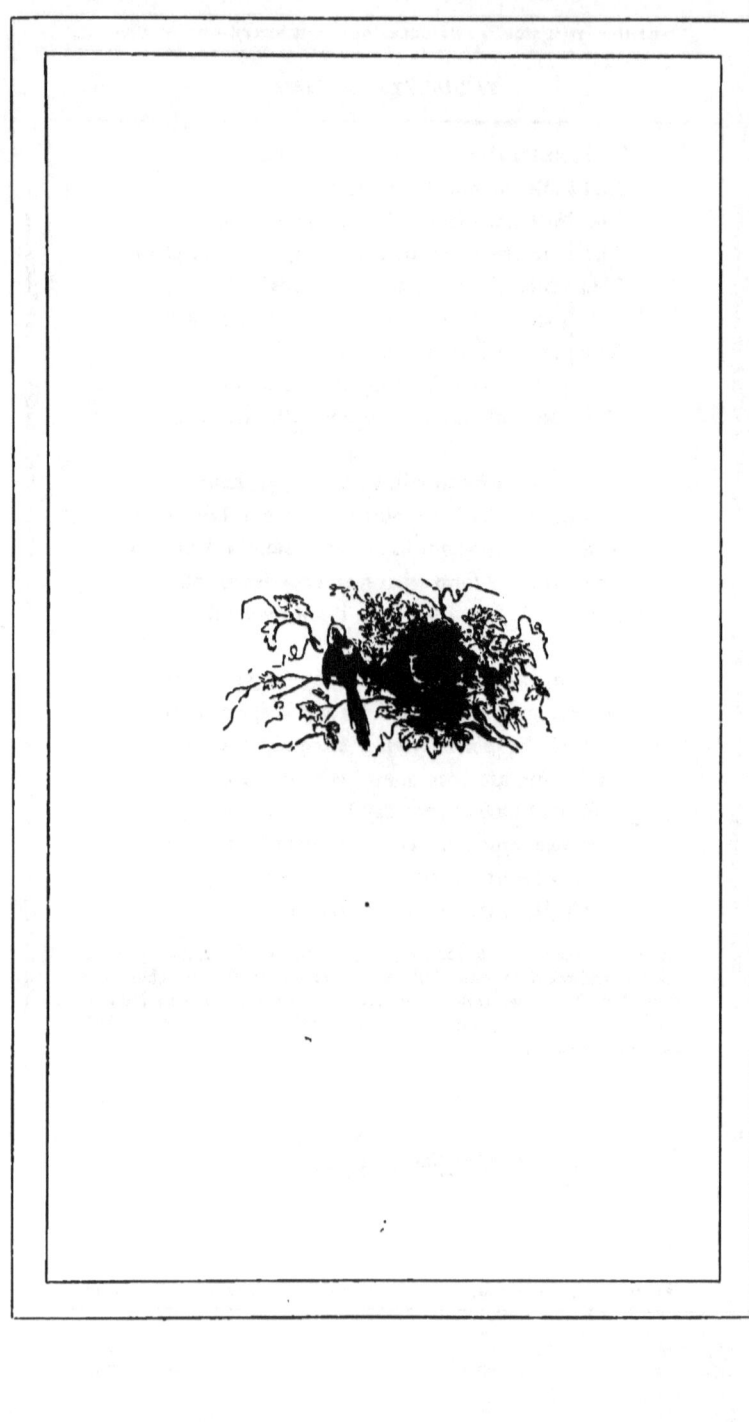

FROM

ALEXANDER POPE, A.D. 1688,

TO

ALEXANDER SMITH, A.D. 1830.

PART III.

A CHARACTER.

THE PHILANTHROPIST.

BUT all our praises why should lords engross?
    Rise, honest Muse! and sing the Man of Ross:
    Pleased Vaga* echoes through her winding bounds,
And rapid Severn hoarse applause resounds.
Who hung with woods yon mountain's sultry brow?
From the dry rock who bade the waters flow?
Not to the skies in useless columns tost,
Or in proud falls magnificently lost;
But clear and artless, pouring through the plain,
Health to the sick, and solace to the swain.
Whose causeway parts the vâle with shady rows?
Whose seats the weary traveller repose?
Who taught the heaven-directed spire to rise?
"The Man of Ross," each lisping babe replies.
Behold the market-place with poor o'erspread!
The Man of Ross divides the weekly bread:
He feeds yon almshouse, neat, but void of state,
Where Age and Want sit smiling at the gate:

* The Latin name of the river Wye.

A CHARACTER.

Him portioned maids, apprenticed orphans blessed,
The young who labour, and the old who rest.
Is any sick? the Man of Ross relieves,
Prescribes, attends, the med'cine makes, and gives.
Is there a variance? enter but his door,
Balked are the courts, and contests are no more:
Despairing quacks with curses fled the place,
And vile attorneys, now a useless race.
—Thrice happy man! enabled to pursue
What all so wish, but want the power to do!
Oh, say, what sums that generous hand supply?
What mines to swell that boundless charity?
—Of debts and taxes, wife and children clear,
This man possessed—five hundred pounds a-year.
Blush, Grandeur, blush! proud courts, withdraw your blaze!
Ye little stars, hide your diminished rays!*
—And what? no monument, inscription, stone?
His race, his form, his name almost unknown?

   Who builds a church to God, and not to fame,
Will never mark the marble with his name;
Go, search it there,† where to be born and die,
Of rich and poor makes all the history;
Enough, that virtue filled the space between,
Proved by the ends of being to have been.
When Hopkins dies,‡ a thousand lights attend
The wretch who, living, saved a candle's end;
Shouldering God's altar a vile image stands,
Belies his features, nay, extends his hands;

* " All the stars
    Hide their diminished heads."—MILTON.
† That is, in the Parish Register.
‡ Matthew Hopkins, a notorious miser who lies buried in Wimbledon churchyard. The "Man of Ross" was one Mr. John Kyrle, who died in 1724, aged 90, after a career of noble and self-denying benevolence. He was buried at Ross, in Herefordshire.

That live-long wig, which Gorgon's self might own,
Eternal buckle takes in Parian stone.
Behold what blessings wealth to life can lend!
And see what comfort it affords our end!

[ALEXANDER POPE, born at London in 1688. died 1744. This great master of versification, this polished satirist, and clear if superficial thinker, hardly now enjoys the estimation to which, I venture to think, his eminent abilities entitle him. That as a poet he stands foremost in the second rank, and only second to Milton, Spenser, Wordsworth, and the other "kings of song," must surely be admitted by every judicious critic who has studied his "Rape of the Lock," and his "Moral Essays." His other works are, "Eloisa to Abelard," "Elegy on an Unfortunate Lady," "Windsor Forest," "The Temple of Fame," "Satires," "The Dunciad," his translation of the Homeric poems, and some minor odes, prologues, epitaphs, and epigrams. The foregoing extract is from the "Moral Essays," Epistle iii.]

A FOREST SCENE.

NOT proud Olympus yields a nobler sight,
Though gods assembled grace his towering height,
Than what more humble mountains offer here,
Where, in their blessings, all those gods appear.
See Pan with flocks, with fruits Pomona crowned,
Here blushing Flora paints the enamelled ground,
Here Ceres' gifts in waving prospect stand,
And nodding tempt the joyful reaper's hand.

. . . . .

See! from the brake the whirring pheasant springs,
And mounts exulting on triumphant wings:
Short is his joy; he feels the fiery wound,
Flutters in blood, and panting beats the ground.
Ah, what avail his glossy varying dyes,
His purple crest, and scarlet-circled eyes,
The vivid green his shining plumes unfold,
His painted wings, and breast that flames with gold?

A FOREST SCENE.

Nor yet when moist Arcturus clouds the sky,
The woods and fields their pleasing toils deny.
To plains with well-breathed beagles we repair,
And trace the mazes of the circling hare
(Beasts, urged by us, their fellow beasts pursue,
And learn of man each other to undo):
With slaughtering guns th' unweary fowler roves,
When frosts have whitened all the naked groves;
Where doves in flocks the leafless trees o'ershade,
And lonely woodcocks haunt the watery glade.

He lifts the tube, and levels with his eye;
Straight a short thunder breaks the frozen sky:
Oft, as in airy rings they skim the heath,
The clamorous lapwings feel the leaden death;
Oft as the mounting larks their holes prepare,
They fall, and leave their little lives in air.
 In genial spring, beneath the quivering shade,
Where cooling vapours breathe along the mead,
The patient fisher takes his silent stand,
Intent, his angle trembling in his hand:
With looks unmoved, he hopes the scaly breed,
And eyes the dancing cork and bending reed.
Our plenteous streams a various race supply:
The bright-eyed perch, with fins of Tyrian dye;
The silver eel, in shining volume rolled;
The yellow carp, in scales bedropped with gold;
Swift trouts, diversified with crimson stains;
And pikes, the tyrants of the watery plains.

[ALEXANDER POPE. From "Windsor Forest," l. 111 to l. 146.]

---o---

THE CARAVAN IN THE DESERT.

BREATHED hot
 From all the boundless furnace of the sky,
 And the wide glittering waste of burning sand,
A suffocating wind the pilgrim smites
With instant death. Patient of thirst and toil,
Son of the Desert! e'en the camel feels,
Shot through his withered heart, the fiery blast.
Or from the black-red ether, bursting broad,
Sallies the sudden whirlwind. Straight the sands
Commoved around, in gathering eddies play;

THE CARAVAN IN THE DESERT.

Nearer and nearer still they darkening come,
Till, with the general all-involving storm
Swept up, the whole continuous wilds arise;
And by their noonday fount dejected thrown,
Or sunk at night in sad disastrous sleep,
Beneath descending hills, the caravan
Is buried deep.   In Cairo's crowded streets
The impatient merchant, wondering, waits in vain,
And Mecca saddens at the long delay.

[JAMES THOMSON, born 1700, died 1748, will always hold a high rank among the English minstrels from his singularly great powers of description. He observed nature closely, and painted her with equal truth and vigour. His finest work is "The Seasons," a poem which sketches the varying aspects of earth during the revolving year; but his "Castle of Indolence" is scarcely inferior in true poetic spirit.   The above extract is from "The Seasons."]

RULE BRITANNIA.

WHEN Britain first, at Heaven's command,
    Arose from out the azure main,
This was the charter of the land,
    And guardian angels sung the strain :
Rule Britannia, Britannia rules the waves !
    Britons never shall be slaves.

The nations not so blest as thee,
    Must in their turn to tyrants fall,
Whilst thou shalt flourish great and free,
    The dread and envy of them all.
Rule Britannia, Britannia rules the waves !
    Britons never shall be slaves.

Still more majestic shalt thou rise,
    More dreadful from each foreign stroke ;
As the loud blast that tears the skies,
    Serves but to root thy native oak.
Rule Britannia, Britannia rules the waves !
    Britons never shall be slaves.

Thee haughty tyrants ne'er shall tame ;
    All their attempts to bend thee down
Will but arouse thy generous flame,
    And work their woe and thy renown.
Rule Britannia, Britannia rules the waves !
    Britons never shall be slaves.

To thee belongs the rural reign ;
    Thy cities shall with commerce shine ;

All thine shall be the subject main,
  And every shore it circles thine.
Rule Britannia, Britannia rules the waves!
  Britons never shall be slaves.

The Muses, still with Freedom found,
  Shall to thy happy coast repair;
Blest Isle, with matchless beauty crowned,
  And manly hearts to guard the fair.
Rule Britannia, Britannia rules the waves!
  Britons never shall be slaves.

[JAMES THOMSON. From the masque of "King Arthur." The music to this noble song, which has deservedly become our national hymn, was composed by Dr. Arne.]

―o―

A ROYAL MADMAN.

CHARLES XII. OF SWEDEN.

ON what foundation stands the warrior's pride,
  How just his hopes, let Swedish Charles decide;
  A frame of adamant, a soul of fire,
No dangers fright him, and no labours tire;
O'er love, o'er fear, extends his wide domain;
Unconquered lord of pleasure and of pain;
No joys to him pacific sceptres yield,
War sounds the trump, he rushes to the field;
Behold surrounding kings their powers combine,
And one capitulate, and one resign;
Peace courts his hand, but spreads her charms in vain;
"Think nothing gained," he cries, "till nought remain;
On Moscow's walls till Gothic banners fly,
And all be mine beneath the Polar sky."

The march begins in military state,
And nations on his eye suspended wait;
Stern Famine guards the solitary coast,
And Winter barricades the realms of frost;
He comes, nor Want and Cold his course delay;
Hide, blushing Glory, hide Pultowa's day : *
The vanquished hero leaves his broken bands,
And shows his miseries in distant lands;
Condemned a needy supplicant to wait;
While ladies interpose, and slaves debate.
But did not chance at length her error mend?
Did no subverted empire mark his end?
Or hostile millions press him to the ground?
His fall was destined to a barren strand,
A petty fortress, and a dubious hand; †
He left a name at which the world grew pale,
To point a moral, or adorn a tale.

[SAMUEL JOHNSON, 1709-1784, better known to posterity as the author of "The Lives of the Poets," "Rasselas," and "The Rambler," than as the author of "The Vanity of Human Wishes" (from which the foregoing lines are quoted), and "London"—two didactic poems of great merit.]

---o---

ODE TO THE SPRING.

O! where the rosy-bosomed hours,
    Fair Venus' train appear,
Disclose the long-expecting flowers,
    And wake the purple year!

* Charles XII. was totally defeated by Peter the Great of Russia on the field of Pultowa, or Pultava, July 8, 1709.
† He was killed by a chance shot while besieging the small town of Frederickshald, in Norway, December 11, 1718.

ODE TO THE SPRING.

The Attic warbler* pours her throat
Responsive to the cuckoo's note,
The untaught harmony of spring:
While, whispering pleasure as they fly,
Cool zephyrs through the clear blue sky
    Their gathered fragrance fling.

Where'er the oak's thick branches stretch
    A broader, browner shade,
Where'er the rude and moss-grown beech
    O'er-canopies the glade,
Beside some water's rushy brink
With me the Muse shall sit, and think,—
(At ease reclined in rustic state),—
How vain the ardour of the crowd,
How low, how little are the proud,
    How indigent the great!

Still is the toiling hand of care;
    The panting herds repose:

* That is, Philomela, the nightingale, a bird frequently heard among the groves of Attica, and much celebrated by the Greek poets.

ODE TO THE SPRING.

Yet hark, how through the peopled air
    The busy murmur glows!
The insect youth are on the wing,
Eager to taste the honied spring
And float amid the liquid noon:
Some lightly o'er the current skim,
Some show their gaily gilded trim
    Quick-glancing to the sun.

To Contemplation's sober eye
    Such is the race of Man:
And they that creep, and they that fly,
    Shall end where they began.
Alike the busy and the gay
But flutter through life's little day,
In Fortune's varying colours drest:
Brushed by the hand of rough Mischance,
Or chilled by Age, their airy dance
    They leave, in dust to rest.

Methinks I hear in accents low
    The sportive kind reply:
Poor moralist! and what art thou?
    A solitary fly!
Thy joys no glittering female meets,
No hive hast thou of hoarded sweets,
No painted plumage to display:
On hasty wings thy youth is flown:
Thy sun is set, thy spring is gone—
    We frolic while 'tis May.

[T. GRAY, author of "The Bard," "Elegy in a Country Churchyard," and other immortal poems, born 1716, died 1771. His specialty is a remarkable richness and felicity of diction.]

AN EPITAPH FOR HEROIC WARRIORS.

HOW sleep the brave who sink to rest
 By all their country's wishes blest!
 When Spring, with dewy fingers cold,
Returns to deck their hallowed mould,
She there shall dress a sweeter sod
Than fancy's feet have ever trod.

By fairy hands their knell is rung,
By forms unseen their dirge is sung;
There Honour comes, a pilgrim gray,
To bless the turf that wraps their clay;
And Freedom shall awhile repair,
To dwell a weeping hermit there!

[W. COLLINS, author of some fine "Eclogues," or "Pastoral Poems," and of the most vigorous lyrical poetry in our language, born 1720, died 1756.]

---o---

HASSAN; OR, THE CAMEL-DRIVER.

Scene—The Desert. Time—Mid-day.

IN silent horror, o'er the boundless waste,
 The driver Hassan with his camels past;
 One cruise of water on his back he bore,
And his light scrip contained a scanty store;
A fan of painted feathers in his hand,
To guard his shaded face from scorching sand.
The sultry sun had gained the middle sky,
And not a tree and not an herb was nigh;
The beasts with pain their dusty way pursue,
Shrill roared the winds, and dreary was the view!

HASSAN; OR, THE CAMEL-DRIVER.

With desperate sorrow wild, the affrighted man
Thrice sighed, thrice struck his breast, and thus began:
"Sad was the hour, and luckless was the day,
When first from Schiraz' walls I bent my way!

Ah, little thought I of the blasting wind,
The thirst or pinching hunger that I find!
Bethink thee, Hassan, where shall thirst assuage,
When fails this cruise, his unrelenting rage?
Soon shall this scrip its precious load resign,
Then what but tears and hunger shall be thine?

Ye mute companions of my toils, that bear
In all my griefs a more than equal share!
Here, where no springs in murmurs break away,
Or moss-crowned fountains mitigate the day,
In vain ye hope the green delights to know,
Which plains more blest or verdant vales bestow;
Here rocks alone and tasteless sands are found,
And faint and sickly winds for ever howl around.

    Sad was the hour, and luckless was the day,
    When first from Schiraz' walls I bent my way!

Cursed be the gold and silver which persuade
Weak men to follow far fatiguing trade!
The lily peace outshines the silver store,
And life is dearer than the golden ore;
Yet money tempts us o'er the desert brown,
To every distant mart and wealthy town.
Full oft we tempt the land, and oft the sea;
And are we only yet repaid by thee?
Ah, why was ruin so attractive made,
Or why fond man so easily betrayed?
Why heed we not, while mad we haste along,
The gentle voice of Peace, or Pleasure's song?
Or wherefore think the flowery mountain's side,
The fountain's murmurs, and the valley's pride—

Why think we these less pleasing to behold
Than dreary deserts, if they lead to gold!
   Sad was the hour, and luckless was the day,
   When first from Schiraz' walls I bent my way!
Oh, cease, my fears! All frantic as I go,
When thought creates unnumbered scenes of woe,
What if the lion in his rage I meet!
Oft in the dust I view his printed feet;
And fearful oft when Day's declining light
Yields her pale empire to the mourner Night,
By hunger roused he scours the groaning plain,
Gaunt wolves and sullen tigers in his train;
Before them Death with shrieks directs their way,
Fills the wild yell, and leads them to their prey.
   Sad was the hour, and luckless was the day,
   When first from Schiraz' walls I bent my way!
At that dead hour the silent asp shall creep,
If aught of rest I find, upon my sleep;
Or some swoln serpent twist his scales around,
And wake to anguish with a burning wound.
Thrice happy they, the wise contented poor,
From lust of wealth and dread of death secure!
They tempt no deserts, and no griefs they find;
Peace rules the day where reason rules the mind.
   Sad was the hour, and luckless was the day,
   When first from Schiraz' walls I bent my way!
O hapless youth! for she thy love hath won,
The tender Zara! will be most undone.
Big swelled my heart, and owned the powerful maid,
When fast she dropped her tears, as thus she said:
'Farewell the youth whom sighs could not detain,
Whom Zara's breaking heart implored in vain!
Yet as thou go'st may every blast arise
Weak and unfelt as these rejected sighs!

Safe o'er the wild no pearls mayst thou see,
No griefs endure, nor weep, false youth, like me.'
Oh, let me safely to the fair return,
Say with a kiss, she must not, shall not mourn;
Oh, let me teach my heart to lose its fears,
Recalled by Wisdom's voice and Zara's tears."

He said, and called on Heaven to bless the day
When back to Schiraz' walls he bent his way.

[WILLIAM COLLINS. From the "Persian Eclogues."]

ENGLISH COUNTRY LIFE.

THE VILLAGE SCHOOLMASTER AND THE VILLAGE INN.

BESIDE yon straggling fence that skirts the way,
With blossomed furze unprofitably gay,
There, in his noisy mansion, skilled to rule,
The village master taught his little school;
A man severe he was, and stern to view—
I knew him well, and every truant knew;
Well had the boding tremblers learned to trace
The day's disasters in his morning face;
Full well they laughed with counterfeited glee
At all his jokes, for many a joke had he;
Full well the busy whisper circling round,
Conveyed the dismal tidings when he frowned;
Yet he was kind, or if severe in aught,
The love he bore to learning was in fault;
The village all declared how much he knew;
'Twas certain he could write and cypher too;
Lands he could measure, times and tides presage,
And even the story ran that he could gauge;

"LET SCHOOL-TAUGHT PRIDE DISSEMBLE ALL IT CAN;

102   ENGLISH COUNTRY LIFE.

In arguing, too, the parson owned his skill,
For e'en though vanquished, he could argue still;
While words of learnèd length, and thund'ring sound,
Amazed the gazing rustics ranged around,
And still they gazed, and still the wonder grew,
That one small head could carry all he knew.
But past is all his fame.   The very spot
Where many a time he triumphed, is forgot.

Near yonder thorn, that lifts its head on high,
Where once the sign-post caught the passing eye,
Low lies that house where nut-brown draughts inspired,
Where grey-beard mirth and smiling toil retired,

THESE LITTLE THINGS ARE GREAT TO LITTLE MAN."—GOLDSMITH.

"BUT SMALL THE BLISS THAT SENSE ALONE BESTOWS."—GOLDSMITH.

ENGLISH COUNTRY LIFE.

Where village statesmen talked with looks profound,
And news much older than their ale went round.
Imagination fondly stoops to trace
The parlour splendours of that festive place;
The white-washed hall, the nicely sanded floor,
The varnished clock that clicked behind the door;

"EVEN HIS FAILINGS LEANED TO VIRTUE'S SIDE."—GOLDSMITH.

The chest contrived a double debt to pay,
A bed by night, a chest of drawers by day;
The pictures placed for ornament and use,
The twelve good rules, the royal game of goose;
The hearth, except when winter chilled the day,
With aspen boughs and flowers and fennel gay,
While broken tea-cups, wisely kept for show,
Ranged o'er the chimney, glistened in a row.

[OLIVER GOLDSMITH, poet, novelist, essayist—a man of delicate genius and tender sympathies—was born in 1728, died 1774. His best works are, "The Vicar of Wakefield," "Citizen of the World," "She Stoops to Conquer," "The Traveller," and "The Deserted Village." Our extract is from the latter.]

---o---

BOADICEA.*

WHEN the British warrior queen,
 Bleeding from the Roman rods,
Sought, with an indignant mien,
 Counsel of her country's gods,

Sage beneath the spreading oak
 Sat the Druid, hoary chief;
Every burning word he spoke
 Full of rage, and full of grief.

"Princess! if our aged eyes
 Weep upon thy matchless wrongs,
'Tis because resentment ties
 All the terrors of our tongues.

* Boadicea, or Bonduca, was Queen of the Iceni, an ancient British nation, and offered an heroic resistance to the Roman invaders, by whose orders she had been cruelly scourged. She attacked and captured the Roman colony of Camalodunum (Maldon), in Essex, destroyed Londinium and Verulamium (St. Albans), but was finally defeated by Suetonius (A.D. 62). In despair she committed suicide.

BOADICEA.

"Rome shall perish—write that word
    In the blood that she has spilt;
Perish, hopeless and abhorred,
    Deep in ruin as in guilt.

"Rome, for empire far renowned,
    Tramples on a thousand states;
Soon her pride shall kiss the ground—
    Hark! the Gaul is at her gates!

"Other Romans shall arise,
    Heedless of a soldier's name;
Sounds, not arms, shall win the prize,
    Harmony the path to fame.

BOADICEA.

"Then the progeny that springs
  From the forests of our land,
Armed with thunder, clad with wings,
  Shall a wider world command.

"Regions Cæsar never knew
  Thy posterity shall sway;
Where his eagles never flew,
  None invincible as they."

Such the bard's prophetic words,
  Pregnant with celestial fire,
Bending as he swept the chords
  Of his sweet but awful lyre.

She, with all a monarch's pride,
  Felt them in her bosom glow;
Rushed to battle, fought, and died;
  Dying, hurled them at the foe.

"Ruffians, pitiless as proud,
  Heaven awards the vengeance due;
Empire is on us bestowed,
  Shame and ruin wait for you."

[WILLIAM COWPER, a descriptive and didactic poet of deserved repute, who is endeared to our sympathies by the melancholy story of his life. Born 1731, died 1800. Wrote "The Task," "Conversation," "Retirement," "Table Talk," and numerous minor poems.]

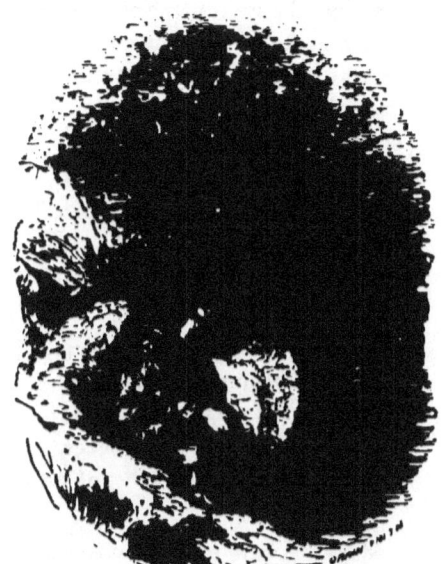

THE SOLITUDE OF ALEXANDER SELKIRK.*

I AM monarch of all I survey,
    My right there is none to dispute,
    From the centre all round to the sea,
I am lord of the fowl and the brute.
O Solitude! where are the charms,
    That sages have seen in thy face?
Better dwell in the midst of alarms
    Than reign in this horrible place.

I am out of humanity's reach,
    I must finish my journey alone,

---

* Alexander Selkirk, whose curious history may possibly have suggested to Daniel Defoe his romance of "Robinson Crusoe," was left on the desolate island of Juan Fernandez, in the Pacific Ocean, by his captain, in 1704. It was his misfortune to spend upwards of four years in solitude.

THE SOLITUDE OF ALEXANDER SELKIRK.

Never hear the sweet music of speech;
    I start at the sound of my own.
The beasts that roam over the plain
    My form with indifference see;
They are so unacquainted with man,
    Their tameness is shocking to me.

Society, Friendship, and Love,
    Divinely bestowed upon man,
Oh, had I the wings of a dove,
    How soon would I taste you again!
My sorrows I then might assuage
    In the ways of religion and truth;
Might learn from the wisdom of age,
    And be cheered by the sallies of youth.

Ye winds that have made me your sport,
    Convey to this desolate shore
Some cordial endearing report
    Of a land I shall visit no more.
My friends, do they now and then send
    A wish or a thought after me?
Oh, tell me I yet have a friend,
    Though a friend I am never to see.

How fleet is a glance of the mind!
    Compared with the speed of its flight,
The tempest itself lags behind,
    And the swift-wingèd arrows of light.
When I think of my own native land,
    In a moment I seem to be there;
But, alas! recollection at hand
    Soon hurries me back to despair.

"ALL TRUTH IS PRECIOUS,—IF NOT ALL DIVINE:—

AND WHAT DILATES THE POWERS, MUST NEEDS REFINE."—COWPER.

"THE BAND OF COMMERCE WAS DESIGNED, TO ASSOCIATE ALL THE BRANCHES OF MANKIND."—COWPER.

"EACH CLIMATE NEEDS WHAT OTHER CLIMES PRODUCE, AND OFFERS SOMETHING TO THE GENERAL USE."—COWPER.

But the sea-fowl has gone to her nest,
    The beast is laid down in his lair;
Even here is a season of rest,
    And I to my cabin repair.
There's a mercy in every place,
    And mercy, encouraging thought!
Gives even affliction a grace,
    And reconciles man to his lot.

[WILLIAM COWPER.]

LOSS OF THE ROYAL GEORGE.[*]

TOLL for the brave!
    The brave that are no more!
All sunk beneath the wave
Fast by their native shore!

Eight hundred of the brave
    Whose courage well was tried,
Had made the vessel heel,
    And laid her on her side.

A land-breeze shook the shrouds,
    And she was overset;
Down went the *Royal George*,
    With all her crew complete.

[*] The *Royal George* was a British man-of-war of 100 guns, which heeled over while lying at Spithead, near Portsmouth, to have some injuries repaired. Of twelve hundred men, women, and children then on board of her, nearly six hundred perished (August 29, 1782).

"WHAT IS BASE, NO POLISH CAN MAKE STERLING."—COWPER.

LOSS OF THE ROYAL GEORGE.

    Toll for the brave!
        Brave Kempenfeldt* is gone;
    His last sea-fight fought,
        His work of glory done.

    It was not in the battle;
        No tempest gave the shock;
    She sprang no fatal leak,
        She ran upon no rock.

    His sword was in its sheath,
        His fingers held the pen,
    When Kempenfeldt went down
        With twice four hundred men.

* Vice-Admiral Kempenfeldt, a gallant and distinguished seaman, in command of the *Royal George*, was writing in his cabin when the catastrophe occurred.

"THE LAURELS THAT A CÆSAR REAPS ARE WEEDS."—COWPER.

Weigh the vessel up
 Once dreaded by our foes!
And mingle with the cup
 The tear that England owes.

Her timbers yet are sound,
 And she may float again
Full charged with England's thunder,
 And plough the watery main:

But Kempenfeldt is gone,
 His victories are o'er;
And he and his eight hundred
 Shall plough the wave no more.

[WILLIAM COWPER.]

———o———

A WINTER EVENING.

NOW stir the fire, and close the shutters fast,
 Let fall the curtains, wheel the sofa round,
 And while the bubbling and loud hissing urn
Throws up a steamy column, and the cups
That cheer but not inebriate, wait on each,
So let us welcome peaceful evening in.
Not such his evening, who with shining face
Sweats in the crowded theatre, and squeezed
And bored with elbow points through both his sides,
Outscolds the ranting actor on the stage;
Nor his, who patient stands till his feet throb,
And his head bumps, to feed upon the breath
Of patriots, bursting with heroic rage,
Or placemen, all tranquillity and smiles.

"FAULTS IN THE LIFE BREED ERRORS IN THE BRAIN."—COWPER.

A WINTER EVENING.

This folio of four pages, happy work!
Which not even critics criticise; that holds
Inquisitive attention while I read,
Fast bound in chains of silence, which the fair,
Though eloquent themselves, yet fear to break;
What is it but a map of busy life,
Its fluctuations and its vast concerns?
Here runs the mountainous and craggy ridge
That tempts ambition. On the summit, see,
The seals of office glitter in his eyes;
He climbs, he pants, he grasps them. At his heels,
Close at his heels, a demagogue ascends,

"THERE IS IN SOULS A SYMPATHY WITH SOUNDS."—COWPER.

And with a dexterous jerk soon twists him down,
And wins them, but to lose them in his turn.
Here rills of oily eloquence in soft
Meanders lubricate the course they take;
The modest speaker is ashamed and grieved
To engross a minute's notice, and yet begs,
Begs a propitious ear for his poor thoughts,
However trivial all that he conceives.
Sweet bashfulness! it claims, at least, this praise;
The dearth of information and good sense,
That it foretells us, always comes to pass.
Cataracts of declamation thunder here,
There forests of no meaning spread the page
In which all comprehension wanders lost;
While fields of pleasantry amuse us there,
With merry descants on a nation's woes.
The rest appears a wilderness of strange
But gay confusion; roses for the cheeks
And lilies for the brow of faded age,
Teeth for the toothless, ringlets for the bald,
Heaven, earth, and ocean plundered of their sweets,
Nectareous essences, Olympian dews,
Sermons and city feasts, and favourite airs,
Æthereal journeys, submarine exploits,
And Katerfelto* with his hair on end
At his own wonders, wondering for his bread.
   'Tis pleasant through the loopholes of retreat
To peep at such a world; to see the stir
Of the great Babel, and not feel the crowd;
To hear the roar she sends through all her gates,

---

* Dr. Katerfelto was a notorious quack who figured in London in 1782, and, by aid of the solar microscope, astonished his audiences with a variety of wonders. He was also a conjurer, and in his performances was attended by several black cats.

A WINTER EVENING.

At a safe distance, where the dying sound
Falls a soft murmur on the uninjured ear.
Thus sitting, and surveying thus at ease
The globe and its concerns, I seem advanced
To some secure and more than mortal height
That liberates and exempts me from them all.
It turns submitted to my view, turns round
With all its generations; I behold
The tumult, and am still.   The sound of war
Has lost its terrors ere it reaches me;
Grieves, but alarms me not.   I mourn the pride
And avarice that make man a wolf to man,
Hear the faint echo of those brazen throats,
By which he speaks the language of his heart,
And sigh, but never tremble at the sound.
He travels and expatiates, as the bee
From flower to flower, so he from land to land;
The manners, customs, policy of all
Pay contribution to the store he gleans;
He sucks intelligence in every clime,
And spreads the honey of his deep research
At his return, a rich repast for me.
He travels, and I too.   I tread his deck,
Ascend his topmast, through his peering eyes
Discover countries, with a kindred heart
Suffer his woes, and share in his escapes;
While fancy, like the finger of a clock,
Runs the great circuit, and is still at home.

[WILLIAM COWPER. From "The Task," Book IV. The opening lines of this beautiful domestic piece are frequently quoted. The whole is a very favourable specimen of Cowper's vigorously graphic style and quiet humour.]

THE SHORES OF GREECE.

IMMORTAL Athens first, in ruin spread,
  Contiguous lies at Port Liono's head;
  Great source of science! whose immortal name
Stands foremost in the glorious roll of fame:
Here god-like Socrates* and Plato† shone,
And firm to truth eternal honour won;
The first, in virtue's cause his life resigned,
By Heaven pronounced the wisest of mankind:
The last, proclaimed the spark of vital fire,
The soul's fine essence, never could expire;
Here Solon‡ dwelt, the philosophic sage
That fled Pisistratus'§ vindictive rage;
Just Aristides|| here maintained the cause
Whose sacred precepts shine through Solon's
    laws:
Of all her towering structures, now alone
Some columns stand, with mantling weeds o'er-
    grown;
The wandering stranger near the port descries
A milk-white lion of stupendous size,

---

* Socrates, the great Athenian philosopher, "who of all with whom we are acquainted [in Ancient History] was in death the noblest, in life the wisest and most just," was born about B.C. 468, died B.C. 399.

† Plato, the most poetical of philosophers, was born about B.C. 428, died B.C. 347.

‡ Solon remodelled the laws and government of Athens, and inaugurated a system of polity which endured for centuries. He is supposed to have been born in B.C. 638. He died about B.C. 515.

§ Pisistratus, the great ruler of Athens, was born in B.C. 612, died in B.C. 527. The power which he won by violence he exercised with consummate ability; and we owe to his care the preservation of the Homeric poems.

|| Aristides, a statesman and general, illustrious through his integrity, died about B.C. 468.

THE SHORES OF GREECE.

Of antique marble; hence the haven's name,
Unknown to modern natives whence it came.
 Next, in the Gulf of Engia, Corinth lies,
Whose gorgeous fabrics seemed to strike the skies;
Whom, though by tyrant victors oft subdued,
Greece, Egypt, Rome, with awful wonder viewed:
Her name, for Pallas'* heavenly art renowned,
Spread like the foliage which her pillars crowned;

* Pallas, a surname of Athena, one of the great divinities of the Greeks.
"Pallas' heavenly art" is that of architecture, but she was the patron of all

THE SHORES OF GREECE.

But now, in fatal desolation laid,
Oblivion o'er it draws a dismal shade.
   Then further westward, on Morea's land,
Fair Misitra! thy modern turrets stand:
Ah! who unmoved with secret woe, can tell
That there great Lacedæmon's glory fell!
Here once she flourished, at whose trumpet's sound
War burst his chains, and nations shook around;
Here brave Leonidas* from shore to shore,
Through all Achaia, bade her thunders roar;

the useful and elegant arts; invented numbers, the chariot, the trumpet, and navigation; and was, in fact, recognized as the goddess of wisdom and knowledge.

* Who does not know the story of Leonidas, the Spartan king;—how with a small body of Spartans he held the narrow pass of Thermopylæ against the Persian host, and by his valour stimulated the enthusiasm of Greece, and afforded its children time to rally to the defence of their country? This famous event occurred in B.C. 480.

He, when imperial Xerxes from afar
Advanced with Persia's sumless hosts to war,
Till Macedonia shrunk beneath his spear,
And Greece dismayed beheld the chief draw near;
He, at Thermopylæ's immortal plain,
His force repelled with Sparta's glorious train;
Tall Œta saw the tyrant's conquered bands
In gasping millions bleed on hostile lands:
Thus vanquished Asia, trembling, heard thy name,
And Thebes and Athens sickened at thy fame;
Thy State, supported by Lycurgus'* laws,
Gained, like thine arms, superlative applause;
Even great Epaminondas† strove in vain
To curb thy spirit with a Theban chain:
But ah! how low that free-born spirit now!
Thy abject sons to haughty tyrants bow;
A false, degenerate, superstitious race,
Infest thy region, and thy name disgrace.
    Westward of these, beyond the isthmus, lies
The long-sought Isle of Ithacus the wise;
Where fair Penelope,‡ her absent lord,
Full twice ten years, with faithful love deplored.

* Lycurgus, the legislator of Sparta, flourished in the ninth century before Christ. After imposing his laws on his countrymen, he made them swear not to make any alteration in them until his return, and immediately withdrew from Sparta to finish his life in voluntary exile. "Where and how he died, nobody could tell. He vanished from the earth like a god, leaving no traces behind but his spirit; and he was honoured as a god at Sparta with a temple and yearly sacrifices down to the latest times."

† Epaminondas was a Theban general of splendid ability. He won the great battle of Leuctra, in which the Spartans suffered a most severe and crushing defeat; and in B.C. 362 crowned his fame by the remarkable victory of Mantineia, in which, however, he received a mortal wound. He was buried on the battle-field.

‡ Penelope is reputed to have been the wife of Odysseus (or Ulysses), king of Ithaca, who accompanied the Greeks to Troy, served in the ten years' war against that city, and afterwards wandered over sea and land for a protracted period. There were many suitors for Penelope's hand, but

Though many a princely heart her beauty won,
She, guarded only by a stripling son,
Each bold attempt of suitor-kings repelled,
And undefiled the nuptial contract held;
With various arts to win her love they toiled,
But all their wiles by virtuous fraud she foiled;
True to her vows, and resolutely chaste,
The beauteous princess triumphed at the last.

PLAIN OF ARGOS.

Argos, in Greece forgotten and unknown,
Still seems her cruel fortune to bemoan;

she remained faithful to her husband's memory, and eventually was rewarded by his return to Ithaca.

THE SHORES OF GREECE.

Argos, whose monarch* led the Grecian hosts
Across the Ægean main to Dardan coasts:
Unhappy prince! who on a hostile shore,
Toil, peril, anguish, ten long winters bore;
And when to native realms restored at last,
To reap the harvest of thy labours past,
There found a perjured friend, and faithless wife,
Who sacrificed to impious lust thy life:
Fast by Arcadia stretch these desert plains,
And o'er the land a gloomy tyrant reigns.

[WILLIAM FALCONER, one of the self-taught men who have risen to eminence in our English literature, was the son of an Edinburgh wig-maker, and born on the 11th of February 1732. His life was chiefly spent on board ship, and the experience he thus acquired, and the scenes he witnessed, form the subject-matter of his fine poem of "The Shipwreck," published in May 1762. He afterwards compiled a work of very different character, but, of its kind, of not inferior value, the well-known "Marine Dictionary." In 1769 he was appointed purser of the *Aurora* frigate, bound for East India on an important mission, but which never reached her destination. She is believed to have been wrecked in the Mozambique Channel—probably in January 1770.]

* Agamemnon, king of Argos, was appointed generalissimo of the Greek army which waged the famous ten years' war against Troy—the subject of Homer's "Iliad." On his return home he was murdered by his treacherous friend Ægisthus, and his false wife Clytemnestra.

DOMESTIC HAPPINESS.

O make a happy fireside clime,
    To weans and wife—
That's the true pathos and sublime
    Of human life.

[ROBERT BURNS, 1754-1796, like Cowper, commands our interest by his misfortunes as well as our admiration by his genius. He is the greatest of modern Scottish poets, though he left behind him no sublime epic or majestic drama. His songs, however, are "gems of purest ray serene;" and his "Tam O'Shanter," "All Hallowe'en," and "Cotter's Saturday Night," are splendid examples of his versatility.]

———o———

THE PEASANT'S EVENING PRAYER.

THE cheerfu' supper done, wi' serious face,
    They round the ingle form a circle wide;
The sire turns o'er, wi' patriarchal grace,
    The big ha'-Bible, ance his father's pride:
His bonnet rev'rently is laid aside,
    His lyart haffets* wearing thin an' bare;
Those strains that once did sweet in Zion glide,
    He wales† a portion with judicious care;
And, "Let us worship God!" he says, with solemn air.

They chant their artless notes in simple guise;
    They tune their hearts, by far the noblest aim:
Perhaps "Dundee's" wild, warbling measures rise,
    Or plaintive "Martyrs," worthy of the name;
Or noble "Elgin" beets‡ the heav'nward flame,
    The sweetest far of Scotia's holy lays;
Compared with these, Italian trills are tame;

* *Lyart haffets*—gray locks over the temples.
† *Wales*—selects.   ‡ *Beets*—feeds, or stimulates.

THE PEASANT'S EVENING PRAYER.

The tickled ears no heart-felt raptures raise;
Nae unison hae they with our Creator's praise.

The priest-like father reads the sacred page,
    How Abram was the friend of God on high;
Or Moses bade eternal warfare wage
    With Amalek's ungracious progeny;
Or how the royal Bard did groaning lie
    Beneath the stroke of Heaven's avenging ire;
Or Job's pathetic plaint, and wailing cry;
    Or rapt Isaiah's wild, seraphic fire;
Or other holy Seers that tune the sacred lyre.

Perhaps the Christian volume is the theme,
    How guiltless blood for guilty man was shed;
How He, who bore in Heaven the second name,
    Had not on earth whereon to lay his Head;

THE PEASANT'S EVENING PRAYER.

How His first followers and servants sped ;
  The precepts sage they wrote to many a land ;
How he, who lone in Patmos banishèd,
  Saw in the sun a mighty angel stand ;
And heard great Bab'lon's doom pronounced by
    Heaven's command.

Then, kneeling down, to Heaven's eternal King
  The saint, the father, and the husband prays :
Hope "springs exulting on triumphant wing,"
  That thus they all shall meet in future days :
There ever bask in uncreated rays,
  No more to sigh, or shed the bitter tear,
Together hymning their Creator's praise,
  In such society, yet still more dear ;
While circling Time moves round in an eternal sphere.

Compared with this, how poor Religion's pride,
  In all the pomp of method and of art,
When men display to congregations wide
  Devotion's ev'ry grace, except the heart !
The Power, incensed, the pageant will desert,
  The pompous strain, the sacerdotal stole :
But haply, in some cottage far apart,
  May hear, well-pleased, the language of the soul ;
And in His Book of Life the inmates poor enrol.

[ROBERT BURNS. From the beautiful domestic idyll of "The Cotter's Saturday Night."]

TO A MOUNTAIN DAISY.

ON TURNING ONE DOWN WITH THE PLOUGH IN APRIL 1786.

WEE, modest, crimson-tippèd flower,
    Thou's met me in an evil hour;
    For I maun crush amang the stoure*
        Thy slender stem:
To spare thee now is past my power,
        Thou bonnie gem.

Alas! it's no thy neebor sweet,
The bonnie lark, companion meet!
Bending thee 'mang the dewy weet!
        Wi' spreckled breast,
When upward-springing, blythe, to greet
        The purpling east.

Cauld blew the bitter-biting north
Upon thy early, humble birth;
Yet cheerfully thou glinted forth
        Amid the storm,
Scarce reared above the parent-earth
        Thy tender form.

The flaunting flowers our gardens yield,
High shelt'ring woods and wa's maun shield,
But thou, beneath the random bield †
        O' clod or stane,
Adorns the histie ‡ stubble-field,
        Unseen, alane.

There, in thy scanty mantle clad,
Thy snawie bosom sunward spread,

---

* *Stoure*—dust.   † *Bield*—shelter.   ‡ *Histie*—dry.

TO A MOUNTAIN DAISY.

Thou lifts thy unassuming head
    In humble guise;
But now the share uptears thy bed,
    And low thou lies!

Such is the fate of artless Maid,
Sweet flow'ret of the youthful shade!
By love's simplicity betrayed,
    And guileless trust,
Till she, like thee, all soiled, is laid
    Low i' the dust.

Such is the fate of simple Bard,
On life's rough ocean luckless starred!
Unskilful he to note the card
    Of prudent lore,
Till billows rage, and gales blow hard,
    And whelm him o'er!

Such fate to suffering worth is given,
Who long with wants and woes has striven,
By human pride or cunning driven
    To misery's brink,
Till, wrenched of every stay but Heaven,
    He, ruined, sink!

Even thou who mourn'st the Daisy's fate,
That fate is thine—no distant date;
Stern Ruin's ploughshare drives, elate,
    Full on thy bloom,
Till, crushed beneath the furrow's weight,
    Shall be thy doom.

[ROBERT BURNS. The reader may compare this fine poem with Wordsworth's on the same subject.]

"WHERE CROUCHING TIGERS WAIT THEIR HAPLESS PREY."—GOLDSMITH.

THE TIGER.

THE TIGER.

TIGER, tiger, burning bright
   In the forests of the night,
   What immortal hand or eye
   Framed thy fearful symmetry?

In what distant deeps or skies
Burned that fire within thine eyes?
On what wings dared he aspire?
What the hand dared seize the fire?

And what shoulder, and what art,
Could twist the sinews of thy heart?
When thy heart began to beat,
What dread hand formed thy dread feet?

What the hammer, what the chain,
Knit thy strength and forged thy brain?
What the anvil? what dread grasp
Dared thy deadly terrors clasp?

"AN HIDEOUS BEAST, OF HORRIBLE ASPECT, THAT COULD THE STRONGEST COURAGE HAVE APPALLED."—SPENSER.

"THE WILD BEAST WHERE HE WONS—IN FOREST WILD, IN THICKET, BRAKE, OR DEN."—JOHN MILTON.

"WITH THOUSAND SPOTS OF COLOURS QUAINT ELECT."—SPENSER.

When the stars threw down their spears,
And watered heaven with their tears,
Did he smile his work to see?
Did He who made the lamb make thee?

[WILLIAM BLAKE, born 1757, died 1827, was distinguished, both as an artist and a poet, by the originality of his genius, and the weird power of his imagination.]

THE DYING SAILOR.

HE called his friend, and prefaced with a sigh
A lover's message:—"Thomas, I must die:
Would I could see my Sally, and could rest
My throbbing temples on her faithful breast,
And gazing, go!—if not, this trifle take,
And say, till death I wore it for her sake;
Yes, I must die!—blow on, sweet breeze, blow on!
Give me one look before my life be gone,
Oh, give me that, and let me not despair,
One last fond look—and now repeat the prayer."

He had his wish, had more: I will not paint
The lovers' meeting: she beheld him faint—
With tender fears, she took a nearer view,
Her terrors doubling as her hopes withdrew;
He tried to smile, and, half succeeding, said,
"Yes, I must die;" and hope for ever fled.

Still, long she nursed him; tender thoughts, meantime,
Were interchanged, and hopes and views sublime.
To her he came to die, and every day
She took some portion of the dread away:
With him she prayed, to him his Bible read,
Soothed the faint heart, and held the aching head;

THE DYING SAILOR.

She came with smiles the hour of pain to cheer;
Apart, she sighed; alone, she shed a tear;
Then, as if breaking from a cloud, she gave
Fresh light, and gilt the prospect of the grave.

One day he lighter seemed, and they forgot
The care, the dread, the anguish of their lot;
They spoke with cheerfulness, and seemed to think,
Yet said not so—"Perhaps he will not sink;"
A sudden brightness in his look appeared,
A sudden vigour in his voice was heard;—
She had been reading in the Book of Prayer,
And led him forth, and placed him in his chair;
Lively he seemed, and spoke of all he knew,
The friendly many, and the favourite few;
Nor one did he to mind that day recall,
But she has cherished, and she loves them all;
When in her way she meets them, they appear
Peculiar people—death has made them dear.
He named his friend, but then his hand she prest,
And fondly whispered, "Thou must go to rest;"
"I go," he said; but, as he spoke, she found
His hand more cold, and fluttering was the sound!
Then gazed affrightened; but she caught a last,
A dying look of love, and all was past!

[Rev. GEORGE CRABBE, 1754-1832, author of "The Village Register," "The Borough," "The Library," and other domestic poems of a peculiar but powerful order. "Crabbe is distinguished from all other poets, both by the choice of his subjects, and by his manner of treating them. By the mere force of his art, and the novelty of his style, he forces us to attend to objects that are usually neglected, and to enter into feelings from which in general we are but too eager to escape."]

"SHE WALKS THE WATERS LIKE A THING OF LIFE."—BYRON.

A SAILOR'S SONG.

A SAILOR'S SONG.

WHILE clouds on high are riding,
    The wintry moonshine hiding,
    The raging blast abiding,
        O'er mountain waves we go.
With hind the dry land reaping,
With townsman shelter keeping,
With lord on soft down sleeping,
        Change we our lot? Oh, no!

On stormy waves careering,
Each sea-mate sea-mate cheering,

"ROLL ON, THOU DARK AND DEEP-BLUE OCEAN, ROLL!"—BYRON.

With dauntless helmsman steering,
Our forthward course we hold.
Their sails with sunbeams whitened,
Themselves with glory brightened,
From care their bosom lightened,
Who shall return? The bold.

[JOANNA BAILLIE, born at Bothwell, Lanarkshire, in 1762; died at Hampstead, near London, 1851. A simple and energetic style, and considerable power of portraying the passions, distinguish her dramatic and poetical works, of which the best are "De Montfort" and "Count Basil."]

A SERENADE.

UP! quit thy bower! late wears the hour;
Long have the rooks cawed round the tower,
O'er flower and tree loud hums the bee,
And the wild kid sports merrily.
The sun is bright, the sky is clear;
Wake, lady, wake! and hasten here.

Up, maiden fair! and bind thy hair,
And rouse thee in the breezy air;
The lulling stream that soothed thy dream,
Is dancing in the sunny beam.
Waste not these hours, so fresh, so gay;
Leave thy soft couch, and haste away.

Up! time will tell; the morning-bell
Its service-sound* has chimèd well;
The agèd crone keeps house alone;
The reapers to the fields are gone.

* *Service-sound*—sound for matins, or morning prayers.

A SERENADE. 131

"FOND WORDS HAVE OFT BEEN SPOKEN TO THEE, SLEEP.—

"SPRINGLETS IN THE DAWN ARE STREAMING, DIAMONDS ON THE BRAKE ARE GLEAMING."—SIR W. SCOTT.

"I HAVE SONG OF WAR FOR KNIGHT, AND LAY OF LOVE FOR LADY BRIGHT."—SIR WALTER SCOTT.

Lose not these hours, so cool and gay;
Lo! while thou sleep'st, they haste away.

[JOANNA BAILLIE. From her "Fugitive Verses."]

AND THOU HAST HAD THY STORE OF TEND'REST NAMES."—WORDSWORTH.

A WISH.

MINE be a cot beside the hill;
    A bee-hive's hum shall soothe my ear;
A willowy brook that turns a mill,
    With many a fall shall linger near.

The swallow, oft, beneath my thatch,
    Shall twitter from her clay-built nest;
Oft shall the pilgrim lift the latch,
    And share my meal, a welcome guest.

Around my ivied porch shall cling
    Each fragrant flower that drinks the dew;
And Lucy, at her wheel, shall sing,
    In russet gown and apron blue.

The village church among the trees,
    Where first our marriage-vows were given,
With merry peals shall swell the breeze,
    And point with taper spire to heaven.

[SAMUEL ROGERS, author of "The Vision of Columbus," "Italy," "Human Life," "The Pleasures of Memory;" born 1763, died 1855.]

GINEVRA.

F thou shouldst ever come by choice or chance
    To Modena, where still religiously
      Among the ancient trophies is preserved
  Bologna's bucket*. . . . .
Stop at a Palace near the Reggio-gate,
Dwelt in of old by one of the Orsini.
Its noble gardens, terrace above terrace,
And rich in fountains, statues, cypresses,
Will long detain thee; but, ere thou go,
Enter the house—prythee, forget it not—
And look awhile upon a picture there.

'Tis of a lady in her earliest youth,
The very last of that illustrious race.
He who observes it,—ere he passes on,
Gazes his fill, and comes and comes again,
That he may call it up, when far away.

She sits, inclining forward as to speak,
Her lips half open, and her finger up,
As though she said "Beware!" her vest of gold
Broidered with flowers, and clasped from head to foot,
An emerald stone in every golden clasp;
And on her brow, fairer than alabaster,
A coronet of pearls. But then, her face,
So lovely, yet so arch, so full of mirth,
The overflowings of an innocent heart,—
It haunts me still, though many a year has fled,
Like some wild melody!

* Reputed to have been the bucket which once caused a war between Bologna and Modena.

GINEVRA.

                Alone it hangs,
Over a mouldering heirloom, its companion,
An oaken chest, half eaten by the worm,
But richly carved by Antony of Trent
With Scripture stories from the life of Christ.

She was an only child; from infancy
The joy, the pride of an indulgent sire;
The young GINEVRA was his all in life,
Still as she grew, for ever in his sight;
And in her fifteenth year became a bride,
Marrying an only son, Francesco Doria,
Her playmate from her birth, and her first love.
Just as she looks there in her bridal dress,
She was all gentleness, all gaiety,
Her pranks the favourite theme of every tongue.
But now the day was come, the day, the hour;
Now frowning, smiling, for the hundredth time,
The nurse, that ancient lady, preached decorum;
And, in the lustre of her youth, she gave
Her hand, with her heart in it, to Francesco.

Great was the joy. But at the bridal feast,
When all sat down, the Bride was wanting there.
Nor was she to be found! Her father cried,
"'Tis but to make a trial of our love!"
And filled his glass to all; but his hand shook,
And soon from guest to guest the panic spread.
'Twas but that instant she had left Francesco,
Laughing and looking back, and flying still,
Her ivory tooth imprinted on his finger.
But now, alas! she was not to be found;
Nor from that hour could anything be guessed,
But that she was not!—

GINEVRA.

Weary of his life,
Francesco fled to Venice, and forthwith
Flung it away in battle with the Turks.
Orsini lived; and long might you have seen
An old man wandering as in quest of something,
Something he could not find—he knew not what.
When he was gone, the house remained awhile
Silent and tenantless—then went to strangers.

Full fifty years were past, and all forgot,
When, on an idle day, a day of search
'Mid the old lumber in the Gallery,
That mouldering chest was noticed; and 'twas said
By one as young, as thoughtless as Ginevra,
"Why not remove it from its lurking-place?"
'Twas done as soon as said; but on the way
It burst, it fell; and, lo! a skeleton,
With here and there a pearl, an emerald-stone,
A golden clasp, clasping a shred of gold.
All else had perished,—save a nuptial ring,
And a small seal, her mother's legacy,
Engraven with a name, the name of both,
"GINEVRA."
              There, then, had she found a grave!
Within that chest had she concealed herself,
Fluttering with joy, the happiest of the happy;
When a spring lock, that lay in ambush there,
Fastened her down for ever!

[SAMUEL ROGERS. From his poem of "Italy." This story is said to be founded on fact, and resembles the legend immortalized in the popular song of "The Mistletoe Bough."]

"'TWAS MORN,—THE SKYLARK O'ER THE FURROW SUNG."—ROGERS.

THE SKYLARK.

"LEAVE TO THE NIGHTINGALE HER SHADY WOOD, A PRIVACY OF GLORIOUS LIGHT IS THINE,"—(WORDSWORTH)

"WHENCE THOU DOST POUR UPON THE WORLD A FLOOD OF HARMONY, WITH INSTINCT MORE DIVINE."—WORDSWORTH.

BIRD of the wilderness,
    Blithesome and cumberless,
Sweet be thy matin o'er moorland and lea!
    Emblem of happiness,
    Blest is thy dwelling-place—
Oh, to abide in the desert with thee!
    Wild is thy lay and loud,
    Far in the downy cloud;
Love gives it energy, love gave it birth.
    Where, on thy dewy wing,
    Where art thou journeying?
Thy lay is in heaven, thy love is on earth.

    O'er fell and fountain sheen,
    O'er moor and mountain green,
O'er the red streamer that heralds the day,

"ETHEREAL MINSTREL! PILGRIM OF THE SKY!"—WORDSWORTH.

MELROSE ABBEY.

Over the cloudlet dim,
Over the rainbow's rim,
Musical cherub, soar, singing, away!
Then, when the gloaming comes,
Low in the heather blooms,
Sweet will thy welcome and bed of love be!
Emblem of happiness,
Blest is thy dwelling-place—
Oh, to abide in the desert with thee!

[JAMES HOGG, a Scotch poet of considerable genius, better known as "The Ettrick Shepherd," was born at Ettrick, in Selkirkshire, in 1770; died in 1835. His "Kilmeny" is a fairy tale of great beauty; and his prose works possess a distinctive and peculiar merit.]

MELROSE ABBEY.

IF thou wouldst view fair Melrose aright,
Go, visit it by the pale moonlight;
For the gay beams of gladsome day
Gild, but to flout, the ruins gray.
When the broken arches are black in night,
And each shafted oriel glimmers white;

When the cold light's uncertain shower
Streams on the ruined central tower;
When buttress and buttress, alternately,
Seem framed of ebony and ivory;
When silver edges the imagery,
And the scrolls that teach thee to live and die;
When distant Tweed is heard to rave,
And the owlet to hoot o'er the dead man's grave;
Then go—but go alone the while—
Then view St. David's ruined pile;
And home returning, soothly swear,
Was never scene so sad and fair!

. . . . .

Spreading herbs and flowerets bright,
Glistened with the dew of night;
Nor herb nor floweret glistened there,
But was carved on the cloister-arches as fair.

. . . . .

Full many a scutcheon and banner riven,
Shook to the cold night-wind of heaven,
   Around the screenèd altar's pale;
And there the dying lamps did burn
Before thy low and lonely urn,
O gallant chief of Otterburne!
   And thine, dark knight of Liddesdale!
Oh, fading honours of the dead!
Oh, high ambition, lowly laid!

. . . . .

The moon on the east oriel shone,
Through slender shafts of shapely stone,
   By foliaged tracery combined;
Thou wouldst have thought some fairy's hand
'Twixt poplars straight the ozier wand,
   In many a freakish joint, had twined;

MARMION AND THE DOUGLAS.

Then framed a spell, when the work was done,
And changed the willow wreaths to stone.
The silver light, so pale and faint,
Showed many a prophet and many a saint,
  Whose image on the glass was dyed;
Full in the midst, his Cross of Red
Triumphant Michael brandishèd,
  And trampled the Apostate's pride.
The moonbeam kissed the holy pane,
And threw on the pavement a bloody stain.

[Sir WALTER SCOTT, born 1771; died 1832. Our extract is from his stirring ballad-poem of "The Lay of the Last Minstrel," and shows how admirable was his mastery over its rapid and spirited rhythm, how keen his observation, and how graphic his description. Scott, however, is better known as the greatest of English novelists than as the successful writer of poetical romances, which, bright and vigorous as they are, nowhere display the higher qualities of his genius.]

THE QUARREL BETWEEN MARMION AND THE DOUGLAS.

NOT far advanced was morning day,
  When Marmion did his troop array
    To Surrey's camp to ride;
He had safe-conduct for his band,
Beneath the royal seal and hand,
    And Douglas gave a guide:
The ancient Earl, with stately grace,
Would Clara on her palfrey place,
And whispered, in an under tone,
"Let the hawk stoop, his prey is flown."
The train from out the castle drew;
But Marmion stopped to bid adieu.

"Though something I might plain," he said,
"Of cold respect to stranger guest,
Sent hither by your King's behest,
　While in Tantallon's towers I stayed;
Part we in friendship from your land,
And, noble Earl, receive my hand."
But Douglas round him drew his cloak,
Folded his arms, and thus he spoke :—
"My manors, halls, and bowers shall still
Be open, at my sovereign's will,
To each one whom he lists, howe'er
Unmeet to be the owner's peer.
My castles are my King's alone,
From turret to foundation-stone—
The hand of Douglas is his own;
And never shall in friendly grasp,
The hand of such as Marmion clasp."

Burned Marmion's swarthy cheek like fire,
And shook his very frame for ire,
　And, "This to me!" he said.
"An 'twere not for thy hoary beard,
Such hand as Marmion's had not spared
　To cleave the Douglas' head!
And, first, I tell thee, haughty peer,
He who does England's message here,
Although the meanest in her state,
May well, proud Angus, be thy mate:
And, Douglas, more I tell thee here,
　Even in thy pitch of pride,
Here in thy hold, thy vassals near
(Nay, never look upon your lord,
And lay your hands upon your sword),
　I tell thee, thou 'rt defied!

MARMION AND THE DOUGLAS.

And if thou said'st I am not peer
To any lord in Scotland here,
Lowland or Highland, far or near,
  Lord Angus, thou hast lied!"
On the Earl's cheek the flush of rage
O'ercame the ashen hue of age:
Fierce he broke forth—"And darest thou then
To beard the lion in his den,
  The Douglas in his hall?
And hopest thou hence unscathed to go?
No, by Saint Bride of Bothwell, no!
Up drawbridge, grooms! What, warder, ho!
  Let the portcullis fall!"
Lord Marmion turned—well was his need—
And dashed the rowels in his steed,
Like arrow through the archway sprung,
The ponderous grate behind him rung:
To pass there was such scanty room,
The bars, descending, razed his plume.
The steed along the drawbridge flies,
Just as it trembled on the rise;
Nor lighter does the swallow skim
Along the smooth lake's level brim:
And when Lord Marmion reached his band,
He halts, and turns with clenchèd hand,
And shout of loud defiance pours,
And shook his gauntlet at the towers.
"Horse! horse!" the Douglas cried, "and
    chase!"
But soon he reined his fury's pace:
"A royal messenger he came,
Though most unworthy of the name.—
A letter forged! Saint Jude to speed!
Did ever knight so foul a deed!

At first in heart it liked me ill,
When the King praised his clerkly skill.
Thanks to Saint Bothan, son of mine,
Save Gawain, ne'er could pen a line :
So swore I, and I swear it still,
Let my boy-bishop fret his fill.
Saint Mary, mend my fiery mood !
Old age ne'er cools the Douglas blood—
I thought to slay him where he stood.
'Tis pity of him, too," he cried :
" Bold can he speak, and fairly ride ;
I warrant him a warrior tried."
With this his mandate he recalls,
And slowly seeks his castle halls.

[Sir WALTER SCOTT. From his poem of "Marmion."]

THE ALBATROSS.

ND now there came both mist and snow,
And it grew wondrous cold :
And ice, mast-high, came floating by,
As green as emerald.

And through the drifts the snowy clifts
Did send a dismal sheen :
Nor shapes of men nor beasts we ken—
The ice was all between.

The ice was here, the ice was there,
The ice was all around ;
It cracked and growled, and roared and howled,
Like noises in a swound.

THE BEST PRAYER.

At length did cross an Albatross—
Through the fog it came;
As if it had been a Christian soul,
We hailed it in God's name.

It ate the food it ne'er had eat,
And round and round it flew.
The ice did split with a thunder-fit;
The helmsman steered us through!

And a good south wind sprung up behind;
The Albatross did follow,
And every day, for food or play,
Came to the mariners' hollo!

In mist or cloud, on mast or shroud,
It perched for vespers nine:
Whiles all the night, through fog-smoke white,
Glimmered the white moon-shine.

[SAMUEL TAYLOR COLERIDGE, born 1772, died 1834, author of "The Friend," "Aids to Reflection," "Confessions of an Inquiring Spirit," "Schiller's 'Wallenstein,'" "Remorse," "Legend of Christabel," and other works in prose and poetry. The extract is from "The Ancient Mariner" (Part I.)—a wild romantic poem of great beauty.]

THE BEST PRAYER.

HE prayeth best who loveth best
All things both great and small;
For the dear Lord who loveth us,
He made and loveth all.

[SAMUEL TAYLOR COLERIDGE. From "The Ancient Mariner."]

A PERFECT WOMAN.

SHE was a phantom of delight
When first she gleamed upon my sight;
A lovely apparition, sent
To be a moment's ornament;
Her eyes as stars of twilight fair,
Like twilight's, too, her dusky hair;
But all things else about her drawn
From Maytime and the cheerful dawn;
A dainty shape, an image gay,
To haunt, to startle, and waylay.

I saw her, upon nearer view,
A spirit, yet a woman too!
Her household motions light and free,
And steps of virgin liberty;
A countenance in which did meet
Sweet records, promises as sweet;
A creature not too bright or good
For human nature's daily food,
For transient sorrows, simple wiles,
Praise, blame, love, kisses, tears, and smiles.

And now I see with eye serene
The very pulse of the machine;
A being breathing thoughtful breath,
A traveller betwixt life and death;
The reason firm, the temperate will,
Endurance, foresight, strength, and skill:
A perfect woman, nobly planned,
To warn, to comfort, and command;

THE DANISH BOY.

*And yet a spirit still and bright,
With something of an angel-light.*

[WILLIAM WORDSWORTH, author of "The Excursion," "Sonnets," "Laodamia," "Ruth," and numerous poems in which depth of thought is nobly combined with splendour of language, was born 1770, died 1850.]

THE DANISH BOY.

BETWEEN two sister moorland rills
There is a spot that seems to lie
Sacred to flowerets of the hills,
And sacred to the sky.
And in this smooth and open dell
There is a tempest-stricken tree;
A corner-stone by lightning cut,
The last stone of a lonely hut;
And in this dell you see
A thing no storm can e'er destroy—
The shadow of a Danish boy.

In clouds above the lark is heard,
But drops not here to earth for rest;
Within this lonesome nook the bird
Did never build her nest.
No beast, no bird hath here his home;
Bees, wafted on the breezy air,
Pass high above those fragrant bells
To other flowers; to other dells
Their burdens do they bear.
The Danish boy walks here alone:
The lovely dell is all his own.

THE DANISH BOY.

A spirit of noon-day is he,
Yet seems a form of flesh and blood;
Nor piping shepherd shall he be,
Nor herd-boy of the wood.
A regal vest of fur he wears,
In colour like a raven's wing;
It fears not rain, nor wind, nor dew;
But in the storm 'tis fresh and blue
As budding pines in spring;
His helmet has a vernal grace,
Fresh as the bloom upon his face.

A harp is from his shoulder hung;
Resting the harp across his knee,
To words of a forgotten tongue
He suits its melody.
Of flocks upon the neighbouring hills
He is the darling and the joy;
And often, when no cause appears,
The mountain-ponies prick their ears, . . .
They hear the Danish boy,
While in the dell he sings alone
Beside the tree and corner-stone.

There sits he: in his face you spy
No trace of a ferocious air;
Nor ever was a cloudless sky
So steady or so fair.
The lovely Danish boy is blest,
And happy in his flowery cove:
From bloody deeds his thoughts are far;
And yet he warbles songs of war,
That seem like songs of love,

For calm and gentle is his mien;
Like a dead boy he is serene.

[WILLIAM WORDSWORTH.]

THE FOUNTAIN.

WE talked with open heart and tongue,
    Affectionate and true,
A pair of friends, though I was young,
    And Matthew seventy-two.

We lay beneath a spreading oak,
    Beside a mossy seat;
And from the turf a fountain broke,
    And gurgled at our feet.

"Now, Matthew, let us try to match
    This water's pleasant tune
With some old border song, or catch,
    That suits a summer noon.

Or of the church-clock and the chimes
    Sing here beneath the shade,
That half-mad thing of witty rhymes
    Which you last April made."

In silence Matthew lay, and eyed
    The spring beneath the tree;
And thus the dear old man replied,
    The gray-haired man of glee:

THE FOUNTAIN.

"Down to the vale this water steers;
　How merrily it goes!
'Twill murmur on a thousand years,
　And flow as now it flows.

"And here, on this delightful day,
　I cannot choose but think
How oft, a vigorous man, I lay
　Beside this fountain's brink.

"My eyes are dim with childish tears,
　My heart is idly stirred,
For the same sound is in my ears
　Which in those days I heard.

"Thus fares it still in our decay;
　And yet the wiser mind
Mourns less for what age takes away
　Than what it leaves behind.

"The blackbird in the summer trees,
　The lark upon the hill,
Let loose their carols when they please,
　Are quiet when they will.

"With Nature never do *they* wage
　A foolish strife: they see
A happy youth, and their old age
　Is beautiful and free;

"But we are pressed by heavy laws,
　And often, glad no more,
We wear a face of joy because
　We have been glad of yore.

THE FOUNTAIN.

"If there is one who need bemoan
    His kindred laid in earth,
The household hearts that were his own,
    It is the man of mirth.

"My days, my friend, are almost gone,
    My life has been approved,
And many love me; but by none
    Am I enough beloved."

"Now both himself and me he wrongs,
    The man who thus complains!
I live and sing my idle songs
    Upon these happy plains;

"And, Matthew, for thy children dead
    I'll be a son to thee!"
At this he grasped my hand, and said,
    "Alas! that cannot be."

We rose up from the fountain side,
    And down the smooth descent
Of the green sheep-track did we glide,
    And through the woods we went;

And, ere we came to Leonard's Rock,
    He sang those witty rhymes
About the crazy old church-clock,
    And the bewildered chimes.

[WILLIAM WORDSWORTH.]

WE ARE SEVEN.

 SIMPLE child,
   That lightly draws its breath,
And feels its life in every limb,
   What should it know of death?

I met a little cottage girl:
   She was eight years old, she said;
Her hair was thick with many a curl
   That clustered round her head.

She had a rustic, woodland air,
   And she was wildly clad;
Her eyes were fair, and very fair:
   —Her beauty made me glad.

"Sisters and brothers, little maid,
   How many may you be?"
"How many? Seven in all," she said;
   And wondering looked at me.

"And where are they? I pray you tell."
   She answered: "Seven are we;
And two of us at Conway dwell,
   And two are gone to sea;

"Two of us in the churchyard lie,
   My sister and my brother;
And, in the churchyard cottage, I
   Dwell near them, with my mother."

"You say that two at Conway dwell,
   And two are gone to sea,

WE ARE SEVEN.

Yet ye are seven!—I pray you tell,
  Sweet maid, how this may be?"

Then did the little maid reply,
  " Seven boys and girls are we;
Two of us in the churchyard lie,
  Beneath the churchyard tree."

" You run about, my little maid,
  Your limbs they are alive;
If two are in the churchyard laid,
  Then ye are only five."

" Their graves are green, they may be seen,"
  The little maid replied,
" Twelve steps or more from my mother's door,
  And they are side by side.

" My stockings there I often knit,
  My kerchief there I hem;
And there upon the ground I sit—
  I sit and sing to them.

" And often after sunset, sir,
  When it is light and fair,
I take my little porringer,
  And eat my supper there.

" The first that died was little Jane:
  In bed she moaning lay,
Till God released her of her pain;
  And then she went away.

" So in the churchyard she was laid;
  And all the summer dry

TO THE DAISY.

Together round her grave we played,
  My brother John and I.

"And when the ground was white with snow,
  And I could run and slide,
My brother John was forced to go,
  And he lies by her side."

"How many are you, then," said I,
  "If they two are in heaven?"
The little maiden did reply,
  "Oh, master, we are seven!"

"But they are dead—those two are dead!
  Their spirits are in heaven!"
'Twas throwing words away; for still
The little maid would have her will,
  And said, "Nay, we are seven!"

[WILLIAM WORDSWORTH.]

―――o―――

TO THE DAISY.*

WITH little here to do or see
  Of things that in the great world be,
  Sweet daisy! oft I talk to thee,
For thou art worthy:
Thou unassuming commonplace
Of Nature, with that homely face,

---

* This delightful ode the reader may advantageously compare with the poem on the same subject by Robert Burns. He will not fail to observe how in each the individuality of the poet strongly displays itself, and though both are beautiful, yet how different they are in sentiment and tone.

TO THE DAISY.

And yet with something of a grace
    Which love makes for thee !

Oft do I sit by thee at ease,
And weave a web of similes,
Loose types of things through all degrees,
    Thoughts of thy raising ;
And many a fond and idle name
I give to thee, for praise or blame,
As is the humour of the game,
    While I am gazing.

A nun demure, of lowly port ;
Or sprightly maiden of love's court,
In thy simplicity the sport
    Of all temptations ;
A queen in crown of rubies dressed ;
A starveling in a scanty vest ;
Are all, as seem to suit thee best,
    Thy appellations.

A little Cyclops, with one eye
Staring to threaten and defy—
That thought comes next ; and instantly
    The freak is over.
The shape will vanish, and, behold !
A silver shield with boss of gold,
That spreads itself, some fairy bold
    In fight to cover.

I see thee glittering from afar,—
And then thou art a pretty star :
Not quite so fair as many are
    In heaven above thee ;

TO A BUTTERFLY.

Yet like a star, with glittering crest,
Self-poised in air, thou seem'st to rest;—
May peace come never to his nest
    Who shall reprove thee!

Sweet flower! for by that name at last,
When all my reveries are past,
I call thee, and to that cleave fast,—
    Sweet silent creature!
That breathest with me in sun and air,
Do thou, as thou art wont, repair
My heart with gladness, and a share
    Of thy meek nature!

[WILLIAM WORDSWORTH.]

TO A BUTTERFLY.

I'VE watched you now a full half-hour
  Self-poised upon that yellow flower;
  And, little Butterfly, indeed,
I know not if you sleep or feed:
How motionless!—not frozen seas
  More motionless! and then
What joy awaits you, when the breeze
Hath found you out among the trees,
    And calls you forth again!

This plot of orchard ground is ours;
My trees they are, my sister's flowers;
Here rest your wings when they are weary;
Here lodge as in a sanctuary!

THE REDBREAST AND THE BUTTERFLY.

Come often to us, fear no wrong,
   Sit near us on the bough;
We'll talk of sunshine and of song;
And summer days, when we were young;
Sweet childish days, that were as long
   As twenty days are now.

[WILLIAM WORDSWORTH.]

THE REDBREAST AND THE BUTTERFLY.

ART thou the bird whom man loves best,
   The pious bird with the scarlet breast,
      Our little English Robin;
The bird that comes about our doors
   When autumn winds are sobbing?

"BY OUR OWN SPIRITS ARE WE DEIFIED."—WORDSWORTH.

156   THE REDBREAST AND THE BUTTERFLY.

> Art thou the "Peter" of Norway boors?
> Their "Thomas" in Finland,
> And Russia far inland?
> The bird, who by some name or other,
> All men who know thee call thee brother,
> The darling of children and men?
> Could Father Adam open his eyes,
> And see this sight beneath the skies,
> He'd wish to close them again.

> If the butterfly knew but his friend,
> Hither his flight he would bend;
> And find his way to me.
> Under the branches of the tree,
> In and out, he darts about;
> Can this be the bird, to men so good,
> That after their bewildering,

"THE HOLY TIME IS QUIET AS A NUN BREATHLESS WITH ADORATION."—WILLIAM WORDSWORTH.

"'TIS SENSE, UNBRIDLED WILL, AND NOT TRUE LOVE, WHICH KILLS THE SOUL."—WORDSWORTH.

"SWEET LOOKS, BY HUMAN KINDNESS BRED."—WORDSWORTH.

THE REDBREAST AND THE BUTTERFLY.

Did cover with leaves the little children,
So painfully in the wood?

What ailed thee, Robin, that thou couldst pursue
    A beautiful creature,
    That is gentle by nature?
Beneath the summer sky
From flower to flower let him fly;
'Tis all that he wishes to do.
The cheerer thou of our indoor sadness,
He is the friend of our summer gladness:
What hinders, then, that ye should be
Playmates in the sunny weather,
And fly about in the air together?
His beautiful wings in crimson are dressed,
A crimson as bright as thine own!
If thou would'st be happy in thy nest,
O pious bird! whom man loves best,
Love him, or leave him alone!

[WILLIAM WORDSWORTH.]

TO THE SMALL CELANDINE.

ANSIES, lilies, kingcups, daisies,
    Let them live upon their praises;
    Long as there's a sun that sets,
Primroses shall have their glory;
Long as there are violets,
They will have a place in story:
There's a flower that shall be mine,—
'Tis the little Celandine.

Eyes of some men travel far
For the finding of a star;
Up and down the heavens they go,
Men that keep a mighty rout!
I'm as great as they, I trow,
Since the day I found thee out,
Little flower!—I'll make a stir,
Like a great astronomer.

Modest, yet withal an elf
Bold, and lavish of thyself;
Since we needs must first have met
I have seen thee, high and low,
Thirty years or more, and yet
'Twas a face I did not know;
Thou hast now, go where I may,
Fifty greetings in a day.

Ere a leaf is on a bush,
In the time before the thrush
Has a thought about its nest,
Thou wilt come with half a call,

TO THE SMALL CELANDINE.

Spreading out thy glossy breast
Like a careless prodigal;
Telling tales about the sun,
When we've little warmth, or none.

Poets, vain men in their mood!
Travel with the multitude;
Never heed them; I aver
That they all are wanton wooers.
But the thrifty cottager,
Who stirs little out of doors,
Joys to spy thee near her home:
Spring is coming—thou art come!

Comfort have thou of thy merit,
Kindly, unassuming spirit!
Careless of thy neighbourhood,
Thou dost show thy pleasant face
On the moor, and in the wood,
In the lane—there's not a place,
Howsoever mean it be,
But 'tis good enough for thee.

Ill befall the yellow flowers,
Children of the flaring hours!
Buttercups, that will be seen,
Whether we will see or no:
Others, too, of lofty mien;
They have done as worldlings do,
Taken praise that should be thine,
Little, humble Celandine!

Prophet of delight and mirth,
Scorned and slighted upon earth!

Herald of a mighty band,
Of a joyous train ensuing,
Singing at my heart's command,
In the lanes my thoughts pursuing,
I will sing, as doth behove,
Hymns in praise of what I love!

[WILLIAM WORDSWORTH. This poem is a notable example of the way in which genius turns the humblest and meanest things to high advantage. What thousands have gazed on the Celandine, yet to how few can the lowly flower have suggested the ideas which Wordsworth has embodied! Here is a pregnant reason for gratitude to our poets: without their aid Nature would remain to most of us a sealed book.]

SIMON LEE THE OLD HUNTSMAN.

IN the sweet shire of Cardigan,
    Not far from pleasant Ivor Hall,
    An old man dwells, a little man,—
I've heard he once was tall.
Of years he has upon his back,
No doubt, a burthen weighty;
He says he is threescore and ten,
But others say he's eighty.

A long blue livery coat has he,
That's fair behind, and fair before;
Yet, meet him where you will, you see
At once that he is poor.
Full five-and-twenty years he lived
A running huntsman merry;
And though he has but one eye left,
His cheek is like a cherry.

SIMON LEE THE OLD HUNTSMAN.

No man like him the horn could sound,
And no man was so full of glee;
To say the least, four counties round
Had heard of Simon Lee.
His master's dead, and no one now
Dwells in the hall of Ivor;
Men, dogs, and horses, all are dead;
He is the sole survivor.

And he is lean and he is sick,
His dwindled body's half awry;
His ankles too are swoln and thick;
His legs are thin and dry.
When he was young, he little knew
Of husbandry or tillage,
And now is forced to work, though weak,
—The weakest in the village.

He all the country could outrun,
Could leave both man and horse behind;
And often, ere the race was done,
He reeled and was stone blind.
And still there's something in the world
At which his heart rejoices;
For when the chiming hounds are out,
He dearly loves their voices!

His hunting feats have him bereft
Of his right eye, as you may see;
And then, what limbs those feats have left
To poor old Simon Lee!
He has no son, he has no child;
His wife, an aged woman,
Lives with him, near the waterfall,
Upon the village common.

SIMON LEE THE OLD HUNTSMAN.

Old Ruth works out of doors with him,
And does what Simon cannot do;
For she, not over stout of limb,
Is stouter of the two.
And, though you with your utmost skill
From labour could not wean them,
Alas, 'tis very little, all
Which they can do between them.

Beside their moss-grown hut of clay,
Not twenty paces from the door,
A scrap of land they have, but they
Are poorest of the poor.
This scrap of land he from the heath
Inclosed when he was stronger;
But what avails the land to them,
Which they can till no longer?

Few months of life has he in store,
As he to you will tell,
For still, the more he works, the more
Do his weak ankles swell.
My gentle reader, I perceive
How patiently you've waited,
And I'm afraid that you expect
Some tale will be related.

Oh, reader! had you in your mind
Such stores as silent thought can bring,
Oh, gentle reader! you would find
A tale in everything.*

* Compare with Shakspeare:
"Our life
Finds tongues in trees, books in the running brooks,
Sermons in stones, and good in everything."

SIMON LEE THE OLD HUNTSMAN.

What more I have to say is short,
I hope you'll kindly take it:
It is no tale; but, should you think,
Perhaps a tale you'll make it.

One summer day I chanced to see
This old man doing all he could
To unearth the root of an old tree,
A stump of rotten wood.
The mattock tottered in his hand;
So vain was his endeavour,
That at the root of the old tree
He might have worked for ever.

"You're over-tasked, good Simon Lee,
Give me your tool," to him I said;
And at the word right gladly he
Received my proffered aid.
I struck, and with a single blow
The tangled root I severed,
At which the poor old man so long
And vainly had endeavoured.

The tears into his eyes were brought,
And thanks and praises seemed to run
So fast out of his heart, I thought
They never would have done.
—I've heard of hearts unkind, kind deeds
With coldness still returning,
Alas! the gratitude of men
Has oft'ner left me mourning.

(WILLIAM WORDSWORTH.)

LORD ULLIN'S DAUGHTER.

CHIEFTAIN to the Highlands bound,
    Cries, "Boatman, do not tarry!
And I'll give thee a silver pound
    To row us o'er the ferry!"

"Now who be ye would cross Lochgyle,*
    This dark and stormy water?"
"Oh, I'm the chief of Ulva's isle,
    And this, Lord Ullin's daughter.

"And fast before her father's men
    Three days we've fled together,
For should he find us in the glen,
    My blood would stain the heather.

"His horsemen hard behind us ride;
    Should they our steps discover,
Then who will cheer my bonny bride
    When they have slain her lover?"

Out spake the hardy Highland wight:
    "I'll go, my chief—I'm ready:—
It is not for your silver bright,
    But for your winsome lady:

"And by my word! the bonny bird
    In danger shall not tarry;
So though the waves are raging white
    I'll row you o'er the ferry."

* Loch Goil, a lake which lies embosomed among wild precipitous mountains, in the south of Argyleshire. It opens into Loch Long.

LORD ULLIN'S DAUGHTER.

By this the storm grew loud apace,
    The water-wraith* was shrieking;
And in the scowl of heaven each face
    Grew dark as they were speaking.

But still as wilder blew the wind,
    And as the night grew drearer,
Adown the glen rode armèd men;
    Their trampling sounded nearer.

"Oh, haste thee, haste!" the lady cries,
    "Though tempests round us gather,
I'll meet the raging of the skies;
    But not an angry father."

The boat has left a stormy land,
    A stormy sea before her,—
When, oh! too strong for human hand
    The tempest gathered o'er her.

And still they rowed amidst the roar
    Of waters fast prevailing:
Lord Ullin reached that fatal shore,
    His wrath was changed to wailing.

For, sore dismayed, through storm and shade,
    His child he did discover:—
One lovely hand she stretched for aid,
    And one was round her lover.

"Come back! come back!" he cried in grief,
    "Across this stormy water:
And I'll forgive your Highland chief,
    My daughter!—oh, my daughter!"

* The water-spirit.

"TO BEAR IS TO CONQUER OUR FATE."—THOMAS CAMPBELL.

BATTLE OF THE BALTIC.

'Twas vain: the loud waves lashed the shore,
Return or aid preventing:
The waters wild went o'er his child,—
And he was left lamenting.

[THOMAS CAMPBELL, author of "The Pleasures of Hope," "Gertrude of Wyoming," and several famous lyrics, born 1777, died 1844.]

———o———

BATTLE OF THE BALTIC.*

OF Nelson and the North
  Sing the glorious day's renown,
    When to battle fierce came forth
All the might of Denmark's crown,
And her arms along the deep proudly shone;
By each gun the lighted brand,
In a bold determined hand,
And the Prince of all the land
Led them on.

Like leviathans afloat,
Lay their bulwarks on the brine;
While the sign of battle flew
On the lofty British line:
It was ten of April morn by the chime:
As they drifted on their path,
There was a silence deep as death;
And the boldest held his breath,
For a time.

* On the 2nd of April 1801, Copenhagen was bombarded by the English under Lord Nelson and Admiral Sir Hyde Parker, and in their engagement with the Danish fleet of twenty-three ships of the line, eighteen were taken or destroyed.

"THE SENTINEL STARS SET THEIR WATCH IN THE SKY."—CAMPBELL.

But the might of England flushed
To anticipate the scene;
And her van the fleeter rushed
O'er the deadly space between.
"Hearts of oak!" our captains cried! when
    each gun
From its adamantine lips
Spread a death-shade round the ships,
Like the hurricane eclipse
Of the sun.

Again! again! again!
And the havoc did not slack,
Till a feeble cheer the Dane
To our cheering sent us back;—
Their shots along the deep slowly boom:—
Then ceased—and all is wail,
As they strike the shattered sail;
Or, in conflagration pale,
Light the gloom.

Out spoke the victor then,
As he hailed them o'er the wave:
"Ye are brothers! ye are men!
And we conquer but to save:—
So peace instead of death let us bring;
But yield, proud foe, thy fleet,
With the crews, at England's feet,
And make submission meet
To our King."

Then Denmark blessed our chief,
That he gave her wounds repose;

And the sounds of joy and grief
From her people wildly rose;
As Death withdrew his shades from the day,
While the sun looked smiling bright
O'er a wide and woeful sight,
Where the fires of funeral light
Died away.

Now joy, Old England, raise!
For the tidings of thy might,
By the festal cities' blaze,
Whilst the wine-cup shines in light;
And yet amidst that joy and uproar,
Let us think of them that sleep,
Full many a fathom deep,
By thy wild and stormy steep,
Elsinore! *

Brave hearts! to Britain's pride
Once so faithful and so true,
On the deck of fame that died,—
With the gallant good Riou; †
Soft sigh the winds of Heaven o'er their grave!
While the billow mournful rolls,
And the mermaid's song condoles,
Singing glory to the souls
Of the brave!

[THOMAS CAMPBELL.]

* Elsinore—a seaport twenty-four miles north of Copenhagen.
† Captain Riou, an able and gallant seaman, was killed in the action

MEN OF ENGLAND.

MEN of England! who inherit
    Rights that cost your sires their blood!
Men whose undegenerate spirit
    Has been proved on land and flood :—

By the foes ye've fought uncounted,
    By the glorious deeds ye've done,
Trophies captured—breaches mounted,
    Navies conquered—kingdoms won!

Yet, remember, England gathers
    Hence but fruitless wreath of fame,
If the freedom of your fathers
    Glow not in your hearts the same.

What are monuments of bravery,
    Where no public virtues bloom?
What avail, in lands of slavery,
    Trophied temples, arch and tomb?

Pageants!—Let the world revere us
    For our people's rights and laws,
And the breasts of civic heroes
    Bared in Freedom's holy cause.

Yours are Hampden's, Russel's glory,
    Sydney's matchless shade is yours—[*]
Martyrs in heroic story,
    Worth a hundred Agincourts!

---

[*] John Hampden, the great patriot leader of the opposition to Charles I. Lord William Russel and Algernon Sydney were both executed in the reign of Charles II., for their resistance to the arbitrary measures of his government.

We're the sons of sires that baffled
Crowned and mitred tyranny :—
They defied the field and scaffold
For their birthrights—so will we !

[THOMAS CAMPBELL.]

―――o―――

HOHENLINDEN.*

N Linden, when the sun was low,
All bloodless lay the untrodden snow,
And dark as winter was the flow
Of Iser, rolling rapidly.

But Linden saw another sight,
When the drum beat, at dead of night,
Commanding fires of death to light
The darkness of her scenery.

By torch and trumpet fast arrayed,
Each horseman drew his battle blade,
And furious every charger neighed,
To join the dreadful revelry.

Then shook the hills with thunder riven,
Then rushed the steed to battle driven,
And louder than the bolts of heaven,
Far flashed the red artillery.

* Hohenlinden—a village in Bavaria. Its name signifies the "high lime-trees." Here was fought a great battle, December 3, 1800, between the Austrians under the Archduke John, and the French under General Moreau. The former were completely defeated.

But redder yet that light shall glow
On Linden's hills of stainèd snow,
And bloodier yet the torrent flow
Of Iser, rolling rapidly.

'Tis morn, but scarce yon level sun
Can pierce the war-clouds, rolling dun,
Where furious Frank, and fiery Hun,
Shout in their sulph'rous canopy.

The combat deepens. On, ye brave,
Who rush to glory, or the grave!
Wave, Munich! all thy banners wave,
And charge with all thy chivalry!

Few, few, shall part where many meet!
The snow shall be their winding-sheet,
And every turf beneath their feet
Shall be a soldier's sepulchre.

[THOMAS CAMPBELL.]

TO THE RAINBOW.

TRIUMPHAL arch, that fill'st the sky
    When storms prepare to part,
I ask not proud philosophy
    To teach me what thou art.

Still seem as to my childhood's sight
    A midway station given,
For happy spirits to alight
    Betwixt the earth and heaven.

TO THE RAINBOW.

"COME, BRIGHT IMPROVEMENT, ON THE CAR OF TIME,

Can all that optics teach, unfold
    Thy form to please me so,
As when I dreamt of gems and gold
    Hid in thy radiant bow?

When Science from Creation's face
    Enchantment's veil withdraws,
What lovely visions yield their place
    To cold material laws?

And yet, fair bow, no fabling dreams,
    But words of the Most High,

AND RULE THE SPACIOUS WORLD FROM CLIME TO CLIME!"—CAMPBELL.

TO THE RAINBOW.

    Have told why first thy robe of beams
        Was woven in the sky.

When o'er the green undeluged earth
    Heaven's covenant thou didst shine,
How came the world's gray fathers forth
    To watch thy sacred sign?

And when its yellow lustre smiled
    O'er mountains yet untrod,
Each mother held aloft her child,
    To bless the bow of God.

Methinks thy jubilee to keep,
    The first-made anthem rang
On earth delivered from the deep,
    And the first poet sang.

Nor ever shall the Muse's eye,
    Unraptured greet thy beam;
Theme of primeval prophecy,
    Be still the poet's theme.

The earth to thee its increase yields,
    The lark thy welcome sings,
When glittering in the freshened fields,
    The snowy mushroom springs.

How glorious is thy girdle cast
    O'er mountain, tower, and town,
Or mirrored in the ocean vast,
    A thousand fathoms down!

As fresh in yon horizon dark,
   As young thy beauties seem,
As when the raven from the ark
   First sported in thy beam.

For, faithful to its sacred page,
   Heaven still rebuilds thy span,
Nor lets the type grow pale with age,
   That first spoke peace to man.

[THOMAS CAMPBELL.]

THE AURORA BOREALIS.

MIDNIGHT hath told his hour; the moon, yet young
Hangs in the argent west her bow unstrung;
Larger and fairer, as her lustre fades,
Sparkle the stars amidst the deepening shades;
Jewels more rich than night's regalia gem
The distant Ice-Blink's spangled diadem;
Like a new moon from orient darkness, there
Phosphoric splendours kindle in mid-air,
As though from heaven's self-opening portal came
Legends of spirits in an orb of flame,—
Flame that from every point an arrow sends,
Far as the concave firmament extends:
Spun with the tissue of a million lines,
Glistening like gossamer the welkin shines;
The constellations in their pride look pale
Through the quick trembling brilliance of that veil:
Then suddenly converged, the meteors rush
O'er the wide south; one deep vermilion blush

THE AURORA BOREALIS.

O'erspreads Orion glaring on the flood,
And rapid Sirius foams through fire and blood :
Again the circuit of the pole they range ;
Motion and figure every moment change,
Through all the colours of the rainbow run,
Or blaze like wrecks of a dissolving sun :
Wide Ether burns with glory, conflict, flight,
And the glad Ocean dances in the light.

[JAMES MONTGOMERY, born at Irvine, in Ayrshire, in 1771; died in 1854. His feeling is deep and pure, his language picturesque ; but his poems do not belong to the highest ranks of poetic literature. He wrote "The Wanderer in Switzerland," "The World before the Flood," "Greenland," and "The Pelican Island."]

THE MINSTREL BOY.

THE Minstrel Boy to the war is gone,
    In the ranks of death you'll find him ;
His father's sword he has girded on,
    And his wild harp slung behind him.
"Land of song !" said the warrior bard,
    "Though all the world betrays thee,
One sword, at least, thy rights shall guard,
    One faithful harp shall praise thee !"

The Minstrel fell ! but the foeman's chain
    Could not bring his proud soul under ;
The harp he loved ne'er spoke again ;
    For he tore its chords asunder,
And said, "No chains shall sully thee,
    Thou soul of song and bravery !
Thy songs were made for the pure and free—
    They shall never sound in slavery !"

[THOMAS MOORE, an Irish poet and prose writer, author of "Lalla Rookh," "Loves of the Angels," "Irish Melodies," "The Epicurean," and of a host of graceful and polished songs, was born in 1779, died 1852.]

REMEMBRANCE.

AS a beam o'er the face of the waters may glow,
    While the tide runs in darkness and coldness below ;
So the cheek may be tinged with a warm sunny smile,
Though the cold heart to ruin runs darkly the while.

One fatal remembrance, one sorrow that throws
Its bleak shade alike o'er our joys and our woes;
To which life nothing darker or brighter can bring,
For which joy has no balm and affliction no sting.

Oh! this thought in the midst of enjoyment will stay,
Like a dead leafless branch in the summer's bright ray:
The beams of the warm sun play round it in vain;
It may smile in his light, but it blooms not again!

[THOMAS MOORE. From the "Irish Melodies."]

SUMMER.

THE months we used to read of
    Have come to us again,
    With sunniness and sunniness,
And rare delights of rain:
The lark is up, and says aloud,
East and west I see no cloud.

The lanes are full of roses,
    The fields are grassy deep;
The leafiness and floweriness
    Make one abundant heap;
The balmy, blossom-breathing airs
Smell of future plums and pears.

The sunshine at our waking
    Is still found smiling by;
With beamingness and earnestness,
    Like some belovèd eye;

"SUNBEAM OF SUMMER! OH, WHAT IS LIKE THEE,

SUMMER.

"AND 'TIS, AND EVER WAS, MY WISH AND WAY, TO LET ALL FLOWERS LIVE FREELY, AND ALL DIE,"—(LANDON)

"WHENE'ER THEIR GENIUS BIDS, THEIR SOULS DEPART, AMONG THEIR KINDRED IN THEIR NATIVE PLACE."—LANDON.

And all the day it seems to take
Delight in being wide awake.

The lasses in the gardens
  Show forth their heads of hair;
With rosiness and lightsomeness,
  A chasing here and there;
And then they'll hear the birds, and stand,
And shade their eyes with lifted hand.

And then again they're off there,
  As if their lovers came;
With giddiness and gladsomeness,
  Like doves but newly tame.

HOPE OF THE WILDERNESS, JOY OF THE SEA!"—MRS. HEMANS.

Ah! light your cheeks at Nature, do,
And draw the whole world after you.

[LEIGH HUNT. This genial and eloquent writer, whose keen appreciation of all that is tender and beautiful will ever render his works the bosom-friends of lovers of poetry and nature, was born at Southgate, Middlesex, in 1784, died 1859. He will be remembered by his "Legend of Florence," "Francesca of Rimini," "Captain Sword and Captain Pen," and his charming essays in prose.]

ABOU-BEN-ADHEM.

A LESSON ON LOVING OUR FELLOW-MEN.

ABOU-BEN-ADHEM—may his tribe increase!—
Awoke one night from a deep dream of peace,
And saw, within the moonlight of his room,
Making it rich and like a lily's bloom,
An angel writing in a book of gold.
Exceeding peace had made Ben-Adhem bold;
And to the Presence in the room he said,
"What writest thou?" The vision raised his head
And, with a look made of all sweet accord,
Answered, "The names of those who love the Lord."
"And is mine one?" said Abou.—"Nay, not so,"
Replied the angel. Abou spake more low,
But cheerily still, and said, "I pray thee, then,
Write me as one that loves his fellow-men."
The angel wrote, and vanished.—The next night
He came again, with a great wakening light,
And showed the names whom love of God had blest;
And, lo! Ben-Adhem's name led all the rest.

[LEIGH HUNT.]

THE GLOVE AND THE LIONS.

KING FRANCIS was a hearty king, and loved a royal sport ;
And one day, as his lions strove, sat looking on the court :
The nobles filled the benches round, the ladies by their side,
And 'mongst them Count de Lorge, with one he hoped to make his bride.
And truly 'twas a gallant thing to see that crowning show—
Valour and love, and a king above, and the royal beasts below.

Ramped and roared the lions, with horrid laughing jaws ;
They bit, they glared, gave blows like beams, a wind went with their paws ;
With wallowing might and stifled roar, they rolled one on another,
Till all the pit with sand and wind was in a thund'rous smother;
The bloody foam above the bars came whizzing through the air:
Said Francis then, "Good gentlemen, we're better here than there !"

De Lorge's love o'erheard the King—a beauteous, lively dame,
With smiling lips and sharp bright eyes, which always seemed the same.
She thought : "The Count, my lover, is as brave as brave can be ;
He surely would do desperate things to show his love of me !
King, ladies, lovers, all look on—the chance is wond'rous fine ;
I'll drop my glove to prove his love : great glory will be mine !"

She dropped her glove to prove his love—then looked on him and smiled ;
He bowed, and in a moment leaped among the lions wild :

"HEAVEN SHIELD THEE FOR THINE UTTER LOVELINESS!"—KEATS.

The leap was quick, return was quick; he soon regained his place,
Then threw the glove, but not with love, right in the lady's face.

"Well done!" cried Francis; "bravely done!" and he rose
  from where he sat:
"No love," quoth he, "but vanity, sets love a task like that!"

[LEIGH HUNT. This agreeable ballad is founded on an incident related by Brantôme, which has also been poetically treated by the German poet, Schiller, and by our own poet Robert Browning.]

THE CITIES OF THE PAST.

WHERE is Rome?
  She lives but in the tale of other times;
  Her proud pavilions are the hermit's home,
And her long colonnades, her public walks,

Now faintly echo to the pilgrim's feet
Who comes to muse in solitude, and trace,
Through the rank moss revealed, her honoured dust.
But not to Rome alone has fate confined
The doom of ruin; cities numberless—
Tyre, Sidon, Carthage, Babylon, and Troy,
And rich Phœnicia—they are blotted out,
Half razed from memory, and their very name
And being in dispute.

[HENRY KIRKE WHITE, 1785-1806, a poet of great promise, who died of consumption just as his powers were beginning to mature.]

---o---

A SEA-SONG.

  WET sheet and a flowing sea,
  A wind that follows fast,
    And fills the white and rustling sail,
  And bends the gallant mast;
And bends the gallant mast, my boys,
  While, like the eagle free,
Away the good ship flies, and leaves
  Old England on the lee.

Oh, for a soft and gentle wind!
  I heard a fair one cry:
But give to me the snoring breeze,
  And white waves heaving high;
And white waves heaving high, my boys,
  The good ship tight and free—
The world of waters is our home,
  And merry men are we.

A SEA-SONG.

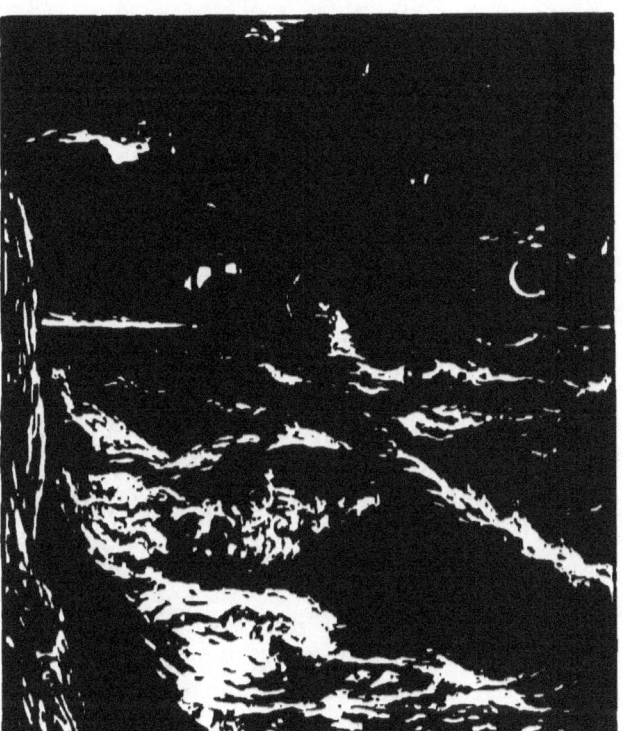

There's tempest in yon hornèd moon,
And lightning in yon cloud;
But, hark! the music, mariners!
The wind is piping loud;
The wind is piping loud, my boys,
The lightning flashing free—
While the hollow oak our palace is,
Our heritage the sea.

[ALLAN CUNNINGHAM, 1785-1842, was an industrious and energetic Scotch *littérateur*, who wrote several novels and biographical works, besides a "rustic epic" and a dramatic poem, but is best remembered by his stirring songs and lays, which breathe much of the old minstrel spirit.]

THE HOLLY-TREE.

H, reader! hast thou ever stood to see
    The Holly-tree?
The eye that contemplates it well perceives
    Its glossy leaves,
Ordered by an Intelligence so wise,
As might confound the atheist's sophistries.

Below, a circling fence, its leaves are seen
    Wrinkled and keen:
No grazing cattle through their prickly round
    Can reach to wound;
But, as they grow where nothing is to fear,
Smooth and unarmed the pointless leaves appear.

I love to view these things with curious eyes,
    And moralize;
And, in this wisdom of the Holly-tree,
    Can emblems see,
Wherewith perchance to make a pleasant rhyme—
One which may profit in the after-time.

Thus, though abroad perchance I might appear
    Harsh and austere;
To those who on my leisure would intrude,
    Reserved and rude:
Gentle at home amid my friends I'd be,
Like the high leaves upon the Holly-tree.

And should my youth—as youth is apt, I know—
    Some harshness show,
All vain asperities I day by day
    Would wear away,

Till the smooth temper of my age should be
Like the high leaves upon the Holly-tree.

And as, when all the summer trees are seen
    So bright and green,
The Holly leaves a sober hue display
    Less bright than they;
But when the bare and wintry woods we see,
What then so cheerful as the Holly-tree?—

So serious should my youth appear among
    The thoughtless throng;
So would I seem among the young and gay,
    More grave than they;
That in my age as cheerful I might be
As the green winter of the Holly-tree.

[ROBERT SOUTHEY, poet-laureate, author of "Madoc," "Joan of Arc," "Thalaba," "The Curse of Kehama," and numerous works in prose and poetry, born 1774, died 1843.]

BISHOP BRUNO.[*]

BISHOP BRUNO awoke in the dead midnight,
  And he heard his heart beat loud with affright:
He dreamt he had rung the Palace-bell,
And the sound it gave was his passing knell.

[*] "Bishop Bruno, the Bishop of Herbipolitanum, sailing in the river of Danube with Henry the Third, then emperor, being not far from a place which the Germans call *Bon Strudel*, or the Devouring Gulf, which is near unto Grinon, a castle in Austria, a spirit was heard clamouring aloud, 'Ho, ho, Bishop Bruno, whither art thou travelling? But dispose of thyself how thou pleasest, thou shalt be my prey and spoil.' At the hearing of these words they were all stupefied, and the bishop, with the rest, crost and blest themselves. The issue was, that within a short time after, the bishop, feasting with the emperor in a castle belonging to the Countess of Esburch,

Bishop Bruno smiled at his fears so vain;
He turned to sleep, and he dreamt again:
He rang at the Palace-gate once more,
And Death was the porter that opened the door.

He started up at the fearful dream,
And he heard at his window the screech-owl scream:
Bishop Bruno slept no more that night,—
Oh, glad was he when he saw the daylight!

Now he goes forth in proud array,
For he with the Emperor dines to-day;
There was not a baron in Germany
That went with a nobler train than he.

Before and behind his soldiers ride;
The people thronged to see their pride;
They bowed the head, and the knee they bent,
But nobody blessed him as he went.

So he went on, stately and proud,
When he heard a voice that cried aloud—
"Ho! ho! Bishop Bruno! you travel with glee,
But I would have you know you travel to me!"

Behind and before, and on either side,
He looked, but nobody he espied;
And the Bishop at that grew cold with fear,
For he heard the words distinct and clear.

And when he rang at the Palace-bell,
He almost expected to hear his knell;

a rafter fell from the roof of the chamber wherein they sate, and struck him dead at the table."—*Thomas Heywood's* "*Hierarchy of the Blessed Angels.*"

And when the porter turned the key,
He almost expected Death to see.

But soon the Bishop recovered his glee,
For the Emperor welcomed him royally;
And now the tables were spread, and there
Were choicest wines and dainty fare.

And now the Bishop had blest the meat,
When a voice was heard as he sat in his seat,—
"With the Emperor now you are dining with glee,
But know, Bishop Bruno, you sup with me!"

The Bishop then grew pale with affright,
And suddenly lost his appetite;
All the wine and dainty cheer
Could not comfort his heart that was sick with fear.

But by little and little recovered he,
For the wine went flowing merrily;
Till at length he forgot his former dread,
And his cheeks again grew rosy red.

When he sat down to the royal fare,
Bishop Bruno was the saddest man there;
But when the masquers entered the hall,
He was the merriest man of all.

Then from amid the masquers' crowd
There went a voice hollow and loud,—
"You have passed the day, Bishop Bruno, in glee;
But you must pass the night with me!"

His cheek grows pale, and his eyeballs glare,
And stiff round his tonsure bristled his hair;

A MOONLIGHT NIGHT.

With that there came one from the masquers' band,
And took the Bishop by the hand.

The bony hand suspended his breath,
His marrow grew cold at the touch of Death;
On saints in vain he attempted to call—
Bishop Bruno fell dead in the Palace-hall.

[Robert Southey.]

A MOONLIGHT NIGHT.

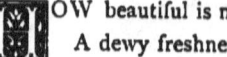OW beautiful is night!
    A dewy freshness fills the silent air;
    No mist obscures, nor cloud, nor speck, nor stain,
Breaks the serene of heaven.

In full-orbed glory yonder moon divine
  Rolls through the dark blue depths :
  Beneath her steady ray
  The desert circle spreads,
Like the round ocean, girdled with the sky :
  How beautiful is night!

[ROBERT SOUTHEY. From the epic poem of "Thalaba."]

---o---

HENRY V. AND THE HERMIT OF DREUX.*

HE passed unquestioned through the camp ;
  Their heads the soldiers bent
  In silent reverence, or begged
  A blessing as he went :
  And so the Hermit passed along
  And reached the royal tent.

King Henry sate in his tent alone,
  The map before him lay ;
Fresh conquests he was planning there
  To grace the future day.

King Henry lifted up his eyes
  The intruder to behold :

* "While Henry V. lay at the siege of Dreux, an honest hermit, unknown to him, came and told him the great evils he brought on Christendom by his unjust ambition, who usurped the kingdom of France, against all manner of right, and contrary to the will of God : wherefore, in His holy name, he threatened him with a severe and sudden punishment if he desisted not from his enterprise. Henry took this exhortation either as an idle whimsey, or a suggestion of the dauphin's, and was but the more confirmed in his design. But the blow soon followed the threatening ; for, within some few months after, he was smitten with a strange and incurable disease."—*Meseray.*

HENRY V. AND THE HERMIT OF DREUX.

With reverence he the Hermit saw,
    For the holy man was old;
His look was gentle as a saint's,
    And yet his eye was bold.

"Repent thee, Henry, of the wrongs
    Which thou hast done this land;
O King, repent in time, for know
    The judgment is at hand.

"I have passed forty years of peace
    Beside the river Blaise;
But what a weight of woe hast thou
    Laid on my latter days!

"I used to see along the stream
    The white sail sailing down,
That wafted food in better times
    To yonder peaceful town.

"Henry! I never now behold
    The white sail sailing down;
Famine, Disease, and Death, and thou
    Destroy that wretched town.

"I used to hear the traveller's voice
    As here he passed along;
Or maiden, as she loitered home,
    Singing her even song.

"No traveller's voice may now be heard—
    In fear he hastens by;
But I have heard the village maid
    In vain for succour cry.

"I used to see the youths row down
  And watch the dripping oar,
As pleasantly their viol's tones
  Came softened to the shore.

"King Henry! many a blackened corpse
  I now see floating down:
Thou bloody man, repent in time,
  And leave this leaguered town!"

"I shall go on," King Henry cried,
  "And conquer this good land;
Seest thou not, Hermit, that the Lord
  Hath given it to my hand?"

The Hermit heard King Henry speak,
  And angrily looked down;
His face was gentle, and for that
  More solemn was his frown.

"What if no miracle from heaven
  The murderer's arm control,
Think you for that the weight of blood
  Lies lighter on his soul?

"Thou conqueror King, repent in time,
  Or dread the coming woe;
For, Henry, thou hast heard the threat,
  And soon shalt feel the blow!"

King Henry forced a careless smile,
  As the Hermit went his way;
But Henry soon remembered him
  Upon his dying day.

[ROBERT SOUTHEY.]

NAPOLEON BONAPARTE.*

'TIS done—but yesterday a king!
    And armed with kings to strive—
And now thou art a nameless thing:
    So abject—yet alive!
Is this the man of thousand thrones,
Who strewed our earth with hostile bones,
    And can he thus survive?
Since he, miscalled the Morning Star,
Nor man nor fiend hath fallen so far.

Ill-minded man! why scourge thy kind
    Who bowed so low the knee?
By gazing on thyself grown blind,
    Thou taught'st the rest to see.
With might unquestioned—power to save—
Thine only gift hath been the grave
    To those that worshipped thee;
Nor till thy fall could mortals guess
Ambition's less than littleness!

   .   .   .   .   .

The triumph, and the vanity,
    The rapture of the strife—
The earthquake voice of Victory,
    To thee the breath of life;
The sword, the sceptre, and that sway
Which man seemed made but to obey,
    Wherewith renown was rife—
All quelled!—Dark Spirit! what must be
The madness of thy memory!

* Written after the abdication of the Emperor Napoleon I. in 1815.

NAPOLEON BONAPARTE.

The Desolator desolate!
 The Victor overthrown!
The Arbiter of others' fate
 A suppliant for his own!
Is it some yet imperial hope,
That with such change can calmly cope?
 Or dread of death alone?
To die a prince—or live a slave—
Thy choice is most ignobly brave!

. . . . . .

Then haste thee to thy sullen Isle,*
 And gaze upon the sea;

VIEW OF ST. HELENA.

That element may meet thy smile—
 It ne'er was ruled by thee!
Or trace with thine all-idle hand,
In loitering mood upon the sand,
 That Earth is now as free!

* St. Helena, in the Atlantic, where Napoleon was confined, and where he died, May 5, 1821.

That Corinth's pedagogue* hath now
Transferred his by-word to thy brow.

Thou Timour! in his captive's cage—†
  What thoughts will there be thine,
While brooding in thy prisoned rage?
  But one—"The world *was* mine!"
Unless, like he of Babylon,‡
All sense is with thy sceptre gone,
  Life will not long confine
That spirit poured so widely forth—
So long obeyed—so little worth!

Or like the thief of fire from heaven,§
  Wilt thou withstand the shock?
And share with him, the unforgiven,
  His vulture and his rock!
Foredoomed by God—by man accurst,
And that last act, thought not thy worst,
  The very fiends arch mock;

---

* Dionysius I., after ruling at Syracuse with tyrannical sway, was constrained to resign his sceptre, and retire to Corinth, where he gained a livelihood as a schoolmaster.

† Timour, the great Tartar chief, having defeated and taken prisoner, at the battle of Angora, the Turkish emir, Bajazet I. (July 28, 1402), imprisoned him in an iron cage until his death, nine months afterwards, at Antioch, in Pisidia. So runs the story.

‡ Nebuchadnezzar (or Nabu-kudari-utsur), the most famous of the kings of Babylon, died about 561 B.C. (See Daniel iii.)

§ According to the ancient legend, the Titan hero, Prometheus, son of Capetus, stole fire from heaven, and taught its use to the sons of men. At this the gods were so enraged that they caused him to be bound to a rock, where a vulture constantly preyed upon his liver. This story—whose esoteric meaning cannot here be developed—suggested to the Greek dramatist Æschylus his finest tragedy. It is also the subject of a poetic drama by Mrs. E. B. Browning, and of the "Prometheus Unbound," of Shelley.

He in his fall preserved his pride,
And, if a mortal, had as proudly died.

[GEORGE GORDON, LORD BYRON, born 1788, died 1824, at Missolonghi, in Greece, whither he had gone to assist the Greeks in their struggle for independence. He has been called, and not inaptly, the Poet of Passion. A misanthropical colouring pervades all his works, which reflect, moreover, in a singular degree, the peculiarities of his own temperament—the faults as well as merits of his own character. He is himself the great sublime he draws. No poet, however, has surpassed him in the force, vigour, and graphic truth with which he has depicted certain moods of nature, and if there mingles in his poems much that is base and mean, there is also much that is lofty and even sublime. His principal works are—"Bride of Abydos," "Giaour," "Lara," "Corsair," "Siege of Corinth," "Parisina," "Childe Harold;" the wild, irregular, but wonderful serio-comic poem of "Don Juan;" the tragedies of "Sardanapalus," "The Two Foscari," and "Marino Faliero;" and the lyric dramas of "Heaven and Earth," "Cain," and "Manfred." His minor poems are very numerous.]

NIGHT BEFORE THE BATTLE OF WATERLOO.

THERE was a sound of revelry by night,
   And Belgium's capital had gathered then
   Her Beauty and her Chivalry, and bright
The lamps shone o'er fair women and brave men;
A thousand hearts beat happily; and when
Music arose with its voluptuous swell,
Soft eyes looked love to eyes which spake again,
And all went merry as a marriage-bell:
But hush! hark! a deep sound strikes like a rising knell!

Did ye not hear it? No; 'twas but the wind,
Or the car rattling o'er the stony street:
On with the dance; let joy be unconfined;
No sleep till morn, when Youth and Pleasure meet
To chase the glowing hours with flying feet:

NIGHT BEFORE THE BATTLE OF WATERLOO.

But, hark! that heavy sound breaks in once more,
As if the clouds its echo would repeat;
And nearer, clearer, deadlier than before!
Arm! arm! it is—it is—the cannon's opening roar!

Within a windowed niche of that high hall
Sate Brunswick's fated Chieftain; he did hear
That sound the first amidst the festival,
And caught its tone with Death's prophetic ear;
And when they smiled because he deemed it near,
His heart more truly knew that peal too well
Which stretched his father on a bloody bier,
And roused the vengeance blood alone could quell;
He rushed into the field, and, foremost fighting, fell.

Ah! then and there was hurrying to and fro,
And gathering tears, and tremblings of distress,
And cheeks all pale, which but an hour ago
Blushed at the praise of their own loveliness;
And there were sudden partings, such as press
The life from out young hearts, and choking sighs
Which ne'er might be repeated; who could guess
If ever more should meet those mutual eyes,
Since upon night so sweet such awful morn could rise?

And there was mounting in hot haste: the steed,
The mustering squadron, and the clattering car,
Went pouring forward with impetuous speed,
And swiftly forming in the ranks of war;
And the deep thunder peal on peal afar;
And near, the beat of the alarming drum
Roused up the soldier ere the morning star;
While thronged the citizens with terror dumb,
Or whispering, with white lips—"The foe! they come! they come!"

NIGHT BEFORE THE BATTLE OF WATERLOO.

And wild and high the "Cameron's Gathering" rose,
The war-note of Lochiel, which Albyn's hills
Have heard—and heard, too, have her Saxon foes:
How in the noon of night that pibroch thrills
Savage and shrill! But with the breath which fills
Their mountain-pipe, so fill the mountaineers
With the fierce native daring which instils
The stirring memory of a thousand years,
And Evan's, Donald's fame rings in each clansman's ears.

And Ardennes waves above them her green leaves,
Dewy with Nature's tear-drops as they pass,
Grieving, if aught inanimate e'er grieves,
Over the unreturning brave—alas!
Ere evening to be trodden like the grass
Which now beneath them, but above shall grow
In its next verdure, when this fiery mass
Of living valour, rolling on the foe,
And burning with high hope, shall moulder cold and low!

Last noon beheld them full of lusty life—
Last eve in Beauty's circle proudly gay;
The midnight brought the signal-sound of strife—
The morn, the marshalling in arms—the day,
Battle's magnificently-stern array!
The thunder-clouds close o'er it, which, when rent,
The earth is covered thick with other clay,
Which her own clay shall cover, heaped and pent,
Rider and horse—friend, foe—in one red burial blent!

[GEORGE GORDON, LORD BYRON. From "Childe Harold," Canto III., stanzas xxi. to xxviii.]

THE BURIAL OF SIR JOHN MOORE.*

NOT a drum was heard, not a funeral note,
    As his corse to the ramparts we hurried ;
Not a soldier discharged his farewell shot
    O'er the grave where our hero we buried.

We buried him darkly, at dead of night,
    The sod with our bayonets turning ;
By the struggling moonbeam's misty light,
    And the lantern dimly burning.

No useless coffin enclosed his breast,
    Nor in sheet nor in shroud we wound him
But he lay like a warrior taking his rest,
    With his martial cloak around him.

Few and short were the prayers we said,
    And we spoke not a word of sorrow ;
But we steadfastly gazed on the face that was dead,
    And we bitterly thought of the morrow.

We thought, as we hollowed his narrow bed,
    And smoothed down his lonely pillow,
That the foe and the stranger would tread o'er his head,
    And we far away on the billow.

Lightly they'll talk of the spirit that's gone,
    And o'er his cold ashes upbraid him ;

---

* The battle of Corunna was fought between the British under Sir John Moore, and the French under Soult, January 16, 1809. The victory remained with the former ; but their gallant leader was mortally wounded, and buried at midnight on the ramparts of Corunna. As no coffin could be procured, the body was simply wrapped in a military cloak and blankets.

But little he'll reck if they let him sleep on
   In the grave where a Briton has laid him.

But half of our heavy task was done
   When the clock struck the hour for retiring;
And we heard the distant and random gun
   That the foe was sullenly firing.

Slowly and sadly we laid him down,
   From the field of his fame fresh and gory;
We carved not a line, and we raised not a stone—
   But we left him alone with his glory.

[Rev. CHARLES WOLFE, born at Dublin 1791, died 1823, owes his fame to this one brief but touchingly-beautiful composition, of which any poet might have been proud. Some of Wolfe's other lyrics, however, are characterized by intense pathos and great power of expression. He died of consumption, hastened by incessant clerical labour, in his thirty-third year.]

TO THE NIGHT.

SWIFTLY walk over the western wave,
   Spirit of Night!
Out of the misty Eastern cave,
Where all the long and lone daylight
Thou wovest dreams of joy and fear,
Which make thee terrible and dear—
   Swift be thy flight!

Wrap thy form in a mantle gray,
   Star-inwrought;
Blind with thine hair the eyes of day,
Kiss her until she is wearied out;

TO THE NIGHT.

Then wander o'er city, and sea, and land,
Touching all with thine opiate wand—
    Come, long-sought!

When I arose and saw the dawn,
    I sighed for thee;
When light rode high, and the dew was gone,
And noon lay heavy on flower and tree,
And the weary day turned to his rest,
Lingering like an unloved guest,
    I sighed for thee.

Thy brother Death came, and cried,
    Would'st thou me?
Thy sweet child Sleep, the filmy-eyed,
Murmured like a noon-tide bee,

Shall I nestle near thy side?
Would'st thou me? And I replied,
   No, not thee!

Death will come when thou art dead,
   Soon, too soon—
Sleep will come when thou art fled;
Of neither would I ask the boon
I ask of thee, belovèd Night:
Swift be thine approaching flight—
   Come soon, come soon!

[PERCY BYSSHE SHELLEY, 1792-1824, author of "Queen Mab," "Hellas," the tragedy of "The Cenci," "Rosalind and Helen," "Alastor," "Adonais, an elegy in memory of the poet Keats," and numerous other works, all displaying a wonderful wealth of imagination and an apparently boundless command of richly poetic language.]

THE CLOUD.

I BRING fresh showers for the thirsting flowers,
   From the seas and the streams;
I bear light shades for the leaves when laid
   In their noonday dreams.
From my wings are shaken the dews that waken
   The sweet buds every one,
When rocked to rest on their mother's breast,
   As she dances about the sun.
I wield the flail of the flashing hail,
   And whiten the green plains under;
And then again I dissolve it in rain,
   And laugh as I pass in thunder.

I sift the snow on the mountains below,
   And their great pines grown aghast;

And all the night 'tis my pillow white,
    While I sleep in the arms of the blast.
Sublime on the towers of my skyey bowers,
    Lightning, my pilot, sits;
In a cavern under is fettered the thunder—
    It struggles and howls at fits:
Over earth and ocean, with gentle motion,
    This pilot is guiding me,
Lured by the love of the genii that move
    In the depths of the purple sea;
Over the rills, and the crags, and the hills,
    Over the lakes and the plains,
Wherever he dream, under mountain or stream,
    The Spirit he loves remains;
And I all the while bask in Heaven's blue smile,
    Whilst he is dissolving in rains.

The sanguine Sunrise, with his meteor eyes,
    And his burning plumes outspread,
Leaps on the back of my sailing rack,
    When the Morning-star shines dead.
As on the jag of a mountain-crag,
    Which an earthquake rocks and swings,
An eagle alit one moment may sit
    In the light of its golden wings.
And when sunset may breathe, from the lit sea beneath,
    Its ardours of rest and love,
And the crimson pall of Eve may fall
    From the depth of heaven above,
With wings folded I rest on mine airy nest,
    As still as a brooding dove.

That orbèd maiden, with white fire laden,
    Whom mortals call the Moon,

THE CLOUD.

Glides glimmering o'er my fleece-like floor,
   By the midnight breezes strewn ;
And wherever the beat of her unseen feet,
   Which only the angels hear,
May have broken the woof of my tent's thin roof,
   The stars peep behind her and peer ;
And I laugh to see them whirl and flee,
   Like a swarm of golden bees,
When I widen the rent in my wind-built tent,
   Till the calm rivers, lakes, and seas,
Like strips of the sky fallen through me on high,
   Are each paved with the moon and these.

I bind the Sun's throne with the burning zone,
   And the Moon's with a girdle of pearl ;
The volcanoes are dim, and the stars reel and swim,
   When the whirlwinds my banner unfurl.
From cape to cape, with a bridge-like shape,
   Over a torrent sea,
Sunbeam proof, I hang like a roof,
   The mountains its columns be.
The triumphal arch through which I march,
   With hurricane, fire, and snow,
When the powers of the air are chained to my chair,
   Is the million-coloured bow ;
The sphere-fire above its soft colours wove,
   While the moist earth was laughing below.

I am the daughter of Earth and Water,
   And the nursling of the Sky :
I pass through the pores of the ocean and shores ;
   I change, but I cannot die.
For after the rain, when with never a stain
   The pavilion of heaven is bare,

And the winds and sunbeams, with their convex gleams,
    Build up the blue dome of the air,
    I silently laugh at my own cenotaph,
    And out of the caverns of rain,
Like a child from the womb, like a ghost from the tomb,
    I arise and unbuild it again.

[PERCY BYSSHE SHELLEY. An admirable example of his rich fancy and remarkable felicity of poetic diction.]

---o---

TO A SKYLARK.

HAIL to thee, blithe Spirit!
    Bird thou never wert,
That from heaven, or near it,
    Pourest thy full heart
In profuse strains of unpremeditated art.

Higher still, and higher,
    From the earth thou springest,
Like a cloud of fire;
    The blue deep thou wingest,
And singing still dost soar, and soaring ever singest.

In the golden lightning
    Of the sunken sun,
O'er which clouds are bright'ning,
    Thou dost float and run;
Like an unbodied Joy whose race has just begun.

The pale purple even
    Melts around thy flight;

TO A SKYLARK. 205

"ODOURS, WHEN SWEET VIOLETS SICKEN,

Like a star of heaven,
In the broad daylight
Thou art unseen, but yet I hear thy shrill delight.

Keen as are the arrows
Of that silver sphere,
Whose intense lamp narrows
In the white dawn clear,
Until we hardly see, we feel that it is there.

All the earth and air
With thy voice is loud,

LIVE WITHIN THE SENSE THEY QUICKEN."—SHELLEY.

"THE SOUL ASPIRES TO HEAVEN, PANTS FOR ITS SEMPITERNAL HERITAGE, WANTONS IN ENDLESS BEING."—SHELLEY.

"SPRING SHALL BLOW HER CLARION O'ER THE EARTH, AND FILL WITH LIVING HUES AND ODOURS PLAIN AND HILL."

As, when night is bare,
  From one lonely cloud
The moon rains out her beams, and heaven is overflowed.

What thou art, we know not:
  What is most like thee?
From rainbow clouds there flow not
  Drops so bright to see,
As from thy presence showers a rain of melody.

Like a poet hidden
  In the light of thought,
Singing hymns unbidden,
  Till the world is wrought
To sympathy with hopes and fears it heeded not:

Like a high-born maiden
  In a palace-tower,
Soothing her love-laden
  Soul in secret hour
With music sweet as love, which overflows her bower:

Like a glowworm golden
  In a dell of dew,
Scattering unbeholden
  Its aërial hue
Among the flowers and grass, which screen it from the view:

Like a rose embowered
  In its own green leaves,
By warm winds deflowered,
  Till the scent it gives
Makes faint with too much sweet these heavy-wingèd thieves.

TO A SKYLARK.

      Sound of vernal showers
         On the tinkling grass,
      Rain-awakened flowers,
         All that ever was
Joyous and clear and fresh, thy music doth surpass.

      Teach us, sprite or bird,
         What sweet thoughts are thine :
      I have never heard
         Praise of love or wine
That panted forth a flood of rapture so divine.

      Chorus hymeneal,
         Or triumphal chaunt,
      Matched with thine would be all
         But an empty vaunt—
A thing wherein we feel there is some hidden want.

      What objects are the fountains
         Of thy happy strain ?
      What fields, or waves, or mountains ?
         What shapes of sky or plain ?
What love of thine own kind ? what ignorance of pain ?

      With thy clear keen joyance
         Languor cannot be ;
      Shadow of annoyance
         Never came near thee :
Thou lovèst, but ne'er knew love's sad satiety.

      Waking or asleep,
         Thou of death must deem
      Things more true and deep
         Than we mortals dream,
Or how could thy notes flow in such a crystal stream ?

TO A SKYLARK.

We look before and after,
    And pine for what is not:
Our sincerest laughter
    With some pain is fraught;
Our sweetest songs are those that tell of saddest thought.*

Yet if we could scorn
    Hate and pride and fear,
If we were things born
    Not to shed a tear,
I know not how thy joy we ever should come near.

Better than all measures
    Of delightful sound,
Better than all treasures
    That in books are found,
Thy skill to poet were, thou scorner of the ground!

Teach me half the gladness
    That thy brain must know,
Such harmonious madness
    From my lips would flow,
The world should listen then, as I am listening now.

[PERCY BYSSHE SHELLEY. This is probably the finest lyric in the English language. Shelley has made the skylark, as Keats has made the nightingale, his own.]

* "We poets in our youth begin in gladness,
  But thereof comes in the end despondency and madness."
                       WORDSWORTH.
    "Most wretched men
Are cradled into poetry by wrong;
They learn in suffering what they teach in song."
                       SHELLEY.

IVAN THE CZAR.

[Ivan the Terrible in his old age besieged Novgorod. The Russian nobles, perceiving his enfeebled state, solicited him to give the command of the assault to his son. So great was his rage at this proposal that nothing could appease it. In vain his son flung himself at his feet; he repulsed him with a blow so violent that two days afterwards the unfortunate young man died. His father then fell a prey to despair, became indifferent equally to war and power, and survived his son but a few months.—*See Madame de Staël's "Dix Années d'Exil."*]

HE sat in silence on the ground,
    The old and haughty Czar,
Lonely, though princes girt him round,
    And leaders of the war;
He had cast his jewelled sabre,
    That many a field had won,
To the earth beside his youthful dead—
    His fair and first-born son.

With a robe of ermine for its bed
    Was laid that form of clay,
Where the light a stormy sunset shed
    Through the rich tent made way;
And a sad and solemn beauty
    On the pallid face came down,
Which the lord of nations mutely watched,
    In the dust, with his renown.

Low tones, at last, of woe and fear,
    From his full bosom broke—
A mournful thing it was to hear
    How then the proud man spoke!
The voice that through the combat
    Had shouted far and high,
Came forth in strange, dull, hollow tones,
    Burdened with agony.

"There is no crimson on thy cheek,
  And on thy lip no breath;
I call thee, and thou dost not speak—
  They tell me this is death!
And fearful things are whispering
  That I the deed have done—
For the honour of thy father's name,
  Look up, look up, my son!

"Well might I know Death's hue and mien—
  But on *thine* aspect, boy!
What, till this moment, have I seen
  Save pride and tameless joy?
Swiftest thou wert to battle,
  And bravest there of all—
How could I think a warrior's frame
  Thus like a flower should fall?

"I will not bear that still, cold look—
  Rise up, thou fierce and free!
Wake as the storm wakes! I will brook
  All, save this calm, from thee!
Lift brightly up, and proudly,
  Once more thy kindling eyes!
Hath my word lost its power on earth?—
  I say to thee, Arise!

"Didst thou not know I loved thee well?
  Thou didst not! and art gone,
In bitterness of soul, to dwell
  Where man must dwell alone.
Come back, young fiery spirit!
  If but one hour, to learn
The secrets of the folded heart
  That seemed to thee so stern.

IVAN THE CZAR.

"Thou art the first, the first, fair child,
    That in mine arms I pressed:
Thou wert the bright one, that has smiled
    Like summer on my breast!
I reared thee as an eagle,
    To the chase thy steps I led,
I bore thee on my battle-horse,
    I look upon thee—dead!

"Lay down my warlike banners here,
    Never again to wave,
And bury my red sword and spear,
    Chiefs! in my first-born's grave!
And leave me!—I have conquered,
    I have slain: my work is done!
Whom have I slain? Ye answer not—
    Thou too art mute, my son!"

And thus his wild lament was poured
    Through the dark resounding night,
And the battle knew no more his sword
    Nor the foaming steed his might.
He heard strange voices moaning
    In every wind that sighed;
From the searching stars of heaven he shrank—
    Humbly the conqueror died.

[FELICIA DOROTHEA HEMANS, author of "The Forest Sanctuary," and numerous songs, ballads, and lyrics, characterized by much grace and tenderness of melody, was born in 1793, died in 1835. "Almost all her poems," says Lord Jeffrey, "are rich with fine descriptions, and studded over with images of visible beauty. But these are never idle ornaments: all her pomps have a meaning; and her flowers and her gems are arranged—as they are said to be among Eastern lovers—so as to speak the language of truth and of passion."]

HENRY I. AFTER THE DEATH OF HIS SON.*

THE bark that held a prince went down,
    The sweeping waves rolled on;
And what was England's glorious crown
    To him that wept a son?
He lived, for life may long be borne
    Ere sorrow break its chain?
Why comes not death to those who mourn?—
    He never smiled again!

There stood proud forms around his throne,
    The stately and the brave,
But which could fill the place of one,
    That one beneath the wave?
Before him passed the young and fair,
    In pleasure's reckless train,
But seas dashed o'er his son's bright hair—
    He never smiled again!

He sat where festal bowls went round,
    He heard the minstrels sing;
He saw the tourney's victor crowned
    Amidst the knightly ring:
A murmur of the restless deep
    Was blent with every strain;
A voice of winds that would not sleep—
    He never smiled again!

Hearts in that time closed o'er the trace
    Of vows once fondly poured,

---

* It is recorded of Henry I., that after the death of his son Prince William, who perished in a shipwreck off the coast of Normandy, he was never seen to smile.

And strangers took the kinsman's place
  At many a joyous board;
Graves which true love had bathed with tears
  Were left to heaven's bright rain,
Fresh hopes were born for other years—
  He never smiled again!

[Mrs. Hemans.]

THE LANDING OF THE PILGRIM FATHERS IN NEW ENGLAND.*

THE breaking waves dashed high
  On a stern and rock-bound coast,
And the woods against a stormy sky
  Their giant branches tossed.

And the heavy night hung dark,
  The hills and waters o'er,
When a band of exiles moored their bark
  On the wild New England shore.

Not as the conqueror comes,
  They, the true-hearted, came;
Not with the roll of the stirring drums,
  And the trumpet that sings of fame:

Not as the flying come,
  In silence and in fear;—

* New England was first settled by the Puritans whom persecution drove from England, in 1620. The vessel which carried them was the famous *Mayflower*.

"YET SHALL OUR HOPE RISE, FANNED BY QUENCHLESS FAITH,

LANDING OF THE PILGRIM FATHERS.

"WE STRIVE, WITH BRIEF ASPIRINGS, AGAINST OUR BONDS IN VAIN;"—(MRS. HEMANS)

"YET, SUMMONED TO BE FREE AT LAST, WE SHRINK—AND CLASP OUR CHAIN."—MRS. HEMANS.

They shook the depths of the desert gloom
   With their hymns of lofty cheer.

Amidst the storm they sang,
   And the stars heard and the sea!
And the sounding aisles of the dim woods rang
   To the anthem of the free.

The ocean-eagle soared
   From his nest by the white wave's foam,
And the rocking pines of the forest roared—
   This was their welcome home!

There were men with hoary hair,
   Amidst that pilgrim band;—
Why had *they* come to wither there
   Away from their childhood's land?

There was woman's fearless eye,
   Lit by her deep love's truth;

AS A FLAME FOSTERED BY SOME WARM WIND'S BREATH."—HEMANS.

There was manhood's brow serenely high,
  And the fiery heart of youth.

What sought they thus afar?
  Bright jewels of the mine!
The wealth of seas, the spoils of war?—
  They sought a faith's pure shrine!

Ay, call it holy ground,
  The soil where first they trode!
They have left unstained what there they found—
  Freedom to worship God.

[MRS. HEMANS.]

———o———

CŒUR DE LION AT THE BIER OF HIS FATHER.*

TORCHES were blazing clear,
    Hymns pealing deep and slow,
  Where a king lay stately on his bier
In the church of Fontivraud.
Banners of battle o'er him hung,
  And warriors slept beneath,
And light, as noon's broad light, was flung
  On the settled face of death.

On the settled face of death
  A strong and ruddy glare;
Though dimmed at times by the censer's breath,
  Yet it still fell brightest there:

* "On the day after King Henry's death, when he was being carried out for burial in the Church of the Nuns at Fontevraud, Earl Richard, his son and heir, came to meet him, and, smitten with remorse, wept bitterly."—*Roger de Hoveden.*

As if each deeply furrowed trace
    Of earthly years to show,—
Alas! that sceptred mortal's race
    Had surely closed in woe!

The marble floor was swept
    By many a long dark stole,
As the kneeling priests round him that slept
    Sang mass for the parted soul;
And solemn were the strains they poured
    Through the stillness of the night,
With the cross above, and the crown and sword,
    And the silent king in sight.

There was heard a heavy clang
    As of steel-girt men the tread,
And the tombs and the hollow pavement rang
    With a sounding thrill of dread;
And the holy chant was hushed awhile,
    As, by the torch's flame,
A gleam of arms, up the sweeping aisle,
    With a mail-clad leader came.

He came with haughty look,
    An eagle glance and clear,
But his proud heart through his breastplate shook,
    When he stood beside the bier!
He stood there still with drooping brow,
    And clasped hands o'er it raised;—
For his father lay before him low;—
    It was Cœur de Lion gazed!

And silently he strove
    With the workings in his breast;

CŒUR DE LION AT THE BIER OF HIS FATHER.

But there's more in late repentant love
 Than steel can keep suppressed!
And his tears broke forth at last like rain;—
 Men held their breath in awe,
For his face was seen by his warrior-train,
 And he recked not that they saw.

He looked upon the dead,
 And sorrow seemed to lie,
A weight of sorrow even like lead,
 Pale on the fast-shut eye.
He stooped, and kissed the frozen cheek,
 And the heavy hand of clay,
Till bursting words, yet all too weak,
 Gave his soul's passion way.

"Oh, father! is it vain,
 This late remorse and deep?
Speak to me, father, once again:
 I weep—behold, I weep!
Alas, my guilty pride and ire!
 Were but this work undone,
I would give England's crown, my sire,
 To have thee bless thy son!

"Speak to me! mighty grief,
 Ere now the dust hath stirred!
Hear me! but hear me, father, chief!
 My king! I must be heard.
Hushed, hushed;—how is it that I call,
 And that thou answerest not?
When was it thus?—woe, woe for all
 The love my soul forgot!

CŒUR DE LION AT THE BIER OF HIS FATHER.

" Thy silver hairs I see,
    So still, so sadly bright !
And father, father ! but for me
    They had not been so white !
I bore thee down, high heart ! at last
    No longer couldst thou strive ;
Oh, for one moment of the past
    To kneel and say, ' Forgive !'

" Thou wert the noblest king
    On royal throne e'er seen ;
And thou didst wear, in knightly ring,
    Of all the stateliest mien ;
And thou didst prove, where spears are proved
    In war, the bravest heart—
Oh, ever the renowned and loved
    Thou wert ;—and there thou art !

" Thou, that my boyhood's guide
    Didst take fond joy to be !—
The times I've sported by thy side,
    And climbed the parent-knee !
And there before the blessed shrine,
    My sire ! I see thee lie ;
How will that still sad face of thine
    Look on me till I die !"

[MRS. HEMANS.]

THE VOICE OF SPRING.

THE VOICE OF SPRING.

COME, I come! ye have called me long;
   I come o'er the mountains with light and song.
   Ye may trace my step o'er the wakening earth,
By the winds which tell of the violet's birth,
By the primrose stars in the shadowy grass,
By the green leaves opening as I pass.

I have breathed on the south, and the chestnut flowers
By thousands have burst from the forest bowers;
And the ancient graves and the fallen fanes
Are veiled with wreaths on Italian plains:
But it is not for me, in my hour of bloom,
To speak of the ruin or the tomb.

I have looked o'er the hills of the stormy north,
And the larch has hung all his tassels forth;
And the fisher is out on the sunny sea,
And the rein-deer bounds o'er the pastures free;
And the pine has a fringe of softer green,
And the moss looks bright, where my foot hath been.

I have sent through the wood-paths a glowing sigh,
And called out each voice of the deep blue sky;

THE VOICE OF SPRING.

From the night-bird's lay through the starry time
In the groves of the soft Hesperian clime,
To the swan's wild note by the Iceland lakes,
Where the dark fir branch into verdure breaks.

From the streams and founts I have loosed the chain:
They are sweeping on to the silvery main.
They are flashing down from the mountain brows,
They are flinging spray o'er the forest boughs,
They are bursting fresh from their sparry caves,
And the earth resounds with the joy of waves.

Come forth, O ye children of gladness, come!
Where the violets lie may be now your home.
Ye of the rose-lip and dew-bright eye,
And the bounding footstep, to meet me fly!
With the lyre, and the wreath, and the joyous lay,
Come forth to the sunshine: I may not stay.

Away from the dwellings of care-worn men,
The waters are sparkling in grove and glen:
Away from the chamber and sullen hearth,
The young leaves are dancing in breezy mirth.
Their light stems thrill to the wild-wood strains,
And youth is abroad in my green domains.

[MRS. HEMANS.]

FACTS FROM FAIRYLAND.

"Oh, then, I see, Queen Mab hath been with you!"—SHAKSPEARE.

OULDST thou know of me
Where our *dwellings* be?
'Tis under this hill,
Where the moonbeam chill
Silvers the leaf and brightens the blade,—
'Tis under this mound
Of greenest ground,
That our crystal palaces are made.

Wouldst thou know of me
What our *food* may be?
'Tis the sweetest breath
Which the bright flower hath
That blossoms in wilderness afar,—

    And we sip it up,
    In a harebell cup,
By the winking light of the towering star.

    Wouldst thou know of me
    What our *drink* may be?
    'Tis the freshest dew,
    And the clearest, too,
That can hang on leaf or flower;
    And merry we skink
    That wholesome drink
Through the quiet of the midnight hour.

    Wouldst thou know of me
    What our *pastimes* be?
    'Tis the hunt and halloo,
    The dim greenwood through;
Oh, bravely we prance it with hound and horn,
    O'er moor and fell,
    And hollow dell,
Till the notes of our woodcraft wake the morn.

    Wouldst thou know of me
    What our *garments* be?
    'Tis the viewless thread
    Which the gossamers spread
As they float in the cool of a summer eve bright,
    And the down of the rose
    Form doublet and hose
For our Squires of Dames on each festal night.

    Wouldst thou know of me
    When our *revelries* be?

'Tis in the still night,
When the moonshine white
Glitters in glory o'er land and sea,
That, with nimble foot,
To tabor and flute,
We whirl with our loves round yon glad old tree.

[WILLIAM MOTHERWELL, a Scotch poet, born at Glasgow in 1797, died 1835. He is chiefly remembered by his fine ballads, in which, as Professor Wilson observes, the style is simple, but in the tenderest movements manly. Frequently it rises to lyrical fervour.]

———o———

ROBIN HOOD.

NO! those days are gone away,
And their hours are old and gray,
And their minutes buried all
Under the down-trodden pall
Of the leaves of many years:
Many times have Winter's shears,
Frozen North and chilly East,
Sounded tempests to the feast
Of the forest's whispering fleeces,
Since men knew not rent nor leases.

No! the bugle sounds no more,
And the twanging bow no more;
Silent is the horn shrill,
Past the heath and up the hill;
There is no mid-forest laugh,
Where lone Echo gives the half
To some wight, amazed to hear
Jesting, deep in forest drear.

"WHENCE THAT COMPLETED FORM OF ALL COMPLETENESS?

224   ROBIN HOOD.

"WHAT IS THERE IN THEE, MOON, THAT THOU SHOULDST MOVE MY HEART SO POTENTLY?"—KEATS.

"WHEN YET A CHILD, I OFT HAVE DRIED MY TEARS WHEN THOU HAST SMILED."—KEATS.

    On the fairest time of June
    You may go, with sun or moon,
    Or the seven stars, to light you,
    Or the polar ray to right you;
    But you never may behold
    Little John or Robin bold—
    Never one of all the clan
    Thrumming on an empty can
    Some old hunting ditty, while
    He doth his green way beguile

WHENCE CAME THAT HIGH PERFECTION OF ALL SWEETNESS?"—KEATS.

ROBIN HOOD.

To fair hostess Merriment,
Down beside the pasture hent ;
For he left the merry tale—
Messenger for spicy ale.

Gone, the merry morris din !
Gone, the song of Gamelyn !
Gone, the tough-belted outlaw
Idling in the " grenè shawe !"
All are gone away and past !
And if Robin should be cast
Sudden from his tufted grave,
And if Marian should have
Once again her forest days,
She would weep and he would craze :
He would swear, for all his oaks,
Fallen beneath the Dockyard strokes,
Have rotted on the briny seas ;
She would weep that her wild bees
Sang not to her—Strange, that honey
Can't be got without hard money !

So it is : yet let us sing
Honour to the old bow-string !
Honour to the bugle-horn !
Honour to the woods unshorn !
Honour to the Lincoln green !
Honour to the archer keen !
Honour to light Little John,
And the horse he rode upon !
Honour to bold Robin Hood,
Sleeping in the underwood !
Honour to Maid Marian,
And to all the Sherwood clan !

Though their days have hurried by,
Let us two a burden try.

[JOHN KEATS, born 1796, died 1821, author of "Hyperion," "Endymion," "Isabella," "Lamia," "Eve of St. Agnes," and other poems, all characterized by a rich imagination, a deep sense of the inner meanings of Nature, and an almost unequalled wealth of poetical language.]

---o---

THE SPANISH ARMADA.
A.D. 1588.

TTEND all ye who list to hear our noble England's praise,
I tell of the thrice famous deeds she wrought in ancient days,
When the great fleet invincible against her bore in vain
The richest stores of Mexico, the stoutest hearts in Spain.

It was about the lovely close of a warm summer's day,
There came a gallant merchant-ship full sail to Plymouth Bay;
Her crew had seen Castile's black fleet beyond Aurigny's isle,
At earliest twilight, on the waves lie heaving many a mile;
At sunset she escaped their van, by God's especial grace;
And the tall *Pinta* * till the noon had held her close in chase.

Forthwith a guard at every gun was placed along the wall;
The beacon blazed upon the roof of Edgcumbe's lofty hall; †
Many a light fishing-barque put out to pry along the coast;
And with loose rein and bloody spur rode inland many a post.

* The *Pinta*, merchant-ship, was a pinnace commanded by one Captain Fleming, who carried the news of the Spanish approach to the Lord High Admiral at Plymouth, July 19, 1588.

† Mount Edgcumbe, near Plymouth, the seat of the Earl of Mount Edgcumbe.

THE SPANISH ARMADA.

With his white hair unbonneted the stout old Sheriff comes;
Behind him march the halberdiers, before him sound the drums;
The yeomen round the market-cross make clear an ample space,
For there behoves him to set up the standard of her Grace.
And haughtily the trumpets peal, and gaily dance the bells,
As slow upon the labouring wind the royal blazon swells.
Look how the lion of the sea lifts up his ancient crown,
And underneath his deadly paw treads the gay lilies down.
So stalked he when he turned to fight on that famed Picard field,*
Bohemia's plume, and Genoa's bow, and Cæsar's eagle shield;
So glared he when at Agincourt in wrath he turned to bay,
And crushed and torn beneath his claws the princely hunters lay.
Ho! strike the flag-staff deep, Sir Knight; ho! scatter flowers, fair maids;
Ho! gunners, fire a loud salute; ho! gallants, draw your blades:
Thou sun, shine on her joyously, ye breezes waft her wide,
Our glorious SEMPER EADEM†—the banner of our pride!
The freshening breeze of eve unfurled that banner's massive fold,
The parting gleam of sunshine kissed that haughty scroll of gold;
Night sank upon the dusky beach, and on the purple sea—
Such night in England ne'er had been, nor ne'er again shall be.

* The "famed Picard field" was the battle of Creçy, won by Edward III. and the Black Prince.
† "Always the same"—Elizabeth's motto.

"THE NOBLEST MIND THE BEST CONTENTMENT HAS."—SPENSER.

THE SPANISH ARMADA.

"POWER, LIKE A DESOLATING PESTILENCE, POLLUTES WHATE'ER IT TOUCHES."—SHELLEY.

"ALL PLACES THAT THE EYE OF HEAVEN VISITS, ARE TO A WISE MAN PORTS AND HAPPY HAVENS."—SHAKSPEARE.

From Eddystone to Berwick bounds, from Lynn to Milford Bay,
That time of slumber was as bright and busy as the day.
For swift to east, and swift to west, the warning radiance spread;
High on St. Michael's Mount it shone—it shone on Beachy Head:
Far on the deep the Spaniard saw, along each southern shire,
Cape beyond cape, in endless range, those twinkling points of fire;

"ILLUSTRIOUS ACTS HIGH RAPTURES DO INFUSE."—WALLER.

THE SPANISH ARMADA.

The fisher left his skiff to rock on Tamar's glittering waves;
The rugged miners poured to war from Mendip's sunless caves:
O'er Longleat's towers,* o'er Cranbourne's oaks, the fiery herald flew;
He roused the shepherds of Stonehenge, the rangers of Beaulieu.
Right sharp and quick the bells all night rang out from Bristol town,
And ere the day three hundred horse had met on Clifton down.
The sentinel on Whitehall gate looked forth into the night,
And saw, o'erhanging Richmond Hill, the streak of blood-red light.
Then bugle's note and cannon's roar the death-like silence broke,
And with one start, and with one cry, the royal city woke:
At once on all her stately gates arose the answering fires;
At once the loud alarum clashed from all her reeling spires;
From all the batteries of the Tower peeled loud the voice of fear,
And all the thousand masts of Thames sent back a louder cheer;
And from the farthest wards was heard the rush of hurrying feet,
And the broad stream of flags and pikes dashed down each roaring street.
And broader still became the blaze, and louder still the din,
As fast from every village round the horse came spurring in:
And eastward straight, from wild Blackheath, the warlike errand went,
And raised in many an ancient hall the gallant squires of Kent;

* Longleat, in Wiltshire, the seat of the Marquis of Bath.

THE SPANISH ARMADA.

Southward, from Surrey's pleasant hills, flew those bright couriers forth;
High on bleak Hampstead's swarthy moor they started for the north.
And on, and on, without a pause, untired they bounded still;
All night from tower to tower they sprang, they sprang from hill to hill,
Till the proud Peak unfurled the flag o'er Darwin's rocky dales—
Till like volcanoes flared to Heaven the stormy hills of Wales—
Till twelve fair counties saw the blaze on Malvern's lonely height—
Till streamed in crimson on the wind the Wrekin's crest of light—
Till, broad and fierce, the star came forth on Ely's stately fane,
And tower and hamlet rose in arms o'er all the boundless plain—
Till Belvoir's lordly terraces the sign to Lincoln sent,
And Lincoln sped the message on o'er the wide vale of Trent—
Till Skiddaw saw the fire that burned on Gaunt's embattled pile,
And the red glare of Skiddaw roused the burghers of Carlisle.

[THOMAS BABINGTON MACAULAY, LORD MACAULAY, born 1800, died 1859, was greatly distinguished as an essayist and an historian, while he also showed no ordinary powers as a statesman, an orator, and a poet. His "Historical Essays" and his picturesque "History of England" will endure as long as the English language.]

THE BATTLE OF IVRY.

NOW glory to the Lord of Hosts, from whom all glories are!
And glory to our sovereign liege, King Henry of Navarre!
Now let there be the merry sound of music and of dance,
Through thy corn-fields green and sunny vines, O pleasant land of France!
And thou, Rochelle, our own Rochelle, proud city of the waters,
Again let rapture light the eyes of all thy mourning daughters!
As thou wert constant in our ills, be joyous in our joy,
For cold, and stiff, and still are they who wrought thy walls annoy.
Hurrah! hurrah! a single field hath turned the chance of war;
Hurrah! hurrah! for Ivry and King Henry of Navarre! *

Oh! how our hearts were beating when at the dawn of day
We saw the army of the League drawn out in long array,
With all its priest-led citizens and all its rebel peers,
And Appenzel's stout infantry and Egmont's Flemish spears!
There rode the blood of false Lorraine, the curses of our land;
And dark Mayenne † was in the midst, a truncheon in his hand.
And, as we looked on them, we thought of Seine's impurpled flood;
And good Coligni's hoary hair, all dabbled with his blood;
And we cried unto the living God, who rules the fate of war,
To fight for His own holy name and Henry of Navarre.

The King is come to marshal us, in all his armour dressed,
And he has bound a snow-white plume upon his gallant crest.

* Henry IV.
† The Duke of Mayenne, who commanded the army of the League.

THE BATTLE OF IVRY.

He looked upon his people, and a tear was in his eye;
He looked upon the traitors, and his glance was stern and high;
Right graciously he smiled on us, as rolled from wing to wing,
Down all our line, a deafening shout, "God save our lord the King!"
"And if my standard-bearer fall, as fall full well he may—
For never saw I promise yet of such a bloody fray—
Press where ye see my white plume shine amidst the ranks of war,
And be your oriflamme to-day the helmet of Navarre!"

Hurrah! the foes are moving! Hark to the mingled din
Of fife and steed, and trump and drum, and roaring culverin!*
The fiery Duke is pricking fast across St. Andre's plain,
With all the hireling chivalry of Guelders and Almayne.
Now, by the lips of those we love, fair gentlemen of France,
Charge for the Golden Lilies now—upon them with the lance!
A thousand spurs are striking deep, a thousand spears in rest—
A thousand knights are pressing close behind the snow-white crest;
And in they burst, and on they rushed, while, like a guiding star,
Amidst the thickest carnage blazed the helmet of Navarre!

Now God be praised! the day is ours! Mayenne hath turned his rein;
D'Aumale † hath cried for quarter; the Flemish Count ‡ is slain:
Their ranks are breaking like thin clouds before a Biscay gale;
The field is heaped with bleeding steeds, and flags, and cloven mail.

* A species of ancient cannon.   † The Governor of Paris.
‡ Count Egmont, commander of the Flemish troops sent by Philip II.

THE BATTLE OF IVRY.

And then we thought of vengeance; and all along our van,
"Remember St. Bartholomew!" was passed from man to man.
But out spoke gentle Henry—"No Frenchman is my foe:
Down, down with every foreigner! but let your brethren go."
Oh! was there ever such a knight, in friendship or in war,
As our sovereign lord King Henry, the Soldier of Navarre?

Ho! maidens of Vienna—ho! matrons of Lucerne,
Weep, weep, and rend your hair for those who never shall return;
Ho! Philip,* send for charity thy Mexican pistoles,
That Antwerp monks may sing a mass for thy poor spearmen's souls;
Ho! gallant nobles of the League, look that your arms be bright;
Ho! burghers of Saint Genevieve,† keep watch and ward to-night.
For our God hath crushed the tyrant, our God hath raised the slave,
And mocked the counsel of the wise and the valour of the brave.
Then glory to His holy name, from whom all glories are!
And glory to our sovereign lord, King Henry of Navarre! ‡

[LORD MACAULAY.]

* Philip II., of Spain.
† Paris, St. Genevieve being the patron saint of the city.
‡ The battle of Ivry (near Evreux, in the north-west of France) was fought on the 14th of March 1590, between the Huguenot forces, under Henry IV., and the army of the Roman Catholic League, led by the Duke of Guise. Henry of Navarre won a complete victory.

HANNIBAL'S OATH.

AND the night was dark and calm,
    There was not a breath of air,
The leaves of the grove were still,
    As the presence of death was there:

Only a moaning sound
    Came from the distant sea;
It was as if, like life,
    It had no tranquillity.

A warrior and a child
    Passed through the sacred wood,
Which, like a mystery,
    Around the temple stood.

The warrior's brow was worn
    With the weight of casque and plume,
And sunburnt was his cheek,
    And his eye and brow were gloom.

The child was young and fair,
    But the forehead large and high,
And the dark eyes flashing light
    Seemed to feel their destiny.

They entered in the temple,
    And stood before the shrine;
It streamed with the victim's blood,
    With incense and with wine.

The ground rocked beneath their feet,
  The thunder shook the dome;
But the boy stood firm, and swore
  Eternal hate to Rome.

There's a page in history
  O'er which tears of blood were wept,
And that page is the record
  How that oath of hate was kept.*

[L. E. LANDON (Mrs. MACLEAN), an English poetess and novelist, born 1802, died 1838, at Cape Coast Castle, on the west coast of Africa, under sorrowful circumstances. Her best works are, "The Improvisatore," "Ethel Churchill," and "Francesca Carrara." She is best known as L. E. L.]

---o---

THE ROMANCE OF THE SWAN'S NEST.

LITTLE Ellie sits alone,
  'Mid the beeches of a meadow,
    By a stream-side on the grass;
    And the trees are showering down
  Doubles of their leaves in shadow
    On her shining hair and face.

She has thrown her bonnet by,
And her feet she has been dipping
  In the shallow water's flow:
Now she holds them nakedly
In her hands, all sleek and dripping,
  While she rocketh to and fro.

* Hannibal was only nine years old when he accompanied his father, Hamilcar, the Carthaginian general, to Spain, and was made to swear upon the altar eternal hostility to Rome, the enemy of his country. "The story was told by Hannibal himself, many years afterwards, to Antiochus, and is one of the best attested in ancient history."—*E. K. Bunbury, in Dr. Smith's "Dictionary of Greek and Roman Biography."*

THE ROMANCE OF THE SWAN'S NEST.

Little Ellie sits alone;
And the smile she softly uses
   Fills the silence like a speech,
   While she thinks what shall be done;
And the sweetest pleasure chooses
   For her future within reach.

Little Ellie, in her smile,
Chooses—"I will have a lover,
   Riding on a steed of steeds;
   He shall love me without guile;
And to *him* I will discover
   The swan's nest among the reeds.

"And the steed shall be red-roan;
And the lover shall be noble,
   With an eye that takes the breath:
   And the lute he plays upon
Shall strike ladies into trouble,
   As his sword strikes men to death.

"And the steed it shall be shod
In silver, housed in azure;
   And the mane shall swim the wind;
   And the hoofs along the sod
Shall flash onward and keep measure,
   Till the shepherds look behind.

"But my lover will not prize
All the glory that he rides in,
   When he gazes in my face:
   He will say, 'O Love, thine eyes
Build the shrine my soul abides in,
   And I kneel here for thy grace.'

"Then, ay, then he shall kneel low,
With the red-roan steed anear him,

Which shall seem to understand,
Till I answer, 'Rise, and go;
For the world must love and fear him
Whom I gift with heart and hand.'

"Then he will arise so pale,
I shall feel my own lips tremble
With a *Yes* I must not say,
Natheless maiden-brave; 'Farewell,'
I will utter and dissemble—
'Light to-morrow with to-day.'

"Then he'll ride among the hills
To the wide world past the river;
There to put away all wrong,
To make straight distorted wills,
And to empty the broad quiver
Which the wicked bear along.

"Three times shall a young foot-page
Swim the stream and climb the mountain,
And kneel down beside my feet—
'Lo, my master sends this gage,
Lady, for thy pity's counting!
What wilt thou exchange for it?'

"And the first time I will send
A white rosebud for a guerdon;
And the second time, a glove;
But the third time—I may bend
From my pride, and answer—'Pardon,
If he comes to take my love.'

"Then the young foot-page will run;
Then my lover will ride faster,
Till he kneeleth at my knee:
'I am a duke's eldest son,

Thousand serfs do call me master;
But, O Love, I love but *thee!*"

"He will kiss me on the mouth
Then, and lead me as a lover
  Through the crowds that praise his deeds:
  And when soul-tied by one troth,
Unto *him* I will discover,
  That swan's nest among the reeds."

Little Ellie, with her smile
Not yet ended, rose up gaily,
  Tied the bonnet, donned the shoe,
  And went homeward round a mile,
Just to see, as she did daily,
  What more eggs were with the two.

Pushing through the elm-tree copse,
Winding up the stream, light-hearted,
  Where the osier pathway leads,
  Past the boughs, she stoops—and stops.
Lo, the wild swan had deserted,
  And a rat had gnawed the reeds!

Ellie went home sad and slow.
If she found the lover ever,
  With his red-roan steed of steeds,
  Sooth I know not; but I know
She could never show him—never,
  That swan's nest among the reeds!

[ELIZABETH BARRETT BROWNING was born in 1809, married to Robert Browning, the poet, in 1846, died in 1861. Her poetical genius was of a lofty order; with the heart of a woman she combined a man's brain. Her principal works are "The Drama of Exile," "Casa Guidi Windows," "Aurora Leigh," and "Poems before Congress." Her minor poems are instinct with the true afflatus.]

SAY NOT, 'WE LOVED THEM ONCE.'"—E. B. BROWNING.

A DEAD ROSE.

 ROSE, who dares to name thee?
  No longer roseate now, nor soft, nor sweet,
  But pale, and hard, and dry as stubble-wheat—
Kept seven years in a drawer, thy titles shame thee.

The breeze that used to blow thee
Between the hedge-row thorns, and take away
An odour up the lane, to last all day—
If breathing now, unsweetened would forego thee.

The sun that used to smite thee,
And mix his glory in thy gorgeous corn,
Till beam appeared to bloom, and flower to burn,—
If shining now, with not a hue would light thee.

The dew that used to wet thee,
And, white first, grew incarnadined, because
It lay upon thee where the crimson was—
If dropping now, would darken where it met thee.

The fly that lit upon thee,
To stretch the tendrils of its tiny feet
Along thy leaf's pure edges after heat—
If lighting now, would coldly overrun thee.

The bee that once did suck thee,
And build thy perfumed ambers up his hive,
And swoon in thee for joy, till scarce alive—
If passing now, would blindly overlook thee.

The *heart* doth recognize thee,
Alone, alone! The heart doth smell thee sweet,

Doth view thee fair, doth judge thee most complete—
Perceiving all those changes that disguise thee.

Yes, and the heart doth owe thee
More love, dead rose! than to such roses bold
Which Julia wears at dances, smiling cold:—
Lie still upon this heart which breaks below thee!

[Elizabeth Barrett Browning.]

---o---

INCITEMENT TO PERSEVERANCE.

AY not, the struggle nought availeth,
   The labour and the wounds are vain;
The enemy faints not, nor faileth,
   And as things have been they remain.

If hopes were dupes, fears may be liars;
   It may be, in yon smoke concealed,
Your comrades chase e'en now the fliers,
   And, but for you, possess the field.

For while the tired waves, vainly breaking,
   Seem here no powerful inch to gain,
Far back, through creeks and inlets making,
   Comes silent, flooding in, the main.

And not by eastern windows only,
   When daylight comes, comes in the light;
In front, the sun climbs slow, how slowly,
   But westward, look, the land is bright.

[Arthur Hugh Clough, author of "The Bothie of Tober-na-Vuolich," a singularly original poem in English hexameters, &c., born 1819, died 1861.]

TO A SLEEPING CHILD.

TO A SLEEPING CHILD.

IPS, lips, open!
    Up comes a little bird that lives inside,
    Up comes a little bird, and peeps and out he flies.

All the day he sits inside, and sometimes he sings,
    Up he comes and out he goes at night to spread his wings.

THE MOUNTAIN AND THE SQUIRREL.

Little bird, little bird, whither will you go?
Round about the world while nobody can know.

Little bird, little bird, whither do you flee?
Far away round the world while nobody can see.

Little bird, little bird, how long will you roam?
All round the world and around again home.

Round the round world, and back through the air,
When the morning comes, the little bird is there.

Back comes the little bird, and looks, and in he flies,
Up wakes the little boy, and opens both his eyes.

Sleep, sleep, little boy, little bird's away,
Little bird will come again, by the peep of day;

Sleep, sleep, little boy, little bird must go
Round about the world, while nobody can know.

Sleep, sleep sound, little bird goes round,
Round and round he goes—sleep, sleep sound.

[Arthur Hugh Clough.]

THE MOUNTAIN AND THE SQUIRREL.

"A place for everybody, and everybody in his place."

THE Mountain and the Squirrel
Had a quarrel,
And the former called the latter, "Little Prig:"

THE MOUNTAIN AND THE SQUIRREL.

Bun replied,
"You are doubtless very big,
But all sorts of things and weather
Must be taken in together
To make up a year,
And a sphere.
And I think it no disgrace
To occupy my place.
If I'm not so large as you,
You are not so small as I,
And not half so spry:
I'll not deny you make
A very pretty squirrel track.
Talents differ; all is well and wisely put;
If I cannot carry forests on my back,
Neither can you crack a nut."

[RALPH WALDO EMERSON, an American writer of great originality, but better known as an essayist than as a poet, born 1803.]

THE HUMBLE-BEE.

BURLY, dozing humble-bee,
  Where thou art is clime for me;
  Let them sail for Porto Rique,
Far-off heats through seas to seek;
I will follow thee alone,
Thou animated torrid zone.
Zig-zag steerer, desert cheerer,
Let me chase thy waving lines:
Keep me nearer, me thy hearer
Singing over shrubs and vines.

Insect lover of the sun,
Joy of thy dominion!
Sailor of the atmosphere;
Swimmer through the waves of air;
Voyager of light and noon;
Epicúrean* of June;
Wait, I prithee, till I come
Within earshot of thy hum—
All without is martyrdom.

* The Epicureans pretended to be followers of Epicurus, and placed all the good of life in pleasure.

When the south wind, in May days,
With a net of shining haze
Silvers the horizon wall,
And, with softness touching all,
Tints the human countenance
With a colour of romance,
And, infusing subtle heats,
Turns the sod to violets,
Thou, in sunny solitudes,
Rover of the underwoods,
The green silence dost displace
With thy mellow, breezy bass.

Hot midsummer's petted crone,
Sweet to me thy drowsy tone..
Tells of countless sunny hours,
Long days, and solid banks of flowers;
Of gulfs of sweetness without bound
In Indian wildernesses found;
Of Syrian peace, immortal leisure,
Firmest cheer, and bird-like pleasure. . . .

Wiser far than human seer,
Yellow-breeched philosopher!
Seeing only what is fair,
Sipping only what is sweet,
Thou dost mock at fate and care,
Leave the chaff and take the wheat.
When the fierce north-western blast
Cools sea and land so far and fast,
Thou already slumberest deep;
Woe and want thou canst outsleep;

Want and woe which torture us,
Thy sleep makes ridiculous.

[RALPH WALDO EMERSON.]

---o---

THE MESSAGE.

HAD a Message to send her,
  To her whom my soul loves best;
But I had my task to finish,
  And *she* had gone to rest:
To rest in the far bright heaven—
  Oh, so far away from here!
It was vain to speak to my darling,
  For I knew she could not hear.

I had a Message to send her,
  So tender, and true, and sweet,
I longed for an angel to hear it,
  And lay it down at her feet.
I placed it, one summer's evening,
  On a little white cloud's breast;
But it faded in golden splendour,
  And died in the crimson west.

I gave it the lark next morning,
  And I watched it soar and soar;
But its pinions grew faint and weary,
  And it fluttered to earth once more.
I cried, in my passionate longing,
  Has the earth no angel friend
Who will carry my love the Message
  My heart desires to send?

Then I heard a strain of music,
  So mighty, so pure, so clear,
That my very sorrow was silent,
  And my heart stood still to hear.
It rose in harmonious rushing
  Of mingled voices and strings,
And I tenderly laid my Message
  On Music's outspread wings.

And I heard it float farther and farther,
  In sound more perfect than speech,
Farther than sight can follow,
  Farther than soul can reach.
And I know that at last my Message
  Has passed through the golden gate;
So my heart is no longer restless,
  And I am content to wait.

[ADELAIDE ANNE PROCTER. This amiable poetess, the daughter of a poet (Bryan Waller Proctor, better known by his *nom de plume* of "Barry Cornwall"), was born in 1825, and died, in the very promise of her powers, in 1864. Her poems, all characterized by delicacy of sentiment and depth of feeling, have been collected in two volumes. "The Message" is given in an abridged form.]

A DOUBTING HEART.

WHERE are the swallows fled?
  Frozen and dead
    Perchance upon some bleak and stormy
      shore.
  Oh, doubting heart!
Far over purple seas,
They wait in sunny ease,
The balmy southern breeze,
To bring them to their northern home once more.

A DOUBTING HEART.

Why must the flowers die?
    Prisoned they lie
In the cold tomb, heedless of tears or rain.
    Oh, doubting heart!
    They only sleep below
    The soft white ermine snow
    While winter winds shall blow,
To breathe and smile upon you soon again.

    The sun has hid its rays
    These many days;
Will dreary hours never leave the earth!
    Oh, doubting heart!
    The stormy clouds on high
    Veil the same sunny sky
    That soon—for spring is nigh—
Shall wake the summer into golden mirth.

    Fair hope is dead, and light
    Is quenched in night.
What sound can break the silence of despair?
    Oh, doubting heart!
    The sky is overcast,
    Yet stars shall rise at last,
    Brighter for darkness past,
And angels' silver voices stir the air.

[ADELAIDE ANNE PROCTER. From her "Legends and Lyrics."]

THE BOOK OF NATURE.

THERE is a book who runs may read,
    Which heavenly truth imparts,
And all the lore its scholars need,
    Pure eyes and Christian hearts.

The works of God above, below,
    Within us and around,
Are pages in that book to show
    How God himself is found.

The glorious sky, embracing all,
    Is like the Maker's love,
Wherewith encompassed, great and small
    In peace and order move.

The dew of heaven is like His grace,
    It steals in silence down;
But where it lights, the favoured place
    By richest fruit is known.

Thou, who hast given me eyes to see
    And love this sight so fair,
Give me a heart to find out Thee,
    And read Thee everywhere.

[Rev. JOHN KEBLE, Vicar of Hursley, in Hampshire, died in 1867. He is best known by his "Lyra Innocentium," and his fine volume of devotional poetry, "The Christian Year."]

BARBARA.

N the Sabbath day,
    Through the churchyard old and gray,
    Over the crisp and yellow leaves I held my rustling way;
And amid the words of mercy, falling on my soul like balms;
'Mong the gorgeous storms of music—in the mellow organ calms,
'Mong the upward streaming prayers, and the rich and solemn psalms,
    I stood heedless, Barbara!

My heart was otherwhere
While the organ filled the air,
And the priest, with outstretched hands, blessed the people with a prayer;
But when rising to go homeward, with a mild and saint-like shine
Gleamed a face of airy beauty with its heavenly eyes on mine—
Gleamed and vanished in a moment. Oh, the face was like to thine,
    Ere you perished, Barbara!

Oh, that pallid face!
Those sweet, earnest eyes of grace!
When last I saw them dearest, it was in another place;
You came running forth to meet me, with my love-gift on your wrist,
And a cursed river killed thee, aided by a murderous mist.
Oh, a purple mark of agony was on the mouth I kissed,
    When last I saw thee, Barbara!

These dreary years eleven
Have you pined within your heaven,
And is this the only glimpse of earth that in that time was
    given?
And have you passed unheeded all the fortunes of your race—
Your father's grave, your sister's child, your mother's quiet face—
To gaze on one who worshipped not within a kneeling place?
        Are you happy, Barbara?

'Mong angels, do you think
Of the precious golden link
I bound around your happy arm while sitting on yon brink?
Or when that night of wit and wine, of laughter and guitars,
Was emptied of its music, and we watched, through lattice-bars,
The silent midnight heaven moving o'er us with its stars,
        Till the morn broke, Barbara?

In the years I've changed;
Wild and far my heart has ranged,
And many sins and errors deep have been on me avenged;
But to you I have been faithful, whatsoever good I've lacked:
I loved you, and above my life still hangs that love intact—
Like a mild consoling rainbow, on a savage cataract.
        Love has saved me, Barbara.

O Love! I am unblest;
With monstrous doubts opprest
Of much that's dark and nether, much that's holiest and best.
Could I but win you for an hour from off that starry shore,
The hunger of my soul were stilled; for Death has told you
    more
Than the melancholy world doth know—things deeper than all
    lore,
        Will you teach me, Barbara?

BARBARA.

In vain, in vain, in vain!
You will never come again,
There droops upon the dreary hills a mournful fringe of rain;
The gloaming closes slowly round, unblest winds are in the tree,
Round selfish shores for ever moans the hurt and wounded sea:
There is no rest upon the earth, peace is with Death and thee—
      I am weary, Barbara!

[ALEXANDER SMITH, born 1830, died 1867. This graceful essayist and true poet died before his powers had fully ripened, being struck down by typhoid fever, acting on an enfeebled nervous system—the result of continuous and excessive literary toil. He had won, however, a high rank among modern poets by his "Life Drama," "Edwin of Deira," and "City Poems;" while his "Dreamthorpe," a volume of essay and criticism, his "Summer in Skýe," and his domestic novel of "Alfred Hagart's Household," show that as a prose writer he would have attained an enduring reputation.]

FROM

B. W. PROCTER, A.D. 1790,

TO

WILLIAM MORRIS.

PART IV.

THE RETURN OF THE ADMIRAL.

HOW gallantly, how merrily
    We ride along the sea!
The morning is all sunshine,
    The wind is blowing free.
The billows are all sparkling
    And bounding in the light,
Like creatures in whose sunny veins
    The blood is running bright.
All nature knows our triumph,
    Strange birds about us sweep;
Strange things come up to look at us,
    The masters of the deep:
In our wake, like any servant,
    Follows ever the bold shark:
Oh, proud must be our Admiral
    Of such a bonny barque!

Proud, proud must be our Admiral,
    (Though he is pale to-day),
Of twice five hundred iron men
    Who all his nod obey;

Who fought for him, and conquered,
    Who've won, with sweat and gore,
Nobility! which he shall have
    Whene'er he touch the shore.
Oh, would I were our Admiral,
    To order, with a word;
To lose a dozen drops of blood,
    And so rise up a lord!
I'd shout e'en to yon shark, there,
    Who follows in our lee,
"Some day I'll make thee carry me
    Like lightning through the sea."

—The Admiral grew paler
    And paler as we flew;
Still talked he to his officers,
    And smiled upon his crew;
And he looked up at the heavens,
    And he looked down on the sea,
And at last he spied the creature
    That kept following in our lee.
He shook—'twas but an instant;
    For speedily the pride
Ran crimson to his heart,
    Till all chances he defied:
It threw boldness on his forehead,
    It gave firmness to his breath;
And he stood like some grim warrior
    New risen up from death.

That night a horrid whisper
    Fell on us where we lay;
And we knew our old fine Admiral
    Was changing into clay;

And we heard the wash of waters,
    Though nothing could we see,
And a whistle and a plunge
    Among the billows in our lee!
'Till dawn we watched the body
    In its dead and ghastly sleep,
And next evening, at sunset,
    It was slung into the deep!
And never, from that moment—
    Save *one* shudder through the sea,
Saw we or heard the shark
    That had followed in our lee!

[BRYAN WALLER PROCTER, better known by his *nom de plume* of "Barry Cornwall," born 1790. He has given to the world numerous works, the best of which are the "Dramatic Scenes," "Marcian Colonna," and "Mirandola;" but is most likely to be remembered by his songs, which are alternately picturesque, pathetic, and sentimental.]

THE OWL.

IN the hollow tree, in the gray old tower,
    The spectral owl doth dwell;
Dull, hated, despised in the sunshine hour,
    But at dusk—he's abroad and well:
Not a bird of the forest e'er mates with him;
    All mock him outright by day;
But at night, when the woods grow still and dim,
    The boldest will shrink away;
    Oh, when the night falls, and roosts the fowl,
    Then, then is the reign of the hornèd owl!

And the owl hath a bride who is fond and bold,
    And loveth the wood's deep gloom;

THE OWL.

And with eyes like the shine of the moonshine cold
    She awaiteth her ghastly groom!
Not a feather she moves, not a carol she sings,
    As she waits in her tree so still;
But when her heart heareth his flapping wing,
    She hoots out her welcome shrill!
    Oh, when the moon shines, and the dogs do howl,
    Then, then is the cry of the hornèd owl!

Mourn not for the owl nor his gloomy plight!
    The owl hath his share of good;
If a prisoner he be in the broad daylight,
    He is lord in the dark green wood!

Nor lonely the bird, nor his ghastly mate;
   They are each unto each a pride—
Thrice fonder, perhaps, since a strange dark fate
   Hath rent them from all beside!
      So when the night falls, and dogs do howl,
      Sing ho! for the reign of the hornèd owl!
   We know not alway who are kings by day,
   But the king of the night is the bold brown owl.

[BARRY CORNWALL. From "English Songs."]

THE STORMY PETREL.

A THOUSAND miles from land are we,
   Tossing about on the roaring sea;
   From billow to bounding billow cast,
Like fleecy snow on the stormy blast:
The sails are scattered abroad, like weeds,
The strong masts shake like quivering reeds;
The mighty cables, and iron chains,
The hull, which all earthly strength disdains,
They strain and they crack, and hearts like stone,
Their natural, hard, proud strength disown.

Up and down! up and down!
From the base of the wave to the billow's crown;
And amidst the flashing and feathery foam
The Stormy Petrel finds a home—
A home, if such a place may be,
For her who lives on the wide, wide sea,
On the craggy ice, in the frozen air,
And only seeketh her rocky lair

THE STORMY PETREL.

To warm her young, and to teach them spring
At once o'er the waves on their stormy wing!

O'er the deep! O'er the deep!
Where the whale, and the shark, and the sword-fish sleep,
Outflying the blast and the driving rain,
The Petrel telleth her tale—in vain:
For the mariner curseth the warning bird,
Who bringeth him news of the storm unheard!
—Ah, thus the prophet, of good or ill,
Meet hate from the creatures he serveth still!
Yet *he* ne'er falters:—So, Petrel! spring
Once more o'er the waves with thy stormy wing!

[BARRY CORNWALL. From "English Songs."]

MARCH.

THE stormy March has come at last,
    With wind, and cloud, and changing skies.
I hear the rustle of the blast
    That through the snowy valley flies.

Ah, passing few are they who speak,
    Wild stormy month, in praise of thee;
Yet, though thy winds are loud and bleak,
    Thou art a welcome month to me.

For thou to northern lands again
    The glad and glorious sun dost bring,
And thou hast joined the gentle train
    And wear'st the gentle name of Spring.

And in thy reign of blast and storm,
    Smile many a long bright sunny day,
When the changèd winds are soft and warm,
    And heaven puts on the blue of May.

Then sing aloud the gushing rills
    And the full springs from frost set free,
That, brightly leaping down the hills,
    Are just set out to meet the sea.

The year's departing beauty hides
    Of wintry storms the sullen threat;
But in thy sternest frown abides
    A look of kindly promise yet.

Thou bring'st the hope of those calm skies,
And that soft time of sunny showers,
When the wide bloom on earth that lies,
Seems of a brighter world than ours.

[WALTER CULLEN BRYANT, born in the state of Massachusetts, in North America, in 1794. His finest poems are the "Thanutopsis" and "Forest Hymn," but many of his minor pieces display a "tender pensiveness" and "moral melancholy" which interest and delight the reader.]

---o---

THE ANGEL AND THE CHILD.

UPON a barren steep,
 Above a stormy deep,
  I saw an angel watching the wild sea;
Earth was that barren steep,
Time was that stormy deep,
And the opposing shore—Eternity!

 "Why dost thou watch the wave?
  Thy feet the waters lave,
The tide engulfs thee if thou dost delay."
 "Unscathed I watch the wave,
 Time not the Angel's grave,
I wait until the ocean ebbs away."

 Hushed on the Angel's breast
 I saw an Infant rest,
Smiling upon the gloomy hell below.
 "What is the infant pressed,
 O Angel, to thy breast?"
"The child God gave me in the long ago:—

"Mine all upon the earth,
 The Angel's angel-birth,
Sweeping each terror from the howling wild."
 Never may I forget
 The dream that haunts me yet,
Of *Patience nursing Hope*—the Angel and the Child.

[LORD LYTTON, one of the most brilliant of living novelists—successful, too, as poet, historian, essayist, and orator—was born in 1805. His principal poem is the epic of "King Arthur."]

---o---

BIRDS IN SUMMER.

HOW pleasant the life of a bird must be,
 Flitting about in each leafy tree;
 In the leafy trees, so broad and tall,
Like a green and beautiful palace-hall,
With its airy chambers, light and boon,
That open to sun, and stars, and moon.
That open unto the bright blue sky,
And the frolicsome winds as they wander by.

They have left their nests in the forest bough;
Those homes of delight they need not now;
And the young and the old they wander out,
And traverse their green world round about:
And hark! at the top of this leafy hall,
How one to the other they lovingly call;
"Come up, come up!" they seem to say,
"Where the topmost twigs in the breezes sway!"

"Come up, come up, for the world is fair,
 Where the merry leaves dance in the summer air!"

BIRDS IN SUMMER.

"HOW BEAUTIFUL IS ALL THIS VISIBLE WORLD!

And the birds below give back the cry,
"We come, we come, to the branches high!"
How pleasant the life of a bird must be,
Flitting about in a leafy tree;
And away through the air what joy to go,
And look on the bright green earth below!

How pleasant the life of a bird must be,
Skimming about on the breezy sea,
Cresting the billows like silvery foam,
And then wheeling away to its cliff-built home!
What joy it must be to sail, upborne
By a strong free wing, through the rosy morn,
To meet the young sun face to face,
And pierce like a shaft the boundless space!

HOW GLORIOUS IN ITS ACTION AND ITSELF!"—BYRON.

THE VOICE OF SPRING.

How pleasant the life of a bird must be,
Wherever it listeth, there to flee;
To go, when a joyful fancy calls,
Dashing adown 'mong the waterfalls,
Then wheeling about with its mate at play,
Above and below, and among the spray,
Hither and thither, with screams as wild
As the laughing mirth of a rosy child!

What joy must it be, like a living breeze,
To flutter about 'mong the flowering trees;
Lightly to soar, and to see beneath
The wastes of the blossoming purple heath,
And the yellow furze, like fields of gold,
That gladdens some fairy regions old!
On mountain tops, on the billowy sea,
On the leafy stems of the forest tree,
How pleasant the life of a bird must be!

[MARY HOWITT, born 18—. This gifted and genial poet, novelist, and essayist, who is so deserved a favourite with the youth of England, is the wife of William Howitt, a well-known man of letters.]

———o———

THE VOICE OF SPRING.

I AM coming, I am coming!
 Hark! the little bee is humming;
 See, the lark is soaring high
In the blue and sunny sky;
And the gnats are on the wing,
Wheeling round in airy ring.

See the yellow catkins cover
All the slender willows over;

THE VOICE OF SPRING.

And on banks of mossy green
Star-like primroses are seen;
And, their clustering leaves below,
White and purple violets blow.

Hark! the new-born lambs are bleating,
And the cawing rooks are meeting

In the elms—a noisy crowd!
All the birds are singing loud;
And the first white butterfly
In the sunshine dances by.

Look around thee—look around!
Flowers in all the fields abound;
Every running stream is bright;
All the orchard trees are white,
And each small and waving shoot
Promises sweet flowers and fruit.

Turn thine eyes to earth and heaven!
God to thee the Spring has given,

Taught the birds their melodies,
Clothed the earth, and cleared the skies
For thy pleasure or thy food :—
Pour thy soul in gratitude !

[MARY HOWITT.]

---o---

THE REAPER AND THE FLOWERS.

THERE is a Reaper, whose name is Death,
  And, with his sickle keen,
He reaps the bearded grain at a breath,
  And the flowers that grow between.

"Shall I have naught that is fair?" said he;
  "Have nought but the bearded grain?
Though the breath of these flowers is sweet to me,
  I will give them all back again."

He gazed at the flowers with tearful eyes,
  He kissed their drooping leaves;
It was for the Lord of Paradise,
  He bound them in his sheaves.

"My Lord has need of these flowerets gay,"
  The Reaper said, and smiled;
"Dear tokens of the earth are they,
  Where He was once a child.

"They shall all bloom in fields of light,
  Transplanted by my care,
And saints, upon their garments white,
  These sacred blossoms wear."

And the mother gave, in tears and pain,
　　The flowers she most did love;
She knew she should find them all again
　　In the fields of light above.

Oh, not in cruelty, not in wrath,
　　The Reaper came that day;
'Twas an angel visited the green earth,
　　And took the flowers away.

[HENRY WADSWORTH LONGFELLOW, the most popular of American poets, was born at Portland, in the United States, in 1807. He was for some time Professor of Modern Languages at Havard College, Cambridge, U.S. He is the author of a host of picturesque ballads and tender lyrics, which are familiar to every English reader; of the poems of "Evangeline," "Hiawatha," and "The Golden Legend;" and the prose romances of "Hyperion" and "Kavanagh."]

THE CHILDREN'S HOUR.

ETWEEN the dark and the daylight,
　　When the night is beginning to lower,
Comes a pause in the day's occupations,
　　That is known as the Children's Hour.

I hear in the chamber above me
　　The patter of little feet,
The sound of a door that is opened,
　　And voices soft and sweet.

From my study I see in the lamp-light,
　　Descending the broad hall-stair,
Grave Alice, and laughing Allegra,
　　And Edith with golden hair.

THE CHILDREN'S HOUR.

A whisper, and then a silence:
  Yet I know by their merry eyes
They are plotting and planning together
  To take me by surprise.

A sudden rush from the stairway,
  A sudden raid from the hall!
By three doors left unguarded
  They enter my castle wall!

They climb up into my turret
  O'er the arms and the back of my chair;
If I try to escape they surround me;
  They seem to be everywhere.

They almost devour me with kisses,
  Their arms about me entwine,
Till I think of the Bishop of Bingen
  In his Mouse-Tower on the Rhine!

Do you think, O blue-eyed banditti,
  Because you have scaled the wall,
Such an old mustache as I am
  Is not a match for you all!

I have you fast in my fortress,
  And I will not let you depart,
But put you down into the dungeon
  In the round-tower of my heart;

And there will I keep you for ever,
  Yes, for ever and a day,
Till the walls shall crumble in ruin,
  And moulder in dust away!

[HENRY WADSWORTH LONGFELLOW.]

THE VILLAGE BLACKSMITH.

THE VILLAGE BLACKSMITH.

UNDER a spreading chestnut tree
    The village smithy stands :
The smith, a mighty man is he,
    With large and sinewy hands ;
And the muscles of his brawny arms
    Are strong as iron bands.

His hair is crisp, and black, and long ;
    His face is like the tan ;
His brow is wet with honest sweat ;
    He earns whate'er he can,

And looks the whole world in the face,
  For he owes not any man.

Week in, week out, from morn till night,
  You can hear his bellows blow;
You can hear him swing his heavy sledge
  With measured beat and slow—
Like a sexton ringing the village bell
  When the evening sun is low.

And children coming home from school
  Look in at the open door:
They love to see the flaming forge,
  And hear the bellows roar,
And catch the burning sparks that fly
  Like chaff from a threshing-floor.

He goes on Sunday to the church,
  And sits among his boys;
He hears the parson pray and preach—
  He hears his daughter's voice
Singing in the village choir,
  And it makes his heart rejoice.

It sounds to him like her mother's voice
  Singing in Paradise:
He needs must think of her once more,
  How in the grave she lies;
And with his hard, rough hand he wipes
  A tear out of his eyes.

Toiling—rejoicing—sorrowing—
  Onward through life he goes:

Each morning sees some task begin,
  Each evening sees it close ;
Something attempted, something done,
  Has earned a night's repose.

Thanks, thanks to thee, my worthy friend,
  For the lessons thou hast taught :
Thus at the flaming forge of life
  Our fortunes must be wrought—
Thus on its sounding anvil shaped
  Each burning deed and thought.

[HENRY WADSWORTH LONGFELLOW.]

———o———

A SPRING LANDSCAPE.

THE green trees whispered low and mild :
  It was a sound of joy ;
  They were my playmates when a child,
And rocked me in their arms so wild,—
Still they looked at me and smiled,
  As if I were a boy ;

And ever whispered, mild and low,
  "Come, be a child once more !"
And waved their long arms to and fro,
And beckoned solemnly and slow :
Oh ! I could not choose but go
  Into the woodlands hoar ;

Into the blithe and breathing air,
  Into the solemn wood—

Solemn and silent everywhere:
Nature with folded hands seemed there,
Kneeling at her evening prayer—
 Like one in prayer I stood.

Before me rose an avenue
 Of tall and sombrous pines;
Abroad their fan-like branches grew,
And where the sunshine darted through,
Spread a vapour soft and blue,
 In long and sloping lines.

And falling on my weary brain,
 Like a fast-falling shower,
The dreams of youth came back again—
Low lispings of the summer rain,
Dropping on the ripened grain,
 As once upon the flower.

[Henry Wadsworth Longfellow.]

THE WRECK OF THE HESPERUS.

IT was the schooner *Hesperus*,
 That sailed the wintry sea;
And the skipper had taken his little daughter,
 To bear him company.

Blue were her eyes as the fairy-flax,
 Her cheeks like the dawn of day,
And her bosom white as the hawthorn buds
 That ope in the month of May.

THE WRECK OF THE HESPERUS.

The skipper he stood beside the helm,
  With his pipe in his mouth,
And watched how the veering flaw did blow
  The smoke now west, now south.

Then up and spake an old sailor,
  Had sailed the Spanish Main—
"I pray thee, put into yonder port,
  For I fear a hurricane.

"Last night the moon had a golden ring,
  And to-night no moon we see."
The skipper he blew a whiff from his pipe,
  And a scornful laugh laughed he.

Colder and louder blew the wind,
  A gale from the north-east;
The snow fell hissing in the brine,
  And the billows frothed like yeast.

Down came the storm, and smote amain
  The vessel in its strength;
She shuddered and paused, like a frighted steed,
  Then leaped her cable's length

"Come hither, come hither, my little daughter,
  And do not tremble so;
For I can weather the roughest gale
  That ever wind did blow."

He wrapped her warm in his seaman's coat,
  Against the stinging blast;
He cut a rope from a broken spar,
  And bound her to the mast.

"O father, I hear the church-bells ring!
  O say, what may it be?"
"'Tis a fog-bell on a rock-bound coast!"—
  And he steered for the open sea.

"O father, I hear the sound of guns!
  O say, what may it be?"
"Some ship in distress, that cannot live
  In such an angry sea!"

"O father, I see a gleaming light!
  O say, what may it be?"
But the father answered never a word—
  A frozen corpse was he!

Lashed to the helm, all stiff and stark,
  With his face to the skies,
The lantern gleamed through the gleaming snow
  On his fixed and glassy eyes.

Then the maiden clasped her hands and prayed
  That savèd she might be;
And she thought of Christ, who stilled the waves
  On the Lake of Galilee.

And fast through the midnight dark and drear,
  Through the whistling sleet and snow,
Like a sheeted ghost, the vessel swept
  Towards the reef of Norman's Woe.

And ever, the fitful gusts between,
  A sound came from the land;
It was the sound of the trampling surf
  On the rocks and the hard sea-sand.

THE WRECK OF THE HESPERUS.

The breakers were right beneath her bows,
 She drifted a dreary wreck,
And a whooping billow swept the crew
 Like icicles from her deck.

She struck where the white and fleecy waves
    Looked soft as carded wool ;
But the cruel rocks they gored her side,
    Like the horns of an angry bull.

Her rattling shrouds, all sheathed in ice,
    With the masts went by the board ;
Like a vessel of glass, she stove and sank—
    Ho ! ho ! the breakers roared !

At daybreak, on the bleak sea-beach,
    A fisherman stood aghast,
To see the form of a maiden fair
    Lashed close to a drifting mast.

The salt sea was frozen on her breast,
    The salt tears in her eyes ;
And he saw her hair, like the brown sea-weed,
    On the billows fall and rise.

Such was the wreck of the *Hesperus*,
    In the midnight and the snow :
Christ save us all from a death like this,
    On the reef of Norman's Woe !

      [HENRY WADSWORTH LONGFELLOW.]

AUTUMN.

HINE, Autumn, is unwelcome lore—
    To tell the world its pomp is o'er :

To whisper in the Rose's ear
    That all her beauty is no more ;

And bid her own the faith how vain,
Which Spring to her so lately swore.

A queen deposed, she quits her state:
The nightingales her fall deplore;

The hundred-voicèd bird may woo
The thousand-leavèd flower no more.

The jasmine sinks its head in shame—
The sharp east wind its tresses shore;

And robbed, in passing, cruelly
The tulip of the crown it wore.

The lily's sword is broken now,
That was so bright and keen before:

And not a blast can blow, but strews
With leaf of gold the Earth's dank floor.

The piping winds sing Nature's dirge,
As through the forest bleak they roar;

Whose leafy screen, like locks of eld,
Each day shows scantier than before.

Thou fadest as a flower, O Man!
Of food for musing here is store.

O Man! thou fallest as a leaf:
Pace thoughtfully, Earth's leaf-strewn floor;

Welcome the sadness of the time,
And lay to heart this natural lore.

[RICHARD CHENEVIX TRENCH, D.D., Archbishop of Dublin, born 1807, a divine and poet of genuine powers, and author of numerous theological, philological, and poetical works.]

ENGLAND.

PEACE, Freedom, Happiness, have loved to wait
On the fair islands, fenced by circling seas;
And ever of such favoured spots as these
Have the wise dreamers dreamed, who would create
That perfect model of a happy state
Which the world never saw. Océana,
Utopia such, and Plato's isle,* that lay
Westward of Cades and the Great Sea's Gate.†
Dreams are they all, which yet have helped to make
That underneath fair politics we dwell,
Though marred in part by envy, faction, hate—
Dreams which are dear, dear England, for thy sake;
Who art, indeed, that sea-girt citadel,
And nearest image of that perfect state.

[RICHARD CHENEVIX TRENCH.]

---

* The poet alludes to the dreams of happy islands and perfect states, which have at all times dazzled the imaginations of men. "Oceana" is the name of a romance by James Harrington (1611-1677), portraying an ideal country, a realm of undisturbed bliss; "Utopia" is a similar romance, by Sir Thomas More (1480-1535); and the island described by Plato was called "Atlantis."

† *Cades*—*i.e.*, Cadiz; and *the Great Sea's Gate*—Gibraltar.

XERXES AT THE HELLESPONT.

"ALM is now that stormy water; it has learned to
  fear my wrath :
    Lashed and fettered, now it yields me for my hosts
      an easy path."
Seven long days did Persia's monarch, on the Hellespontine
  shore,
Throned in state, behold his armies, without pause, defiling o'er;
Only on the eighth the rearward to the further side were past,
Then one haughty glance of triumph, far as eye could reach,
  he cast :
Far as eye could reach he saw them, multitudes equipped for
  war,—
Medians with their bows and quivers, linkèd armour and tiar ;
From beneath the sun of Afric, from the snowy hills of Thrace,
And from India's utmost borders, nations gathered at one
  place :
At a single mortal's bidding all this pomp of war unfurled—
All in league against the freedom and the one hope of the
  world.

"What though once some petty trophies from my captains
  thou hast won,
Think not, Greece, to see another such a day as Marathon :
Wilt thou dare await the conflict, or in battle hope to stand,
When the lord of sixty nations takes himself his cause in hand?
Lo! they come, and mighty rivers, which they drink of once,
  are dried,
And the wealthiest cities beggared, that for them one meal
  provide.
Power of number by their numbers infinite are overborne ;
Lo ! I measure men by measure, as a husbandman his corn.

Mine are all—this sceptre sways them; mine is all in every
    part."
And he named himself most happy, and he blessed himself in
    heart:
Blessed himself; but on that blessing, tears abundant followed
    straight,
For that moment thoughts came o'er him of man's painful brief
    estate—
Ere a hundred years were finished, where would all these
    myriads be?
Hellespont would still be rolling his blue waters to the sea;
But of all these countless numbers not one living would be
    found—
A dead host, with a dead monarch, silent in the silent ground.

[RICHARD CHENEVIX TRENCH.]

---o---

THE SPILT PEARLS.

HIS courtiers of the Caliph crave—
    "Oh, say how this may be,
That of thy slaves this Ethiop slave
    Is best beloved of thee?

"For he is hideous as the night;
    And when has ever chose
A nightingale, for its delight,
    A hueless, scentless rose?"

The Caliph then—"No features fair
    Nor comely mien are his:
Love is the beauty he doth wear,
    And love his glory is.

THE SPILT PEARLS.

"Once when a camel of my train
    There fell in narrow street,
From broken basket rolled amain
    Rich pearls before my feet.

"I, nodding to my slaves, that I
    Would freely give them these;
At once upon the spoil they fly,
    The costly boon to seize.

"One only at my side remained—
    Beside this Ethiop, none;
He, moveless as the steed he reined,
    Behind me sat alone.

"'What will thy gain, good fellow, be,
    Thus lingering at my side?'
'My king, that I shall faithfully
    Have guarded thee,' he cried.

"True servant's title he may wear,
    He only, who has not
For his lord's gifts, how rich soe'er,
    His lord himself forgot."

So thou alone dost walk before
    Thy God with perfect aim,
From Him desiring nothing more
    Beside Himself to claim.

For if thou not to Him aspire,
    But to His gifts alone,
Not love, but covetous desire,
    Has brought thee to His throne.

While such thy prayer, it mounts above
In vain; the golden key
Of God's rich treasure-house of love
Thine own will ever be.

[RICHARD CHENEVIX TRENCH.]

THE LENT JEWELS.

IN schools of wisdom all the day was spent;
His steps at eve the Rabbi homeward bent,
With homeward thoughts, which dwelt upon the wife
And two fair children, who consoled his life.
She, meeting at the threshold, led him in,
And with these words preventing,* did begin:
"Ever rejoicing at your wished return,
Yet am I most so now; for since this morn
I have been much perplexed and sorely tried
Upon one point, which you shall now decide.
Some years ago a friend unto my care
Some jewels gave—rich, precious gems they were:
But having given them in my charge, this friend
Did afterwards nor come for them nor send,
But left them in my keeping for so long,
That now it almost seems to me a wrong
That he should suddenly arrive to-day
To take those jewels which he left away.
What think you? Shall I freely yield them back,
And with no murmuring? so henceforth to lack
Those gems myself which I had learned to see
Almost as mine for ever, mine in fee?"

* That is, anticipating him. The word *preventing* is here used in its original sense, as it is in the English Common Prayer-Book.

"What question can be here? Your own true heart
Must needs advise you of the only part.
That may be claimed again which was but lent,
And should be yielded with no discontent.
Not surely can we find herein a wrong,
That it was left us to enjoy so long."

"Good is the word," she answered: "may we now
And evermore that it is good allow!"
And, rising, to an inner-chamber led,
And there she showed him, stretched upon one bed,
Two children pale: and he the jewels knew,
Which God had lent him, and resumed anew.

[RICHARD CHENEVIX TRENCH.]

HOPE.

HE night is mother of the day,
    The winter of the spring,
And ever upon old decay
    The greenest mosses cling.

Behind the cloud the starlight lurks;
    Through showers the sunbeams fall;
For God, who loveth all his works,
    Has left his hope with all.

[JOHN GREENLEAF WHITTIER, born in 1808, an American poet of high reputation, author of "Snow-bound," and other works.]

THE FROST SPIRIT.

HE comes—he comes—the frost spirit comes!
    You may trace his footsteps now
  On the naked woods, and the blasted fields,
    And the broad hill's withered brow.
He has smitten the leaves of the gray old trees,
    Where their pleasant green came forth,
And the winds which follow where'er he goes,
    Have shaken them down to earth.

He comes—he comes—the frost spirit comes!
    From the frozen Labrador—
From the icy bridge of the Northern Seas,
    Which the white bear wanders o'er—
Where the fisherman's sail is stiff with ice,
    And the luckless forms below
In the sunless cold of the atmosphere
    Into marble statues grow!

He comes—he comes—the frost spirit comes!
    On the rushing northern blast,
And the dark Norwegian pines have bowed
    As his fearful breath went past.
With an unscorched wing he has hurried on,
    Where the fires of Hecla glow
On the darkly beautiful sky above
    And the ancient ice below.

He comes—he comes—the frost spirit comes!
    And the quiet lake shall feel
The torpid touch of his glazing breath,
    And ring to the skater's heel;

THE FROST SPIRIT.

And the streams which danced on the broken rocks,
    Or sang on the leaning grass,
Shall bow again to the winter's chain
    And in mournful silence pass.

He comes—he comes—the frost spirit comes!
    Let us meet him as we may,
And turn with the light of the parlour fire
    His evil power away;
And gather closer the circle round,
    When that fire-light dances high,

And laugh at the shriek of the baffled fiend
As his sounding wing goes by.

[JOHN GREENLEAF WHITTIER.]

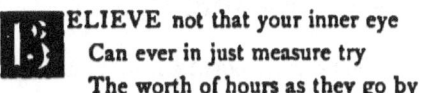

THE VALUE OF THE HOURS.

"Ruit Hora." [The Hour rushes by.]

BELIEVE not that your inner eye
Can ever in just measure try
The worth of hours as they go by;

For every man's weak self, alas!
Makes him to see them while they pass
As through a dim or tinted glass:

But if in earnest care you would
Mete out to each its part of good,
Trust rather to your after mood.

These surely are not fairly spent,
That leave your spirit bowed and bent
In sad unrest, and ill content.

And more—though free from seeming harm,
You rest from toil of mind or arm,
Or slow retire from pleasure's charm—

If then a painful sense comes on,
Of something wholly lost and gone,
Vainly enjoyed, or vainly done—

Of something from your being's chain
Broke off, nor to be linked again
By all mere memory can retain—

Upon your heart this truth may rise—
Nothing that altogether dies
Suffices man's just destinies:

So should we live, that every hour
May die as dies the natural flower—
A self-reviving thing of power;

That every thought and every deed
May hold within itself the seed
Of future good, and future meed;

Esteeming sorrow, whose employ
Is to develop, not destroy,
Far better than a barren joy.

[Lord Houghton, author of "Palm Leaves," and other poems, born 1809.]

———o———

THE LORD OF BURLEIGH.*

IN her ear he whispers gaily,
   "If my heart by signs can tell,
  Maiden, I have watched thee daily,
   And I think thou lovest me well."
She replies, in accents fainter,
   "There is none I love like thee."
He is but a landscape painter,
   And a village maiden she.

* This ballad is founded on a true story.

He to lips, that fondly falter,
    Presses his without reproof;
Leads her to the village altar,
    And they leave her father's roof.
"I can make no marriage-present:
    Little can I give my wife;
Love will make our cottage pleasant,
    And I love thee more than life."
They by parks and lodges going
    See the lordly castles stand:
Summer woods, about them blowing,
    Made a murmur in the land.
From deep thought himself he rouses,
    Says to her that loves him well—
"Let us see these handsome houses
    Where the wealthy nobles dwell."
So she goes by him attended,
    Hears him lovingly converse,
Sees whatever fair and splendid
    Lay betwixt his home and hers;
Parks with oak and chestnut shady,
    Parks and ordered gardens great,
Ancient homes of lord and lady,
    Built for pleasure and for state.
All he shows her make him dearer:
    Evermore she seems to gaze
On that cottage growing nearer,
    Where they twain shall spend their days.
Oh, but she will love him truly!
    He shall have a cheerful home;
She will order all things duly,
    When beneath his roof they come.
Thus her heart rejoices greatly,
    Till a gateway she discerns

THE LORD OF BURLEIGH.

With armorial bearings stately,
    And beneath the gate she turns;
Sees a mansion more majestic
    Than all those she saw before:
Many a gallant, gay domestic
    Bows before him at the door.
And they speak in gentle murmur,
    When they answer to his call,
While he treads with footstep firmer,
    Leading on from hall to hall.
And, while now she wonders blindly,
    Nor the meaning can divine,
Proudly turns he round and kindly,
    "All of this is mine and thine."
Here he lives in state and bounty,
    Lord of Burleigh, fair and free,
Not a lord in all the county
    Is so great a lord as he.
All at once the colour flushes
    Her sweet face from brow to chin:
As it were with shame she blushes,
    And her spirit changed within.
Then her countenance all over
    Pale again as death did prove:
But he clasped her like a lover,
    And he cheered her soul with love.
So she strove against her weakness,
    Though at times her spirit sank:
Shaped her heart with woman's meekness
    To all duties of her rank:
And a gentle consort made he,
    And her gentle mind was such
That she grew a noble lady,
    And the people loved her much.

THE LORD OF BURLEIGH.

But a trouble weighed upon her,
    And perplexed her, night and morn,
With the burden of an honour
    Unto which she was not born.
Faint she grew, and ever fainter,
    And she murmured, "Oh, that he
Were once more that landscape painter
    Which did win my heart from me!"
So she drooped and drooped before him,
    Fading slowly from his side;
Three fair children first she bore him,
    Then before her time she died.
Weeping, weeping late and early,
    Walking up and pacing down,
Deeply mourned the Lord of Burleigh,
    Burleigh House by Stamford town.
And he came to look upon her,
    And he looked at her and said,
"Bring the dress, and put it on her,
    That she wore when she was wed."
Then her people, softly treading,
    Bore to earth her body, drest
In the dress that she was wed in,
    That her spirit might have rest.

[ALFRED TENNYSON, the Poet Laureate, was born in 1810. He has enriched our English literature with some poems "which the world will not willingly let die;" with "The Princess," "The Idylls of the King," "Maud," "In Memoriam," "Enoch Arden," and numerous ballads, odes, lyrics, and songs, which are cherished in the heart of every true lover of poetry.]

LITTLE BIRDIE.

WHAT does little Birdie say
In her nest at peep of day?
Let me fly, says little Birdie,
Mother, let me fly away.
Birdie rest a little longer,
Till the little wings are stronger.
So she rests a little longer,
Then she flies away.

What does little Baby say
In her bed at peep of day?
Baby says, like little Birdie,
Let me rise and fly away.
Baby, sleep a little longer,
Till the little limbs are stronger.
If she sleeps a little longer,
Baby too shall fly away.

[ALFRED TENNYSON. This exquisite songlet occurs in "Enoch Arden, and Other Poems," published in 1864.]

THE CHARGE OF THE LIGHT BRIGADE.*

HALF a league, half a league,
   Half a league onward,
   Into the Valley of Death
     Rode the Six Hundred.
"Forward the Light Brigade ;—
Charge for the guns!" he said :
Into the Valley of Death
   Rode the Six Hundred.

"Forward the Light Brigade!"
Was there a man dismayed?
Not though the soldier knew
   Some one had blundered :
Theirs not to make reply,
Theirs not to reason why,
Theirs but to do or die !
Into the Valley of Death
   Rode the Six Hundred.

Cannon to right of them,
Cannon to left of them,
Cannon in front of them
   Volleyed and thundered :
Stormed at with shot and shell,
Boldly they rode, and well,
Into the jaws of Death,
Into the mouth of Hell,
   Rode the Six Hundred.

* Celebrating a gallant feat of arms which occurred during the war with Russia. About six hundred (607) British cavalry, obeying a mistaken order, charged a greatly superior force of Russians, and cut their way through them, with heavy loss. Only a hundred and ninety-eight returned. October 25, 1854.

Flashed all their sabres bare,
Flashed as they turned in air,
Sabring the gunners there,
Charging an army, while
　All the world wondered:
Plunged in the battery smoke
Right through the line they broke;
Cossack and Russian
Reeled from the sabre-stroke,
　Shattered and sundered.
Then they rode back—but not,
　Not the Six Hundred.

Cannon to right of them,
Cannon to left of them,
Cannon behind them
　Volleyed and thundered:
Stormed at with shot and shell,
While horse and hero fell,
They that had fought so well,
Came through the jaws of Death,
Back from the mouth of Hell,
All that was left of them,
　Left of Six Hundred.

When can their glory fade?
Oh, the wild charge they made!
　All the world wondered.
Honour the charge they made!
Honour the Light Brigade,
　Noble Six Hundred!

[ALFRED TENNYSON. From "Maud, and Other Poems."]

THE TOURNAMENT.

IT was the point of noon,
    The lists were ready.* Empanoplied and plumed
    We entered in, and waited; fifty there
Opposed to fifty; till the trumpet blared
At the barrier like a wild horn in a land
Of echoes, and a moment, and once more
The trumpet, and again: at which the storm
Of galloping hoofs bare on the ridge of spears
And riders front to front, until they closed
In conflict with the crash of shivering points,
And thunder.
  On his haunches rose the steed,
And into fiery splinters leapt the lance,
And out of stricken helmets sprang the fire.
Part sat like rocks: part reeled, but kept their seats:
Part rolled on the earth, and rose again, and drew:
Part stumbled, mixt with floundering horses. Down
From those two bulks at Arac's side, and down
From Arac's arm, as from a giant's flail,
The large blows rained, as here and everywhere
He rode the mellay, lord of the ringing lists,
And all the plain—brand, mace, and shaft, and shield—

---

* In the chivalric spectacle of the Tournament, the place of combat was called the *lists*: an extensive area surrounded by ropes or palings in single or double row. Two opposite entrances were provided, and at these stood the heralds and pursuivants, in sumptuous attire, filling the air with the music of their trumpets. Without the lists were raised tier upon tier of seats, adorned with rich hangings, garlands, and gay streamers, and glittering with lords and ladies, squires and gentles, all decked out in the brightest attire. A gallery, more splendidly decorated than any other, was occupied by the sovereigns and their train; and a conspicuous place was reserved for the lady whom the victor in the *mêlée* might select as Queen of Love and Beauty.

"IF YOU FEAR, CAST ALL YOUR CARES ON GOD."—TENNYSON.

THE TOURNAMENT.

"HIDDEN AS THE MUSIC OF THE MOON SLEEPS IN THE PALE EGGS OF THE NIGHTINGALE."—ALFRED TENNYSON.

"STAR TO STAR VIBRATES LIGHT; MAY SOUL TO SOUL STRIKE THROUGH A FINER ELEMENT OF HER OWN."—IBID.

Shocked, like an iron-clanging anvil banged
With hammers.

. . . . . .

I glanced aside, and saw the palace-front
Alive with fluttering scarfs and ladies' eyes.

"A TRIFLE MAKES A DREAM, A TRIFLE BREAKS."—TENNYSON.

THE TOURNAMENT.

. . . .
   With that I drave
Among the thickest and bore down a prince.

. . . .
   But that large-moulded man,
His visage all agrin as at a wake,*
Made at me through the press, and, staggering back
With stroke on stroke the horse and horseman, came
As comes a pillar of electric cloud,
Flaying the roofs and sucking up the drains,
And shadowing down the champain till it strikes
On a wood, and takes, and breaks, and cracks, and splits,
And twists the grain with such a roar that Earth
Reels, and the herdsmen cry; for everything
Gave way before him: only Florian, he
That loved me closer than his own right eye,
Thrust in between; but Arac rode him down:
And Cyril seeing it, pushed against the prince,
Strong, supple, sinew-corded, apt at arms;
But tougher, heavier, stronger, he that smote
And threw him: last I spurred; I felt my veins
Stretch with fierce heat; a moment, hand to hand
And sword to sword, and horse to horse we hung,
Till I struck out and shouted; the blade glanced;
I did but shear a feather, and dream and truth
Flowed from me; darkness closed me; and I fell.

[ALFRED TENNYSON. From "The Princess: A Medley."]

* At wakes, or country fairs, it was a common amusement for peasants to outvie one another in grinning through a horse collar.

HOW THEY BROUGHT THE GOOD NEWS FROM GHENT TO AIX.

SPRANG to the stirrup, and Joris, and he;
   I galloped, Dirck galloped, we galloped all three;
    "Good speed!" cried the watch, as the gate-bolts
      undrew;
"Speed!" echoed the wall to us galloping through;
Behind shut the postern, the lights sank to rest,
And into the midnight we galloped abreast.

Not a word to each other; we kept the great pace
Neck by neck, stride by stride, never changing our place;
I turned in my saddle, and made its girths tight,
Then shortened each stirrup, and set the pique right,
Rebuckled the cheek-strap, chained slacker the bit,
Nor galloped less steadily Roland a whit.

'Twas moonset at starting; but, while we drew near
Lokeren, the cocks crew and twilight dawned clear;
At Boom, a great yellow star came out to see;
At Düffeld, 'twas morning as plain as could be;
And from Mechlin church-steeple we heard the half-chime,
So Joris broke silence with, "Yet there is time!"

At Aerschot, up leaped of a sudden the sun,
And against him the cattle stood black every one,
To stare through the mist at us galloping past,
And I saw my stout galloper, Roland, at last,
With resolute shoulders each butting away
The haze, as some bluff river headland its spray;

And his low head and crest, just one sharp ear bent back,
For my voice, and the other pricked out on his track;
And one eye's black intelligence—ever that glance
O'er its white edge at me, his own master, askance!
And the thick heavy spume-flakes which aye and anon
His fierce lips shook upwards in galloping on.

By Hasselt Dirck groaned; and cried Joris, "Stay spur!
Your Roos galloped bravely, the fault's not in her,
We'll remember at Aix"—for one heard the quick wheeze
Of her chest, saw the stretched neck, and staggering knees,
And sunk tail, and horrible heave of the flank,
As down on her haunches she shuddered and sank.

So we were left galloping, Joris and I,
Past Loos and past Tongres, no cloud in the sky;
The broad sun above laughed a pitiless laugh,
'Neath our foot broke the brittle bright stubble like chaff;
Till over by Dalhem a dome-tower sprang white,
And "Gallop," cried Joris, "for Aix is in sight!"

"How they'll greet us!" and all in a moment his roan
Rolled neck and croup over, lay dead as a stone;
And there was my Roland to bear the whole weight
Of the news which alone could save Aix from her fate,
With his nostrils like pits full of blood to the brim,
And with circles of red for his eye-sockets' rim.

Then I cast my loose buff-coat, each holster let fall,
Shook off both my jack-boots, let go belt and all,
Stood up in the stirrup, leaned, patted his ear,
Called my Roland his pet name, my horse without peer;

Clapped my hands, laughed and sang, any noise, bad or
    good,
Till at length into Aix Roland galloped and stood.

And all I remember is friends flocking round
As I sate with his head 'twixt my knees on the ground,
And no voice but was praising this Roland of mine,
As I poured down his throat our last measure of wine,
Which (the burgesses voted by common consent)
Was no more than his due who brought good news from
    Ghent.

[ROBERT BROWNING, in some respects the greatest of living poets, and scarcely less remarkable for his wealth of language than his depth of thought, his insight into character, and suggestiveness, is the author of "Paracelsus," "The Blot in the 'Scutcheon," "Dramatis Personæ," "Pippa Passes," "Men and Women," "The Ring and the Book," and numerous lyrics and ballads.]

―――o―――

TUBAL CAIN.

I.

LD Tubal Cain was a man of might
    In the days when Earth was young;
By the fierce red light of his furnace bright
    The strokes of his hammer rung;
And he lifted high his horny hand
    On the glowing iron clear,
Till the sparks rushed out in scarlet showers,
    As he fashioned the sword and the spear.
And he sang—"Hurra for my handiwork!
    Hurra for the spear and the sword!
Hurra for the hand that shall wield them well,
    For he shall be king and lord!"

II.

To Tubal Cain came many a one,
    As he wrought by his roaring fire,
And each one prayed for a strong steel blade
    As the crown of his desire;
And he made them weapons sharp and strong,
    Till they shouted loud for glee,
And gave him gifts of pearl and gold,
    And spoils of the forest free.
And they sang—" Hurra for Tubal Cain,
    Who hath given us strength anew!
Hurra for the smith, hurra for the fire,
    And hurra for the metal true!"

III.

But a sudden change came o'er his heart
    Ere the setting of the sun,
And Tubal Cain was filled with pain
    For the evil he had done;
He saw that men, with rage and hate,
    Made war upon their kind,
That the land was red with the blood they shed
    In their lust for carnage blind.
And he said—"Alas! that ever I made
    Or that skill of mine should plan
The spear and the sword for men whose joy
    Is to slay their fellow-man."

IV.

For many a day old Tubal Cain
    Sat brooding o'er his woe;
And his hand forbore to smite the ore,
    And his furnace smouldered low.

But he rose at last with a cheerful face,
    And a bright courageous eye,
And bared his strong right arm for work,
    While the quick flames mounted high.
And he sang—" Hurra for my handiwork!"
    And the red sparks lit the air;
" Not alone for the blade was the bright steel made!"
    And he fashioned the first ploughshare.

V.

And men, taught wisdom from the past,
    In friendship joined their hands,
Hung the sword in the hall, the spear on the wall,
    And ploughed the willing lands;
And sang—" Hurra for Tubal Cain!
    Our stanch good friend is he;
And for the ploughshare and the plough
    To him our praise should be.
But while oppression lifts its head,
    Or a tyrant should be lord,
Though we may thank him for the plough,
    We'll not forget the sword!"

[DR. CHARLES MACKAY, a justly popular poet, song-writer, and *littérateur*, author of " The Salamandrine," " Egeria," " Under Green Leaves," and various prose works, was born in 1812.]

YOUTH'S WARNING.

BEWARE, exulting youth, beware,
    When life's young pleasures woo,
That ere you yield you shrive your heart,
    And keep your conscience true!

For sake of silver spent to-day,
Why pledge to-morrow's gold?
Or in hot blood implant Remorse,
To grow when blood is cold!
If wrong you do, if false you play,
In summer among the flowers,
You must atone, you shall repay,
In winter among the showers.

To turn the balances of Heaven
Surpasses mortal power;
For every white there is a black,
For every sweet a sour.
For every up there is a down,
For every folly, shame;
And retribution follows guilt,
As burning follows flame.
If wrong you do, if false you play,
In summer among the flowers,
You must atone, you shall repay,
In winter among the showers.

[CHARLES MACKAY.]

―o―

THE SANDS OF DEE.

"OH, Mary, go and call the cattle home,
And call the cattle home,
And call the cattle home,
Across the sands o' Dee."
The western wind was wild and dank wi' foam,
And all alone went she.

THE STARLINGS.

The creeping tide came up along the sand,
    And o'er and o'er the sand,
    And round and round the sand,
        As far as eye could see;
The blinding mist came down and hid the land—
    And never home came she.

"Oh, is it weed, or fish, or floating hair—
    A tress o' golden hair,
    O' drownèd maiden's hair,
        Above the nets at sea?
Was never salmon yet that shone so fair,
    Among the stakes on Dee."

They rowed her in across the rolling foam,
    The cruel crawling foam,
    The cruel, hungry foam,
        To her grave beside the sea:
But still the boatmen hear her call the cattle home,
    Across the sands o' Dee.

[Rev. CHARLES KINGSLEY, M.A., born 1819; author of "Yeast," "Andromeda," "The Saint's Tragedy," "Alton Locke," "Hypatia," "Two Years," "Hereward," "Westward Ho!" "Glaucus," "Sermons," "The Roman and the Teuton," and other works.]

---o---

THE STARLINGS.

ARLY in spring time, on raw and windy mornings,
    Beneath the freezing house-eaves I heard the starlings sing—
"Ah, dreary March month, is this then a time for building wearily?
Sad, sad, to think that the year is but begun."

THE THREE FISHERS.

Late in the autumn, on still and cloudless evenings,
  Among the golden reed-beds I heard the starlings sing—
"Ah, that sweet March month, when we and our mates were
      courting merrily;
Sad, sad, to think that the year is all but done."

[Rev. CHARLES KINGSLEY. From "Andromeda, and Other Poems."]

THE THREE FISHERS.

THREE fishers went sailing away to the west,
    Away to the west as the sun went down;
Each thought on the woman who loved him best,
And the children stood watching them out of the town;
  For men must work, and women must weep,
  And there's little to earn, and many to keep,
    Though the harbour bar be moaning.

Three wives sat up in the lighthouse tower,
    And they trimmed the lamps as the sun went down;
They looked at the squall, and they looked at the shower,
And the night-rack came rolling up ragged and brown;
  But men must work, and women must weep,
  Though storms be sudden, and waters deep,
    And the harbour bar be moaning.

Three corpses lay out on the shining sands
    In the morning gleam as the tide went down,
And the women are weeping and wringing their hands
  For those who will never come home to the town;
  For men must work, and women must weep,
  And the sooner 'tis over, the sooner to sleep,
    And good-bye to the bar and its moaning.

[Rev. CHARLES KINGSLEY. From "Andromeda, and Other Poems."]

EARL HALDAN'S DAUGHTER.

I.

IT was Earl Haldan's daughter,
   She looked across the sea;
   She looked across the water,
   And long and loud laughed she!
"The locks of six princesses
   Must be my marriage fee,
So hey bonny boat, and ho bonny boat!
   Who comes a-wooing me?"

II.

It was Earl Haldan's daughter,
   She walked along the sand;
When she was aware that a knight so fair,
   Come sailing to the land.
His sails were all of velvet,
   His mast of beaten gold,
And, "Hey bonny boat, and ho bonny boat!
   Who saileth here so bold?"

III.

"The locks of five princesses
   I won beyond the sea;
   I clipt their golden tresses
   To fringe a cloak for thee.
One handful yet is wanting,
   But one of all the tale;
So hey bonny boat, and ho bonny boat,
   Furl up thy velvet sail!"

IV.

He leapt into the water,
　That rover young and bold;
He gript Earl Haldan's daughter,
　He clipt her locks of gold;
"Go weep, go weep, proud maiden,
　The tale is full to-day.
Now hey bonny boat, and ho bonny boat!
　Sail westward ho away!"

[Rev. CHARLES KINGSLEY. From "Andromeda, and Other Poems."]

A FAREWELL.

MY fairest child, I have no song to give you;
　No lark could pipe to skies so dull and gray:
Yet, ere we part, one lesson I can leave you
　For every day.
Be good, sweet maid, and let who will be clever;
Do noble things, not *dream* them, all day long;
And so make life, death, and that vast For-ever
　One grand, sweet song.

[Rev. CHARLES KINGSLEY.]

THE FOUNTAIN.

NTO the sunshine,
　Full of light,
Leaping and flashing
　From morn to night!

THE FOUNTAIN.

Into the moonlight,
   Whiter than snow,
Waving so flower-like
   When the winds blow!

Into the starlight,
   Rushing in spray,
Happy at midnight,
   Happy by day!

Ever in motion,
   Blithesome and cheery,
Still climbing heavenward,
   Never a-weary;—

Glad of all weathers,
  Still seeming best,
  Upward or downward,
  Motion thy rest ;—

Full of a nature
  Nothing can tame,
  Changed every moment,
  Ever the same ;—

Ceaseless, aspiring ;
  Ceaseless, content ;
  Darkness or sunshine
  Thy element ;—

Glorious fountain !
  Let my heart be
  Fresh, changeful, constant,
  Upward, like thee !

[JAMES RUSSELL LOWELL, an American poet of original genius, with a bold fancy, liberal and exalted sympathies, and a rich vein of humour, was born in 1819. He is the author of "The Biglow Papers," and other popular productions.]

THE SEASONS.

 BLUE-EYED child, that sits amid the noon,
    O'erhung with a laburnum's drooping sprays,
  Singing her little songs, while softly round
    Along the grass the chequered sunshine plays.

All beauty that is throned in womanhood,
  Pacing a summer-garden's fountained walks,

310   BABY MAY.

That stoops to smooth a glossy spaniel down,
  To hide her blushing cheek from one who talks.

A happy mother with her fair-faced girls,
  In whose sweet spring again her youth she sees,
With shout and dance and laugh and bound and song,
  Stripping in Autumn orchard's laden trees.

An agèd woman in a wintry room—
  Frost on the pane, without the whirling snow—
Reading old letters of her far-off youth,
  Of sorrows past and joys of long ago.

[WILLIAM COX BENNETT, a popular song-writer, born in 1820.]

———o———

BABY MAY.

CHEEKS as soft as July peaches;
  Lips whose dewy scarlet teaches
    Poppies paleness; round large eyes,
Ever great with new surprise;
Minutes filled with shadeless gladness,
Minutes just as brimmed with sadness—
Happy smiles and wailing cries,
Crows and laughs and tearful eyes—
Lights and shadows swifter born
Than on wind-swept autumn corn;
Ever some new tiny notion,
Making every limb all motion—
Catchings up of legs and arms,
Throwings back and small alarms,
Clutching fingers, straightening jerks,
Twining feet whose each toe works,

BABY MAY.

Kickings up and straining risings;
Mother's ever-new surprisings;
Hands all wants, and looks all wonder
At all things the heavens under;
Tiny scorns of smiled reprovings
That have more of love than lovings;
Mischiefs done with such a winning
Archness, that we prize such sinning;
Breakings dire of plate and glasses;
Graspings small at all that passes;
Pullings off of all that's able
To be caught from tray or table;
Silences—small meditations,
Deep as thoughts of cares for nations,

Breaking into wisest speeches,
In a tongue that nothing teaches,
All the thoughts of whose possessing
Must be wooed to light by guessing ;
Slumbers—such sweet angel-seemings,
That we'd ever have such dreamings,
Till from sleep we see thee breaking,
And we'd always have thee waking ;
Wealth for which we know no measure,
Pleasure high above all pleasure,
Gladness brimming over gladness,
Joy in care, delight in sadness,
Loveliness beyond completeness,
Sweetness distancing all sweetness,
Beauty all that beauty may be ;—
That's May Bennett, that's my baby.

[WILLIAM COX BENNETT.]

LITTLE WHITE LILY.*

LITTLE White Lily
    Sat by a stone,
    Drooping and waiting
    Till the sun shone.
Little White Lily
    Sunshine has fed ;
Little White Lily
    Is lifting her head.

* We suppose the poet refers to the lily generally called the "lily of the valley," which lifts its "little green-tipt lamps of white" among the emerald foliage of the spring, like (as Leigh Hunt says) "detected light."

LITTLE WHITE LILY.

Little White Lily
  Said, "It is good—
Little White Lily's
  Clothing and food."
Little White Lily,
  Drest like a bride;
Shining with whiteness,
  And crownèd beside.

Little White Lily
  Droopeth with pain,
Waiting and waiting
  For the wet rain.
Little White Lily
  Holdeth her cup;
Rain is fast falling
  And filling it up.

Little White Lily
  Said, "Good again—
When I am thirsty
  To have nice rain:
Now I am stronger,
  Now I am cool;
Heat cannot burn me,
  My veins are so full."

Little White Lily
  Smells very sweet;
On her head sunshine,
  Rain at her feet.
"Thanks to the sunshine,
  Thanks to the rain,

Little White Lily
Is happy again."

[GEORGE MACDONALD, LL.D., author of "Within and Without," "Guild Court," "Adela Cathcart," "David Elginbrod," "Unspoken Sermons," &c., born 1826.]

THE SHADOWS.

Y little boy, with pale round cheeks,
    And large, brown, dreamy eyes,
Not often, little wisehead, speaks,
    But yet will make replies.

His sister, always glad to show
    Her knowledge, for its praise,
Said yesterday, "God's here, you know;
    He's everywhere, always.

"He's in this room." His large brown eyes
    Went wandering round for God;
In vain he looks, in vain he tries—
    His wits are all abroad.

"He is not here, mamma? No, no;
    I don't see Him at all.
He's not the shadows, is He?" So
    His doubtful accents fall—

Fall on my heart, like precious seed,
    Grow up to flowers of love;
For as my child, in love and need,
    Am I to Him above.

How oft, before the vapours break,
And day begins to be,
In our dim-lighted rooms we take
The shadows, Lord, for thee!

While every shadow lying there,
Slow remnant of the night,
Is but an aching, longing prayer
For thee, O Lord, the Light.

[GEORGE MACDONALD.

THE FIGHTING TEMERAIRE.

TUGGED TO HER LAST BERTH IN PORTSMOUTH HARBOUR.

[The *Temeraire* was one of the men-of-war engaged in the great sea-fight off Trafalgar. The following vigorous lyric appears to have been suggested by Turner's well-known picture.]

IT is a glorious tale to tell,
 When nights are long and mirk,
How well she fought our fight; how well
 She did our England's work.
  Our good ship Temeraire;
  The fighting Temeraire!
 She goeth to her last long home,
  Our grand old Temeraire.*

Bravely over the breezy blue,
 They went to do or die;
And proudly on herself she drew
 The battle's burning eye!

Round her the glory fell in flood,
 From Nelson's loving smile,
When, raked with fire, she ran with blood,
 In England's hour of trial!

* This refrain, or "burden," is repeated at the end of each verse.

THE FIGHTING TEMERAIRE.

And when our darling of the sea
  Sank dying on his deck,
With her revengeful thunders, she
  Struck down his foe—a wreck!

And when our victory stayed the rout,
  And Death had stilled the storm,
How gallantly she led them out—
  Her prize on either arm!

Her day now draweth to its close,
  With solemn sunset crowned;
To death her crested beauty bows;
  The night is folding round.

No more the big heart in her breast
  Will heave from wave to wave;
Weary and war-worn, ripe for rest,
  She glideth to her grave.

In her dumb pathos desolate
  As night among the dead!
Yet wearing an exceeding weight
  Of glory on her head.

Good-bye! good-bye! old Temeraire;
  A sad, a proud good-bye!
The stalwart spirit that did wear
  Your sternness shall not die.

Through battle blast, and storm of shot,
  Your banner we shall bear;
And fight for it, like those who fought
  Your guns, old Temeraire!

[GERALD MASSEY, born 1828, one of our self-taught poets, and the author of "The Ballad of Babe Christabel," "Craigcrook Castle," "Havelock's March," and of a very able work on "Shakspeare's Sonnets."]

"THE SOUL OF MAN IS LARGER THAN THE SKY."—H. COLERIDGE.

ROBIN REDBREAST.

A CHILD'S SONG.

OOD-BYE, good-bye to Summer!
  For Summer's nearly done;
The garden smiling faintly,
  Cool breezes in the sun:
Our thrushes now are silent,
  Our swallows flown away;
But Robin's here, in coat of brown,
  With ruddy breast-knot gay.
    Robin, Robin Redbreast!
    O Robin dear!

"FLOWERS SICKEN WHEN THE SUMMER FLIES."—B. W. PROCTER.

ROBIN REDBREAST.

> Robin sings so sweetly
> In the falling of the year.
>
> Bright yellow, red, and orange,
> The leaves come down in hosts;
> The trees are Indian princes,
> But soon they'll turn to ghosts;
> The leathery pears and apples
> Hang russet on the bough:
> It's Autumn, Autumn, Autumn late,
> 'Twill soon be Winter now.
> Robin, Robin Redbreast!
> O Robin dear!
> And what will this poor Robin do?
> For pinching days are near.
>
> The fireside for the cricket,
> The wheatstack for the mouse,
> When trembling night-winds whistle
> And moan all round the house.
> The frosty ways like iron,
> The branches plumed with snow:
> Alas! in Winter dead and dark,
> Where can poor Robin go?
> Robin, Robin Redbreast!
> O Robin dear!
> And a crumb of bread for Robin,
> His little heart to cheer.

[WILLIAM ALLINGHAM, author of "Day and Night Songs," "The Music Master," "Laurence Bloomfield in Ireland," and other poems.]

NOTE.—The robin's song varies according to the season of the year. It is merry in summer, sweet but sad in autumn, and a jerking, irregular chirp in the winter. At all times, however, we are well content to listen to the music of
> "The bird whom man loves best,
> The pious bird with the scarlet breast,
> Our English Robin."

"FRIENDSHIP IS A SHELTERING TREE."—S. T. COLERIDGE.

OUTWARD BOUND.

OUTWARD BOUND.

C**LINK!** clink! clink! goes our windlass—
"Ahoy!" "Haul in!" "Let go!"
Yards braced and sails set,
Flags uncurl and flow.
Some eyes that watch from shore are wet,
(How bright their welcome shone!)

"HEAVEN LIES ABOUT US IN OUR INFANCY."—WORDSWORTH.

While, bending softly to the breeze,
And rushing through the parted seas,
  Our gallant ship glides on.

Though one has left a sweetheart,
  And one has left a wife,
'Twill never do to mope and fret,
  Or curse a Sailor's life.
See, far away they signal yet!
  They dwindle—fade—they're gone!
For, dashing outward, bold and brave,
And springing light from wave to wave,
  Our merry ship flies on.

Gay spreads the sparkling ocean;
  But many a gloomy night
And stormy morrow must be met
  Ere next we heave in sight.
The parting look we'll ne'er forget,
  The kiss, the benison,
As round the rolling world we go:
God bless you all!—blow, breezes, blow!—
  Sail on, good ship, sail on!

[WILLIAM ALLINGHAM.]

---o---

HOMEWARD BOUND.

EAD the ship for England!
  Shake out every sail!
Blithe leap the billows,
  Merry sings the gale.

HOMEWARD BOUND.

Captain, work the reck'ning;
  How many knots a day?—
Round the world and home again,
  That's the Sailor's way!

We've traded with the Yankees,
  Brazilians, and Chinese;
We've laughed with dusky beauties,
  In shade of tall palm-trees;
Across the Line and Gulf Stream—
  Round by Table Bay—
Everywhere and home again,
  That's the Sailor's way!

Nightly stands the North Star
  Higher on our bow;
Straight we run for England—
  Our thoughts are in it now.
Jolly time with friends ashore,
  When we've drawn our pay!—

All about and home again,
That's the Sailor's way!

Tom will to his parents;
Jack will to his dear;
Joe to wife and children;
Bob to pipes and beer;
Dicky to the dancing-room,
To hear the fiddles play;—
Round the world and home again,
That's the Sailor's way!

[WILLIAM ALLINGHAM.]

SUMMER MOON, O SUMMER MOON.

SUMMER Moon, O Summer Moon, across the west you fly,
    You gaze on half the earth at once, with sweet and steadfast eye;
Summer Moon, O Summer Moon, were I aloft with thee,
I know that I could look upon my boy who sails at sea.

Summer Moon, O Summer Moon, you throw your silver showers
Upon a glassy sea that lies round shores of fruit and flowers;
The blue tide trembles on the shore, with murmuring as of bees,
And the shadow of the ship lies dark near shades of orange-trees.

Summer Moon, O Summer Moon, now wind and storm have fled,
Your light creeps through a cabin-pawl and lights a flaxen head;

SUMMER MOON, O SUMMER MOON.

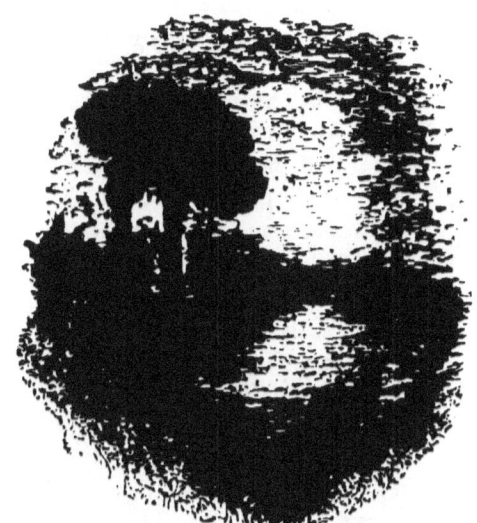

He tosses with his lips apart, lies smiling in your gleam,
For underneath his folded lids you put a pleasant dream.

Summer Moon, O Summer Moon, his head is on his arm;
He stirs with balmy breath and sees the moonlight on the Farm;
He stirs and breathes his mother's name, he smiles and sees once more
The moon above, the fields below, the shadow at the door.

Summer Moon, O Summer Moon, across the lift you go;
Far south you gaze and see my boy, where groves of orange grow !
Summer Moon, O Summer Moon, you turn again to me,
And seem to have the smile of him who sleeps upon the sea.

[ROBERT BUCHANAN—born 1841—author of "Undertones," "Idyls and Legends of Inverburn," "City Poems," "North Coast, and Other Poems," and a volume of graceful prose sketches entitled, "David Gray, and Essays on Poetry and Poets."]

IRIS THE RAINBOW.

'MID the cloud-enshrouded haze
    Of Olympus I arise,*
With the full and rainy gaze
    Of Apollo in mine eyes;
But I shade my dazzled glance
    With my dripping pinions white,
Where the sunlight sparkles dance
    In a many-tinctured light:
My foot upon the woof
    Of a fleecy cloudlet small,
I glimmer through the roof
    Of the paven banquet-hall.
And a soft pink radiance dips
    Through the floating mists divine,
Touching eyes and cheeks and lips
    Of the mild-eyed gods supine,
And the pinky odour rolls
    Round their foreheads, while I stain,
With a blush like wine, the bowls
    Of foam-crusted porcelain:
Till the whole calm place has caught
    A deep gleam of rosy fire—
When I darken to the thought
    In the eyes of Zeus the Sire.†

Then Zeus, arising, stoops
    O'er the ledges of the skies,
Looking downward, through the loops
    Of the starry tapestries,

---

* The Greek poets personified the rainbow under the name of Iris.
† Zeus, the father of gods and men, the supreme divinity of Olympus, transformed by the Romans into Jupiter (that is, *Zeus-pater*).

IRIS THE RAINBOW.

On the evident * dark plain
  Speckled with wood and hill and stream,
On the wrinkled tawny main
  Where the ships, like snowflakes, gleam;
And with finger without swerve,
  Swiftly lifted, swiftly whirled,
He draws a magic curve
  O'er the cirrus † of the world;
When with waving wings displayed,
  On the Sun-god's threshold bright
I upleap, and seem to fade
  In a humid flash of light;
But I plunge through vapours dim
  To the dark low-lying land,
And I tumble, float, and swim
  On the strange curve of the Hand:
From my wings that drip, drip, drip,
  With cool rains, shoot jets of fire,
As across green capes I slip
  With the thought of Zeus the Sire.

Thence, with drooping wings bedewed,
  Folded close about my form,
I alight with feet unviewed
  On the ledges of the storm;
For a moment, cloud-enrolled,
  'Mid the murm'rous rain I stand,
And with meteor eyes behold
  Vapoury ocean, misty land;
Till the thought of Zeus outsprings
  From my ripe mouth with a sigh,

---

* *Evident* (from *e* and *video*)—here used in its primary meaning of "visible."
† *Cirrus*—a form of cloud, consisting of tendril-like fibres.

326   THE WARBLING OF BLACKBIRDS.

  And unto my lips it clings
   Like a shining butterfly;
  When I brighten, gleam, and glow,
   And my glittering wings unfurl,
  And the melting colours flow
   To my foot of dusky pearl;
  And the ocean, mile on mile,
   Gleams through capes and straits and bays,
  And the vales and mountains smile,
   And the leaves are wet with rays,—
  While I wave the humid Bow
   Of my wings with flash of fire,
  And the Tempest, crouched below,
   Knows the thought of Zeus the Sire.

[ROBERT BUCHANAN (see page 318). From his "Undertones," a volume of truly exquisite poetry. The reader may compare the preceding with Shelley's "Cloud," p. 194.]

---o---

THE WARBLING OF BLACKBIRDS.

  WHEN I hear the waters fretting,
   When I see the chestnut letting
  All her lovely blossom falter down, I
   think, "Alas the day!"
  Once with magical sweet singing,
   Blackbirds set the woodland ringing,
That awakes no more while April hours wear themselves away.

  In our hearts fair hope lay smiling,
   Sweet as air, and all-beguiling;
And there hung a mist of blue-bells on the slope and down the dell;

And we talked of joy and splendour
That the years unborn would render,
And the blackbirds helped us with the story, for they knew it
well.

Piping, fluting, bees are humming,
April's here, and summer's coming;
Don't forget us when you walk, a man with men, in pride and
joy;
Think on us in alleys shady,
When you step a graceful lady;
For no fairer day have we to hope for, little girl and boy.

Laugh and play, O lisping waters,
Lull our downy sons and daughters;
Come, O wind, and rock their leafy cradle in thy wanderings
coy;
When they wake we'll end the measure
With a wild sweet cry of pleasure,
And a "Hey down derry, let's be merry! little girl and boy!"

[JEAN INGELOW, born about 1830. From "A Story of Doom, and Other Poems."]

———o———

THE PRIVATE OF THE BUFFS.

[Some Sikhs, and a private of the Buffs, during the last Chinese war, fell into the hands of the enemy. On the next morning they were brought before the authorities, and commanded to prostrate themselves. The Sikhs obeyed; but Moyse, the English soldier, heroically declared he would not humble himself before any Chinaman alive. He was immediately led out and executed.]

LAST NIGHT, among his fellow roughs,
He jested, quaffed, and swore;
A drunken private of the Buffs,
Who never looked before.

THE PRIVATE OF THE BUFFS.

To-day, beneath the foeman's frown,
  He stands in Elgin's* place,
Ambassador from Britain's crown,
  And type of all her race.

Poor, reckless, rude, low-born, untaught,
  Bewildered, and alone,
A heart, with English instinct fraught,
  He yet can call his own.
Ay, tear his body limb from limb,
  Bring cord, or axe, or flame:
He only knows, that not through *him*
  Shall England come to shame.

For Kentish hop-fields round him seemed,
  Like dreams, to come and go;
Bright leagues of cherry-blossom gleamed,
  One sheet of living snow;
The smoke above his father's door,
  In gray soft eddyings hung:
Must he then watch it rise no more,
  Doomed by himself, so young?

Yes, honour calls!—with strength like steel
  He put the vision by;
Let dusky Indians whine and kneel—
  An English lad must die.
And thus, with eyes that would not shrink,
  With knee to man unbent,
Unfaltering on its dreadful brink,
  To his red grave he went.

* The Earl of Elgin accompanied the British army (which was commanded by Sir Hope Grant) as ambassador to the Emperor of China.

Vain, mightiest fleets of iron framed;
   Vain, those all-shattering guns;
Unless proud England keep, untamed,
   The strong heart of her sons.
So, let his name through Europe ring—
   A man of mean estate,
Who died, as firm as Sparta's king,*
   Because his soul was great.

[Sir Francis Hastings Doyle, Professor of Poetry at the University of Oxford. This spirited ballad first appeared in *Macmillan's Magazine*.]

APOLLO AND MARSYAS.

[According to an old Greek legend, Apollo, the god of poetry, contended with Marsyas, a Phrygian faun, for the prize of music, and Marsyas being vanquished, was flayed alive by order of his cruel conqueror. The fable is reproduced in the following stanzas with all the elegance and fine *colouring* of the Greek poetry.]

S the sky-brightening south wind clears the day,
   And makes the massed clouds roll,
The music of the lyre blows away
   The clouds that wrap the soul.

Oh, that Fate had let me see
The triumph of the sweet persuasive lyre!
That famous, final victory
When jealous Pan with Marsyas did conspire!

When, from far Parnassus' side,
Young Apollo, all the pride
Of the Phrygian flutes to tame,
To the Phrygian highlands came!

* Leonidas, king of Sparta, who, with his famous Three Hundred, defended the Pass of Thermopylæ against the Persians.

Where the long green reed-beds sway
In the rippled waters gray
Of that solitary lake
Where Meander's springs are born;*
Where the ridged pine-wooded roots
Of Messogis westward break,
Mounting westward, high and higher.
There was held the famous strife;
There the Phrygian brought his flutes,
And Apollo brought his lyre;
And, when now the westering sun
Touched the hills, the strife was done,
And the attentive Muses said—
"Marsyas! thou art vanquishèd."
Then Apollo's minister
Hanged upon a branching fir
Marsyas, that unhappy faun,
And began to whet his knife.
But the Mœnads, who were there,
Left their friend, and with robes flowing
In the wind, and loose dark hair
O'er their polished bosoms blowing,
Each her ribboned tambourine
Flinging on the mountain-sod,
With a lovely frightened mien
Came about the youthful god.
But he turned his beauteous face
Haughtily another way,
From the grassy sun-warmed place
Where in proud repose he lay,
With one arm over his head,
Watching how the whetting sped.

* A river in Asia Minor, famous for its winding course; whence our word *meandering*. It flows into the Archipelago.

APOLLO AND MARSYAS.

But aloof, on the lake strand,
Did the young Olympus stand,
Weeping at his master's end;
For the faun had been his friend.
For he taught him how to sing,
And he taught him flute-playing.
Many a morning had they gone
To the glimmering mountain lakes,
And had torn up by the roots
The tall crested water reeds
With long plumes, and soft brown seeds,
And had carved them into flutes,
Sitting on a tabled stone
Where the shoreward ripple breaks.
And he taught him how to please
The red-snooded Phrygian girls,
Whom the summer evening sees
Flashing in the dance's whirls
Underneath the starlit trees
In the mountain villages.
Therefore now Olympus stands,
At his master's piteous cries
Pressing fast with both his hands
His white garment to his eyes,
Not to see Apollo's scorn;
Ah, poor faun, poor faun! ah, poor faun!

[MATTHEW ARNOLD, born 1822, son of the late illustrious Dr. Thomas Arnold, Head Master of Rugby School. Mr. Arnold is the author of a tragedy named "Merope," of "Empedocles on Etna"—the poem from which the foregoing extract is taken—and of several minor poems, as well as of various prose essays, remarkable for their elegance of style and keenness of criticism. He was Professor of Poetry at Oxford from 1857-1867.]

A CROSS IN EACH ONE'S LOT.*

WILFUL, headlong river,
    That turned not to left or right;
You might hear the passionate rushing
    Far in the silent night.

" Where was it hasting, the river,
    Flowing so straight and true?"
I cannot tell you, my darling,
    For only the river knew.

Nay, do not smile; to the river
    It was a matter of life and death:
To have watched it hurrying onwards
    Had taken away your breath.

Perchance, in depths of a far blue lake
    Its waters yearned to rest;
Perchance the many-voiced sea had called
    The river home to his breast.

Whatever the dream, it might not be;
    For they laid great stones, and hard,
In the bed of the shining river,
    And all its purpose marred.

And if you had heard the sobbing
    Of waters, the passionate moan,
You would have thought a human heart
    Was breaking against the stone.

* The moral of these verses we take to be, that we cannot always look for the fulfilment of our dearest wishes, but though the disappointment breed great sorrow in our hearts, yet will it assuredly work out some wise and beneficent end.

Yet now, in the thirsty meadows,
    Is water enough and to spare;
The drooping flowers in the gardens
    Raise faces so fresh and fair!

Well—was it well for the river?
    You think, "It was better far."
I cannot tell: is the trailing light
    Sweet to the falling star?

But if you had heard the sobbing
    Of waters, the passionate moan,
You would have thought a human heart
    Was breaking against the stone.

[ELIZABETH D. CROSS (MRS. BULLOCK), author of "An Old Story, and Other Poems," published in 1868.]

A GYPSY ENCAMPMENT.

THIS is Moorish land,
    Where Allah lives unconquered in dark breasts,
    And blesses still the many-nourishing earth
With dark-armed industry. See from the steep
The scattered olives hurry in gray throngs
Down towards the valley, where the little stream
Parts a green hollow 'twixt the gentler slopes;
And in that hollow, dwellings: not white homes
Of building Moors, but little swarthy tents
Such as of old perhaps on Asian plains,
Or wending westward past the Caucasus,
Our fathers raised to rest in. Close they swarm
About two taller tents, and viewed afar

> "BUT TRUE IT IS, ABOVE ALL LAW AND FATE ....

A GYPSY ENCAMPMENT.

Might seem a dark-robed crowd in penitence
That silent kneel; but come now in their midst
And watch a busy, bright-eyed, sportive life!
Tall maidens bend to feed the tethered goat,
The ragged kirtle fringing at the knee
Above the living curves, the shoulder's smoothness
Parting the torrent strong of ebon hair.
Women with babes, the wild and neutral glance
Swayed now to sweet desire of mothers' eyes,
Rock their strong cradling arms and chant low strains
Taught by monotonous and soothing winds
That fall at night-time on the dozing ear.
The crones plait reeds, or shred the vivid herbs
Into the caldron: tiny urchins crawl,
Or sit and gurgle forth their infant joy.
Lads lying sphynx-like with uplifted breast
Propped on their elbows, their black manes tossed back,
Fling up the coin and watch its fatal fall,
Dispute and scramble, run and wrestle fierce,
Then fall to play and fellowship again;
Or in a thieving swarm they run to plague
The grandsires, who return with rabbits slung,
And with the mules fruit-laden from the fields.
Some striplings choose the smooth stones from the
    brook*
To serve the slingers, cut the twigs for snares,
Or trim the hazel wands, or at the bark
Of some exploring dog they dart away
With swift precision towards a moving speck.
These are the brood of Zarca's Gypsy tribe;
Most like an earth-born race bred by the Sun
On some rich tropic soil, the father's light

---

* "And he took his staff in his hand, and chose him five smooth stones out of the brook" (1 Sam. xvii. 40).

> IS FAITH, ABIDING THE APPOINTED DAY."—H. COLERIDGE.

"THUS YESTERDAY, TO-DAY, TO-MORROW COME, THEY BUSTLE ONE ANOTHER, AND THEY PASS;—

BUT ALL OUR BUSTLING MORROWS ONLY MAKE THE SMOOTH TO-DAY OF GOD."—MATTHEW ARNOLD.

Flashing in coal-black eyes, the mother's blood
With bounteous elements feeding their young limbs.

[This vigorous piece of word-painting occurs in "The Spanish Gypsy," a poem of remarkable power and beauty, by which GEORGE ELIOT—or, rather, MISS EVANS—has shown herself possessed of abilities as a poet, equal to those she had already displayed as a novelist. Miss Evans was born about 1820. Her first work, "Scenes of Clerical Life," appeared in *Blackwood's Magazine.* Her later novels are—"Adam Bede," "The Mill on the Floss," "Romola," and "Felix Holt the Radical."]

A SONG OF APRIL.

FAIR mid-spring, besung so oft and oft,
How can I praise thy loveliness enow?
Thy sun that burns not, and thy breezes soft
That o'er the blossoms of the orchard blow,
The thousand things that 'neath the young leaves grow,
The hopes and chances of the growing year,
Winter forgotten long, and summer near.

When Summer brings the lily and the rose,
She brings us fear: her very death she brings
Hid in her anxious heart, the forge of woes;
And, dull with fear, no more the mavis sings.
But thou! thou diest not, but thy fresh life clings
About the fainting Autumn's sweet decay,
When in the earth the hopeful seed they lay.

Ah, life of all the year, why yet do I,
Amid thy snowy blossoms' fragrant drift,
Still long for that which never draweth nigh,

Striving my pleasure from my pain to sift,
Some weight from off my fluttering mirth to lift;
—Now, when far bells are ringing, "Come again,
Come back, past years! why will ye pass in vain?"

[WILLIAM MORRIS, a poet of great and increasing reputation, author of "The Defence of Queen Guenevere," "The Life and Death of Jason," and "The Earthly Paradise." From the latter we have borrowed the foregoing beautiful stanzas.]

---o---

A SCORE OF SONNETS.

[The Sonnet, although originally borrowed from Italy, has taken firm root in English ground; and being successively cultivated by our greatest poets, has developed admirable flower and fruit. Though somewhat rigid in form, consisting always of fourteen lines, it shows a remarkable capability of adapting itself to the genius of the artist making use of it; and the reader will observe the wide difference in music and character of the specimens which follow, notwithstanding an apparent similarity of structure. In the hands of a master, it is a peculiarly graceful and fascinating instrument; and the melody educed from it may be, at will, stirring as the sound of a trumpet, or sweet and soothing as the strain of a lute.]

I.—THE LOVELINESS OF TRUTH.

OH, how much more doth beauty beauteous seem
By that sweet ornament which truth doth give!
The rose looks fair, but fairer we it deem
For that sweet odour which doth in it live.
The canker-blooms * have full as deep a dye
As the perfumèd tincture of the roses,
Hang on such thorns, and play as wantonly
When summer's breath their maskèd buds discloses:
But, for their virtue only is their show,
They live unwooed, and unrespected fade;

* The wild, or dog-rose, is the plant to which Shakspeare here alludes

Die to themselves. Sweet roses do not so;
Of their sweet deaths are sweetest odours made:
And so of you, beauteous and lovely youth,
When that shall fade, by verse distils your truth.

[WILLIAM SHAKSPEARE (see p. 24). The construction of the foregoing is the same as of the Italian sonnet—alternate rhymes, terminating with a couplet. Shakspeare wrote one hundred and fifty-four sonnets, some of which are equal to any in the language, but a mystery attaches to the object of their composition.]

---o---

II.—A COMPARISON AND A MORAL.

LOOK how the flower which lingeringly doth fade,
    The morning's darling late, the summer's queen,
    Spoiled of that juice which kept it fresh and green,
As high as it did raise, bows low the head:
Right so my life, contentments being dead,
Or in their contraries but only seen,
With swifter speed declines than erst it spread,
And, blasted, scarce now shows what it hath been.
As doth the pilgrim therefore, whom the night
Hastes darkly to imprison on his way,
Think on thy home, my soul, and think aright
Of what yet rests thee of life's wasting day;
Thy sun posts westward, passèd is thy morn,
And twice it is not given thee to be born.

[WILLIAM DRUMMOND, of Hawthornden, born 1585, died 1649, was a poet of graceful sentiment, and much force, eloquence, and purity of expression. His principal works are:—"Tears on the Death of Mœliades" (Prince Henry), "Wandering Muses," "Flowers of Zion," and his "Sonnets"—the latter remarkable for pathos, fancy, and harmonious versification.]

SONNETS.

III.—ON THE LATE MASSACRE IN PIEDMONT.*

AVENGE, O Lord, thy slaughtered saints, whose bones
    Lie scattered on the Alpine mountains cold;
Even them who kept thy truth so pure of old,
When all our fathers worshipped stocks and stones,
Forget not: in thy book record their groans
Who were thy sheep, and in their ancient fold

---

* Written on the occasion of the persecution of the Vaudois, inaugurated by the Church of Rome in 1625.

Slain by the bloody Piemontese that rolled
Mother with infant down the rocks. Their moans
The vales redoubled to the hills, and they
To heaven. Their martyred blood and ashes sow
O'er all the Italian fields, where still doth sway
The triple tyrant ; * that from these may grow
A hundred fold, who, having learned thy way,
Early may fly the Babylonian woe.

[JOHN MILTON. See p. 62.]

IV.—DEATH NOT THE CONQUEROR.

DEATH, be not proud, though some have callèd thee
Mighty and dreadful, for thou art not so ; †
For those whom thou think'st thou dost overthrow
Die not, poor Death ; nor yet canst thou kill me.
From rest and sleep, which but thy picture be,
Much pleasure—then from thee much more dost flow :
And soonest our best men with thee do go,
Rest of their bones, and soul's delivery.
Thou'rt slave to fate, chance, kings, and desperate men,
And dost with poison, war, and sickness dwell ;
And poppy or charms can make us sleep as well,
And better than thy stroke. Why swell'st thou then ?

* Alluding to the tiara, or triple crown, worn by the Pope of Rome.
† We may be reminded here of the fine thought of Henry Vaughan (born 1621, died 1695) :—

" Dear, beauteous death—the jewel of the just,
  Shining nowhere but in the dark—
What mysteries do lie beyond thy dust,
  Could man outlook that mark ! "

One short sleep past, we wake eternally;
And Death shall be no more—Death, thou shalt die!

[Dr. JOHN DONNE, born 1573, died 1631. This learned and metaphysical writer overloads his poems with abstruse conceits, and clothes his thoughts with a shroud of obscurity which is not easily penetrated. They contain, however, many noble passages and pregnant sentiments, which may well incline us to forgive the ruggedness of their versification. His principal works are—his "Elegies," "The Pseudo-Martyr," and some remarkable Sermons.]

V.—IN MEMORY OF A DEPARTED FRIEND.

IN vain to me the smiling mornings shine,
   And reddening Phœbus lifts his golden fire;
   The birds in vain their amorous descant join,*
Or cheerful fields resume their green attire.
These ears, alas! for other notes repine,
A different object do these eyes require;
My lonely anguish melts no heart but mine,
And in my breast the imperfect joys expire;
Yet morning smiles the busy race to cheer,
And new-born pleasure brings to happier men;
The fields to all their wonted tribute bear,
To warm their little loves the birds complain;
I fruitless mourn to him that cannot hear,
And weep the more, because I weep in vain.

[THOMAS GRAY. See p. 97. This beautiful sonnet was a tribute to the memory of his friend, Richard West.]

* "Amorous descant."—*Milton.*

VI.—TO THE RIVER LODDON.*

AH, what a weary race my feet have run,
　　Since first I trod thy bank with alders crowned,
　　And thought my way was all through fairy ground,
Beneath thy azure sky and golden sun;
Where first my Muse to lisp her notes begun!
While pensive Memory traces back the round
Which fills the varied interval between,
Much pleasure, more of sorrow, marks the scene.
Sweet native stream! those skies and suns so pure
No more return to cheer my native road;
Yet still one joy remains—that not obscure
Nor useless all my vacant days have flowed,
From youth's gay dawn to manhood's prime mature,
Nor with the Muse's laurel unbestowed.

[Thomas Warton, D.D., born 1728, died 1790. An elegant critic, an accomplished scholar, and a graceful if somewhat feeble poet. He rendered some useful service to English literature. His "History of English Poetry," though incomplete, is not unworthy of the subject, nor of the occupant of the Chair of Poetry at Oxford.]

VII.—EVENING.

IT is a beauteous evening, calm and free;
　　The holy time is quiet as a nun
　　Breathless with adoration; the broad sun
Is sinking down in its tranquillity;
The gentleness of heaven is on the sea:
Listen! the mighty being is awake,

* One of the sweet Berkshire rivers; flows into the Thames.

"WHAT STRONGER BREAST-PLATE THAN A HEART UNTAINTED!—

342   SONNETS.

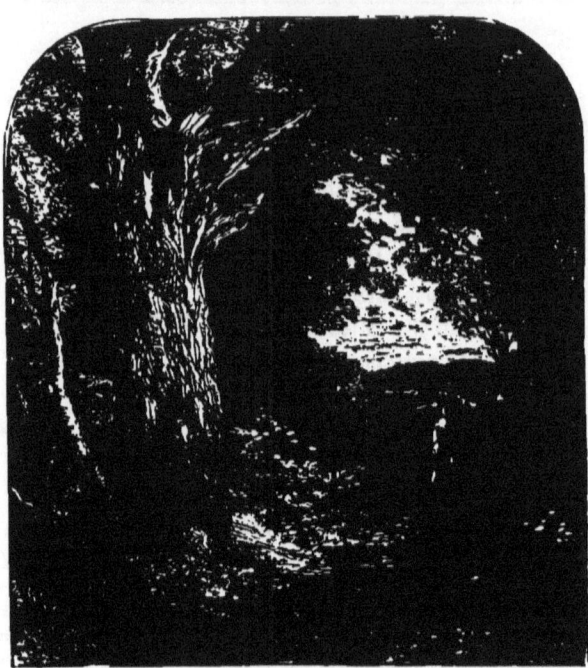

"LIFE IS A DIAL, WHICH POINTS OUT THE SUNSET, AS IT MOVES ABOUT:—(H. KING.

AND SHADOWS OUT IN LINES OF NIGHT THE SUBTLE STAGES OF TIME'S FLIGHT."—H. KING.

And doth with his eternal motion make
A sound like thunder everlastingly.
Dear child! dear girl! that walkest with me here,
If thou appear'st untouched by solemn thought,
Thy nature therefore is not less divine;
Thou liest "in Abraham's bosom" all the year,
And worshipp'st at the temple's inner shrine;
God being with thee when we know it not.

[WILLIAM WORDSWORTH. See p. 139.]

THRICE IS HE ARMED THAT HATH HIS QUARREL JUST."—SHAKSPEARE.

VIII.—WORLDLINESS.

THE world is too much with us; late and soon,
Getting and spending, we lay waste our powers:
Little we see in nature that is ours;
We have given our hearts away—a sordid boon!
This sea that bares her bosom to the moon;
The winds that will be howling at all hours,
And are up-gathered now like sleeping flowers;
For this, for everything, we are out of tune;
It moves us not.   Great God! I'd rather be
A pagan suckled in a creed outworn;
So might I, standing on this pleasant lea,
Have glimpses that would make me less forlorn,
Have sight of Proteus coming from the sea,
Or hear old Triton blow his wreathèd horn.

[WILLIAM WORDSWORTH. See p. 139.]

IX.—THE FIRST MAN.

WHAT was 't awakened first the untried ear
Of that sole man who was all human kind?
Was it the gladsome welcome of the wind,
Stirring the leaves that never yet were sere?*
The four mellifluous streams † which flowed so near,
Their lulling murmurs all in one combined?
The note of bird unnamed?   The startled hind
Bursting the brake—in wonder, not in fear

* A beautiful line, conveying, as it seems to me, a very striking picture of the young and fadeless charms of Eden.
† Pison, Gihon, Hiddekel, Euphrates (Genesis ii. 10–14).

Of her new lord? Or did the holy ground
Send forth mysterious melody to greet
The gracious pressure of immaculate feet?
Did viewless seraphs rustle all around,
Making sweet music out of air as sweet?
Or his own voice awake him with its sound?

[HARTLEY COLERIDGE, son of Samuel Taylor Coleridge, born 1796, died 1849. His life was a sad example of neglected opportunities and misapplied abilities. Of a fine, keen, brilliant genius, a lovable and generous disposition, and with a heart pure and innocent as a child's, he was cursed with the vice of irresolution, and a terrible want of self-control. The fatal habit of intoxication spoiled all his noble gifts, and instead of bequeathing to posterity some great work which the world would not willingly let die, he has left but the shadow of a name—to point a moral and adorn a tale.]

X.—THE BELLS.

HOW sweet the tuneful bells responsive peal!
  As when, at opening morn, the fragrant breeze
  Breathes on the trembling sense of wan disease,
So piercing to my heart their force I feel!
And hark! with lessening cadence now they fall,
And now along the white and level tide
They fling their melancholy music wide,
Bidding me many a tender thought recall
Of summer days, and those delightful years
When by my native streams, in life's fair prime,
The mournful magic of their mingling chime
First waked my wondering childhood into tears;
But seeming now, when all those days are o'er,
The sounds of joy once heard, and heard no more.

[Rev. WILLIAM LISLE BOWLES, born 1762, died 1850. The sonnets of this amiable man and pleasing writer are distinguished by a graceful fancy and a smooth melodious rhythm; but his two great merits are these—that he wrote naturally, and with a true love of nature, at a time when our literature was corrupted by imitations of Pope, and worse imitations of the artificial French style; and that he inspired Coleridge and Byron with a poetical enthusiasm which led in either case to splendid though very unequal results. He survived by many years both of his disciples—disciples who were afterwards, pre-eminently, his masters.]

---o---

XL—THE THRUSH'S NEST.

WITHIN a thick and spreading hawthorn bush
  That overhung a molehill large and round,
  I heard from morn to morn a merry thrush
Sing hymns of rapture, while I drank the sound
With joy; and oft, an unintruding guest,
  I watched her secret toils from day to day;
How true she warped the moss to form her nest,
  And modelled it within with wood and clay.
And by-and-by, like heath-bells gilt with dew,
  There lay her shining eggs as bright as flowers,
Ink-spotted over, shells of green and blue:
  And there I witnessed in the summer hours
A brood of nature's minstrels chirp and fly,
Glad as the sunshine and the laughing sky.

[JOHN CLARE, the "Northamptonshire poet," born 1793, died 1864. The story of his life is a melancholy one:—The son of a poor peasant, and himself a peasant, he sang as the bird sings, literally out of the fulness of his heart; and, worn down by poverty and hard labour, yet contrived to pour out strains of great beauty, fresh and fascinating in their accurate descriptions of rural scenes and sounds. He rises in his poetry to a higher level than Bloomfield, also a peasant-poet, ever attained; and to read his songs is like going out into a bright green meadow, with the odour of flowers and the music of streams about you. His intellect at length gave way beneath the pressure of heavy sorrows and unfulfilled aspirations, and poor Clare spent the last years of his life in a madhouse.]

XII.—THE GRASSHOPPER AND THE CRICKET.

GREEN little vaulter on the sunny grass,
   Catching your heart up at the feel of June,
   Sole voice that's heard amidst the lazy noon,
When even the bees lag at the summoning brass;
And you, warm little housekeeper, who class
With those who think the candles come too soon,
Loving the fire, and with your tricksome tune
Nick the glad silent moments as they pass;
O sweet and tiny cousins, that belong,
   One to the fields, the other to the hearth,
Both have your sunshine; both, though small, are strong
At your clear hearts, and both seem given to earth
To sing in thoughtful ears this natural song,
In doors and out, summer and winter, mirth.

[LEIGH HUNT. See p. 173.]

———o———

XIII.—THE GRASSHOPPER AND THE CRICKET.

THE poetry of earth is never dead:
   When all the birds are faint with the hot sun,
   And hide in cooling trees, a voice will run
From hedge to hedge about the new-mown mead:
That is the grasshopper's—he takes the lead
In summer-luxury—he has never done
With his delights; for when tired out with fun,
He rests at ease beneath some pleasant weed.
The poetry of earth is ceasing never:
On a lone winter-evening, when the frost

Has wrought a silence, from the stove there shrills
The cricket's song, in warmth increasing ever;
And seems to one in drowsiness half lost,
The grasshopper's among some grassy hills.

[JOHN KEATS. See p. 219.]

XIV.—TO AILSA ROCK.

HEARKEN, thou craggy ocean pyramid!*
   Give answer from thy voice, the sea-fowl's screams!
   When were thy shoulders mantled in huge streams?
When from the sun was thy broad forehead hid?
How long is 't since the mighty power bid
   Thee heave to airy sleep from fathom dreams—
   Sleep in the lap of thunder or sunbeams,
Or when gray clouds are thy cold coverlid?
Thou answer'st not, for thou art dead asleep!
   Thy life is but two dead eternities—
   The last in air, the former in the deep;
First with the whales, last with the eagle skies—
   Drowned wast thou till an earthquake made thee steep;
   Another cannot wake thy giant size.

[JOHN KEATS. See p. 219.]

XV.—THE EVENING CLOUD.

A CLOUD lay cradled near the setting sun,
   A gleam of crimson tinged its braided snow:
   Long had I watched the glory moving on
O'er the still radiance of the lake below.

* Ailsa Crag is an isolated rock, of pyramidal outline, situated off the mouth of the river Clyde, and about twenty miles from the Ayrshire coast.

Tranquil its spirit seemed, and floated slow !
Even in its very motion there was rest :
While every breath of eve that chanced to blow
Wafted the traveller to the beauteous West.
Emblem, methought, of the departed soul !
To whose white robe the gleam of bliss is given ;
And by the breath of mercy made to roll
Right onwards to the golden gates of heaven,
Where, to the eye of faith, it peaceful lies,
And tells to man his glorious destinies.

[JOHN WILSON, born 1785, died 1844. His principal poems, which contain many graceful descriptive passages, and are instinct with a very tender and subdued pathos, are "The City of the Plague" and "The Isle of Palms;" but he is more generally known by the remarkable papers which, under the *nom de plume* of "Christopher North," he for many years contributed to *Blackwood's Magazine.* He was also Professor of Moral Philosophy in the University of Edinburgh.]

———o———

XVI.—FALSE POETS AND TRUE.

LOOK how the lark soars upward and is gone,
Turning a spirit as he nears the sky !
His voice is heard, but body there is none
To fix the vague excursions of the eye.
So, poets' songs are with us, though they die
Obscured, and hid by death's oblivious shroud,
And earth inherits the rich melody,
Like raining music from the morning cloud.
Yet few there be who pipe so sweet and loud,
Their voices reach us through the lapse of space ;
The noisy day is deafened by a crowd
Of undistinguished birds, a twittering race ;
But only lark and nightingale forlorn
Fill up the silences of night and morn.

[THOMAS HOOD. See p. 222.]

XVII.—SPRING.

AGAIN the violet of our early days
   Drinks beauteous azure from the golden sun,
   And kindles into fragrance at his blaze:
The streams, rejoiced that winter's work is done,
Talk of to-morrow's cowslips as they run.
Wild apple! thou art bursting into bloom;
Thy leaves are coming, snowy-blossomed thorn!
Wake, buried lily! spirit, quit thy tomb;
And thou, shade-loving hyacinth, be born.
Then haste, sweet rose! sweet woodbine, hymn the morn,
Whose dew-drops shall illume with pearly light
Each grassy blade that thick embattled stands
From sea to sea, while daisies infinite
Uplift in praise their little glowing hands *
O'er every hill that under heaven expands.

[EBENEZER ELLIOTT, popularly known as the "Corn-Law Rhymer," in allusion to his vigorous poetical denunciations of the old Corn Law monopoly, was born in 1781, died in 1841. Though political passions sometimes exacerbated his strains, he was a very sweet true poet, and his love of nature was enthusiastic.]

XVIII.—NOT DEATH, BUT LOVE.

I THOUGHT once how Theocritus † had sung
   Of the sweet years, the dear and wished-for years,
   Who each one, in a gracious hand, appears
To bear a gift for mortals, old and young;

* So Shelley tells us, that—
    "The very worm that creeps beneath the sod
    In love and worship lifts itself to God."

† Theocritus, the Greek pastoral poet, flourished about 360–310 B.C.

Aud as I nursed it in his antique tongue
I saw a gradual vision through my tears—
The sweet sad years, the melancholy years,
Those of my own life, who by turns had flung
A shadow across me.   Straightway I was 'ware,
So weeping, how a mystic shape did move
Behind me, and drew me backwards by the hair,
And a voice said in mastery, while I strove—
"Guess now who holds thee?"—"Death," I said; but there
The silver answer rang—"Not Death, but Love."

[ELIZABETH BARRETT BROWNING. See p. 235.]

XIX.—WORLDLY PLACE.

"EVEN in a palace, life may be led well!"
So spake the inspired sage, purest of men,
Marcus Aurelius.*   But the stifling den
Of common life, where, crowded up pell mell,
Our freedom for a little bread we sell,
And drudge under some foolish master's ken,
Who rates us if we peer outside our pen—
Matched with a palace, is not this a hell?
"Even in a palace!"   On his truth sincere
Who spoke these words, no shadow ever came;
And when my ill-schooled spirit is aflame
Some nobler, ampler stage of life to win,
I'll stop, and say—"There were no succour here!
The aids to noble life are all within."

[MATTHEW ARNOLD. See p. 326.]

* Marcus Aurelius Antoninus, one of the wisest and noblest of the Roman emperors, was born in A.D. 121, died in A.D. 180.

XX.—A PRAYER FOR SUMMER.

WINTER, wilt thou never, never go?
O Summer, but I weary for thy coming;
Longing once more to hear the Luggie flow,*
And frugal bees, laboriously humming.
Now the east wind diseases the infirm,
And I must crouch in corners from rough weather;
Sometimes a winter sunset is a charm—
When the fired clouds, compacted, blaze together,
And the large sun dips red behind the hills.
I, from my window, can behold this pleasure;
And the eternal moon, what time she fills
Her orb with argent, treading a soft measure,
With queenly motions of a bridal mood,
Through the white spaces of infinitude.

[DAVID GRAY, born 1838, died 1861. This young poet, who may claim to be one of Shelley's "inheritors of unfulfilled renown," was the son of a Scotch weaver, and born near Kirkintilloch, in Stirlingshire. He received his education at the parish school; early displayed a strong passion for poetry; and, smitten with an unquenchable longing for fame, boldly launched himself on the great sea of London life, with few friends and no resources but his genius, at the age of twenty. What he might have become we can only surmise from the abundant promise of his youth—for consumption marked him as its own, and, returning to his father's cottage, he lingered through a few months of pain, and died with all his hopes unrealized. His remains have been edited, with a graceful memoir, by Mr. James Hedderwick, under the title of "The Luggie, and Other Poems."]

* A stream near the poet's house at Kirkintilloch, in Stirlingshire.

www.ingramcontent.com/pod-product-compliance
Lightning Source LLC
Chambersburg PA
CBHW030345230426
43664CB00007BB/537